Recreating Men
Postmodern Masculinity Politics

Bob Pease

SAGE Publications
London • Thousand Oaks • New Delhi

First published 2000

SAGE Publications Ltd
6 Bonhill Street
London EC2A 4PU

SAGE Publications Inc
2455 Teller Road
Thousand Oaks, California 91320

SAGE Publications India Pvt Ltd
32, M-Block Market
Greater Kailash – I
New Delhi 110 048

British Library Cataloguing in Publication data

A catalogue record for this book is
available from the British Library

ISBN 0 7619 6205 0
ISBN 0 7619 6206 9 (pbk)

Library of Congress catalog card number available

Typeset by M Rules
Printed in Great Britain by Athenaeum Press, Gateshead

Contents

Acknowledgements

Writing this book has been both an individual and collective effort. Since I began this project I have been supported and encouraged by a number of people. First, I want to express my indebtedness to the participants who devoted their time and energy to sharing their stories, thoughts and feelings throughout the 15 months of the participatory research group. I also want to thank the interlocutors who were prepared to express their support, reservations and criticisms about profeminism for the public record. In particular, I want to acknowledge the conversations with Anthony McMahon about whether it is in men's interests to change.

This book draws on research I completed for my doctoral thesis. I would like to thank Jacques Boulet for his encouragement and support throughout the earlier version of this project. I am indebted to his attention to detail and his commitment to the supervision.

Throughout the course of this research many colleagues and friends have read parts or all of early drafts of my work and have offered thoughtful comments and valuable suggestions. Tricia Moynihan commented helpfully on my beginning attempt to come to terms with postmodernism. Bob Fuller, Wendy Weeks and Yoland Wadsworth read and commented on work-in-progress drafts of the early chapters when my ideas were in their formative stages. Glenda Koutroulis introduced me to the pleasures and pitfalls of memory-work. I thank them all for their support and assistance. I would especially like to thank Silvia Starc, Peter Horsfield, David Tacey, Helen Marshall and Rob Watts for their comments on the full penultimate draft of the thesis manuscript on which this book is based.

In moving from thesis to book, I want to thank my dissertation examiners, Michael Kimmel, John Rowan and Malcolm McCouat. Their enthusiastic response to the thesis, and their belief that this research had value to the general public as well as to academic audiences, encouraged me to take the extra step of moving this work beyond the confines of the academy.

Finally, I want to express my further appreciation to Silvia Starc for her tender support throughout all stages of this project. She, more than anyone, is aware of the blood, sweat and tears involved in the production of this book. Now we can regain the balance that enables these ideas to be more fully lived.

1 Introduction: Men, Masculinities and Feminism

One of the most central issues for women's prospects for equality is whether men can and will change. I believe that men's subjectivity is crucial to gender domination and that changing the social relations of gender will necessitate the transforming of men's subjectivities as well as changing their daily practices. This book will provide an indication of the extent to which this is possible by focusing on the subjectivities and practices of profeminist men, of whom I am one. It is concerned with the questions: What does it mean to be a profeminist man? What is the experience of endeavouring to live out a profeminist commitment? What do these experiences tell us about changing men's subjectivities and practices towards gender equality?

These are questions that have been a personal challenge in my search to understand my place as a white, heterosexual man who is committed to a profeminist position. This commitment arose out of the changes in gender relations that occurred in the 1970s. As someone who was involved in social justice campaigns, I found it relatively easy, at the intellectual level, to see the justice of feminist claims and my own complicity in the oppression of women. At the emotional level, I was deeply threatened by it. Listening to the experiences of women for the first time brought complex reactions from sorrow to outrage and confusion about how to respond. To begin to address these issues, I co-founded an anti-sexist men's consciousness-raising group in 1977. It was during this time that I first started reading feminist theory in an effort to understand what women were saying about men. That was the beginning of a personal, political and intellectual journey in confronting the social construction of white, Western masculinity.

Since 1986 I have been involved in trying to develop a collective profeminist men's politics through co-founding an organization called Men Against Sexual Assault (MASA). MASA has been involved in the organization of forums on gender issues; conducting workshops in schools on anti-sexist masculinity for boys; running workshops and giving public talks educating men about the impact of patriarchy on women's lives; speaking out in the public media about the objectification of women; and organizing campaigns against men's violence. (For a detailed discussion of the development of MASA, see Pease, 1997.)

In giving public lectures on the impact of men's practices on both women and men, I often encounter resistance from men about the validity of feminist analyses. While some of these resistances came from angry anti-feminist men, many of the negative responses came from men who saw themselves as supportive of women's rights while believing that feminism had gone too far. It was this level of resistance by ordinary men to feminism that has been of most concern to me as an educator and an activist.

In 1993 two other men and I designed a two-day patriarchy-awareness workshop to address these resistances. The workshop used small group discussion and experiential exercises to explore such issues as analyses of patriarchal culture, men's experience of power and domination, alternatives to patriarchal power, the impact of men's domination on women, social and personal blocks to men's ability to listen to women and the visions, obstacles and potential for men to change. The experience of facilitating these workshops further led me to recognize the importance of theorizing the processes by which patriarchal belief systems become embedded in men's psyches and the implications for resistance and change.

Men and Feminism

The antipathy of ordinary men towards feminism is deeply entrenched, as surveys of men's attitudes to the changing roles of women demonstrate. While the majority of men espouse support for equal pay and opposition to men's physical violence, they also tend to be critical of feminism and the women's movement. Walczak's (1988: 129) survey demonstrated that while a minority of men in the United Kingdom hold egalitarian views and an equivalent minority hold traditional views, the vast majority hold views somewhere between 'the extremes'. This is consistent with Townsend's (1994: 271) research where 15 per cent of Australian men identified as anti-feminist, 10 per cent as profeminist and 75 per cent indicated broad support for the goal of equality but were critical of how feminism operates in practice.

Men's main criticisms of feminism from these and other surveys are: that exclusion of men from women's groups and women's organizations is discriminatory; that feminism will erode what are perceived to be fundamental differences between men and women; that women are going the wrong way about trying to achieve their objectives; that feminism has gone 'too far'; that women are now better off than men; and that feminism is anti-male (Franks, 1984; Ingham, 1984; Walczak, 1988; Townsend, 1994).

Many white, heterosexual men are thus unaware that their race, sexuality and gender give them privileges which help perpetuate inequalities. Because many men are unaware of how much the social structure advantages them, they take patriarchy for granted, being more aware of both their burdens and responsibilities than their unearned advantages (Goode, 1982: 137).

Not all men are batterers and rapists, but without 'ordinary' men's participation in routine oppressive practices men's subordination of women would not take the form that it does. Furthermore, because many men's oppressive behaviour is socially accepted as 'normal male behaviour', it can be said to impede their awareness of its oppressive aspects. These instances differ from more extreme forms of oppression, in that many individual men may be misguided by social norms that permit some oppressive behaviours (Calhoun, 1989: 389–94).

Awareness of men's privileges and socially legitimated oppressive behaviours constitutes the minimal requirement for a progressive men's politics. But what is a progressive men's politics? Some writers refer to 'progressive' practices by men as the 'profeminist wing' of the men's movement. Others talk about a profeminist men's movement, while still others talk about profeminist men becoming a part of the feminist movement. The constituency and location of profeminist politics remains unclear, as does its potential to reach a larger group of men.

My aims in this book are therefore twofold and operate on two different levels: to *theorize* masculinities to inform a profeminist men's politics at both the levels of changing men's subjectivities and challenging the structures of gender domination; and to *enact* strategies that will promote these processes of change. There is a dialectical relationship between these two levels and between the two sites of change. The theoretical investigations and the reflections on practice influence each other, and the methodical and engaged exploration of profeminist men's subjectivities and the dialogues across difference with other individuals and groups are both attempts to link the process of personal transformation to the collective politics of change in gender relations.

Profeminism

Why is it important to study profeminist men? Will their experience tell us anything about the more general resistances of men to the process of change? I believe that there are a number of reasons why profeminist men's experiences are important to study.

First, profeminist men are not exceptional. They still occupy positions of dominance and they continue to embody much of the internalized domination of ordinary men. They are only different through their attempts to confront both their internalized domination and their dominant position. Secondly, profeminist men's awareness of their privilege and their socially legitimated oppressive behaviours are minimal requirements for a progressive politics of change among men. Thirdly, the attempts of such men to change will give some evidence to women as to whether men can potentially become reliable allies in the struggle to transform gender relations more broadly. Fourthly, because these men are attempting to create a collective politics of gender among men, they are, or can be, at the 'cutting edge' in changing dominant masculinities. Finally, such men's experiences give a useful insight into the determinative factors of gender construction and its associated structural components to see whether men who want to change actually can do so.

Little is known, however, about these men and their politics and the contribution they might make to changes in gender relations. This is in spite of the fact that in recent years there has been considerable empirical research on masculinities and men in gender relations, from both journalistic and academic perspectives. This research has focused on a diverse range of topics including sport, the media, male sexuality, men in families, men at work, men's friendships, intimacy with women, boyhood, adolescence, midlife and ageing and the men's movement.

Significantly though and notwithstanding the fact that studies of fathers and men in the men's movement sometimes express profeminist sentiments, very few empirical studies of explicitly anti-sexist or profeminist men have been undertaken. As I will later demonstrate, most men in these studies are not enacting a profeminist politics. Two exceptions in the literature that most closely parallel my own work are Connell's (1990) study of six anti-sexist men involved in the environment movement and Christian's (1994) life-history interviews with 30 anti-sexist men. While both studies are useful in shedding light on the reasons these individual men became involved in anti-sexist politics, the life-history method does not contribute to a collective politics among such men.

A premise of this research is that profeminist men's experiences constitute a 'submerged voice' within the hegemonic discourses of masculinity. The emergence of profeminist subject positions is an example of what Foucault (1972: 81) calls 'an insurrection of subjugated knowledges'. Profeminist men also constitute a marginal group within patriarchy. Researching the experiences of such a group enables us to identify the formation of new subject positions that provide a 'counter logic to the prevailing modes of domination in society' (Smith, 1992: 496). Thus, the attempts of profeminist men to challenge the patriarchal discourse enable us to clarify aspects of the process of change in gender relations from the perspective of those in the dominant position.

Constructing a Profeminist Men's Standpoint

How valid is a critique of patriarchal dominance from within the experiences of white heterosexual profeminist men? Many currents in feminism argue that we should put more trust in the vantage points of the oppressed and argue that there is good reason to believe that vision is better from below (Haraway, 1988: 583). Theorizing from experience is juxtaposed to the notion that objectivity and distance are the best stances from which to generate knowledge. Instead, it is argued that 'the oppressed can see with clarity not only their own position but also that of the oppressor/privileged and indeed the shape of social systems as a whole' (Frankenberg, 1993: 8). Thus, feminist standpoint theory asserts that to start from women's experiences decreases the partiality and distortion of our images of nature and social relations (Harding, 1992: 181).

For Swigonski (1993: 172, 179), a standpoint involves a level of awareness about an individual's social location, from which certain features of reality come into prominence and from which others are obscured. According to her, a researcher's standpoint 'emerges from one's social position with respect to gender, culture, colour, ethnicity, class and sexual orientation and the way in which these factors interact and affect one's everyday world'. Researchers are required to reflect upon the implications of their social position for both their motives for undertaking the research and the consequences for the conduct of their research.

There are a variety of standpoint theories that range from essentialist expressions and materialist analyses to postmodern variations. While earlier versions of standpoint theory did have an essentializing tendency, more recent interpretations have located women's experience in concrete, historical contexts. Furthermore, postmodern developments have led to the rejection of a single female perspective and to the acknowledgement of a plurality of female standpoints (Grant, 1993: 91). Thus, there is considerable convergence between recent versions of standpoint theory and postmodernism in that both emphasize multiple interpretations and multiple subjectivities.

What are the implications of postmodern revisions of standpoint theory for profeminist male researchers? If where one 'stands' shapes what one can see and how one can understand it, from what standpoint can profeminist men study masculinity? If, as Harding argues, men also can create anti-sexist knowledge (1992: 178), is it possible to formulate a profeminist men's standpoint to study men and masculinities?

According to Morgan (1992: 29), when dominant groups research their own position in society 'these considerations may be more in terms of justifications than in terms of critical analysis [and] their investigations may always be suspect'. He goes on to raise questions about the extent to which it is possible for men to develop those forms of self-knowledge which could lead to the erosion of male power and privileges.

If, however, men are seen to be locked into an ontological position within patriarchy, what space is left for us to explore our own masculinity? While we cannot individually or as a group 'escape' our material position in the social structure, I believe that we *can* change our ideological and discursive position. The advantage of the notion of standpoint is that it relates to both structural location as well as the discursive construction of subjectivity, allowing us to distinguish between 'men's standpoint' and 'profeminist men's standpoint'. Following Frankenberg (1993: 265), I recognize that there is a substantial difference between the self-conscious engagements of oppressed groups with their own positioning and the self-conscious and self-critical engagement with a dominant position in the gender order. Nevertheless, I still believe that it is possible for men to change their subjectivities and practices to constitute a profeminist men's standpoint.

The process of change is itself a requirement in formulating a profeminist men's standpoint. Men have to change their vantage point if they want to see the world from a different position and this entails more than just a theoretical shift. It also requires men to actively engage in profeminist struggles in both the private and public arenas, translating in the possibility of a change towards more equal gender positionings.

There is feminist support for the view that it is possible for some men to change in the ways I have outlined and thus escape biological and structural determinism. Harding (1987: 10–11) argues that men can make important contributions to feminist research and she does not believe that the ability or the willingness to contribute to feminist understanding are sex-linked traits. Men can learn to see the world from the perspective of experiences and lives that are not their own and can thus generate knowledge from the perspective of women's lives. If women are not the sole generators of feminist knowledge, men are obligated to contribute to feminist analyses and, in doing so, they must learn to take responsibility for the position from which they speak (Harding, 1992: 183, 188).

While men can contribute to feminist theoretical work, there is a danger that the dominance of men will begin to assert itself on feminist knowledge by theoretical justification as a right. I believe that the most appropriate stance for profeminist men to take is the following: to hear feminist critiques of patriarchy, to research men in light of feminist theoretical insights and developments in methodology, to understand the origins and dynamics of these critiques from 'within' and to make the results of this research available for dialogue and critique, as a basis for working in alliance with women against men's social dominance.

The basis of men's contribution to feminist knowledge (and to their struggles) will be from our specific situation. Men have access to some areas of male behaviour and thought that women do not have. In this sense, women cannot know the 'content of the deliberate strategies that men and male dominated institutions use to maintain their power' (Kelly et al., 1994: 33). When men do research on men, it potentially enables the reader to eavesdrop on privileged consciousness and it reveals how men construct themselves in a dominant position.

On the other hand, there are further dangers when men engage with feminist issues. Reinharz (1992: 16) is appropriately concerned that feminist scholarship is sometimes taken more seriously when men discuss it than when women do. Morgan (1992: 183) has also pointed to the danger of men becoming so successful at deploying feminist methods that they may attract research funding, set up centres and organize journals at the cost of women's endeavours. Such dangers indeed exist but, given that men value masculine authority more highly, I believe that they *should* use it to resocialize men.

In light of the above, while men can support feminism, we cannot *be* feminists because we do not have women's experience (Reinharz, 1992: 14–15). I prefer Wadsworth and Hargreaves's (1993: 5) premise that men can do *profeminist* research if they can fulfil certain conditions, including making their work accountable to a critical reference group of women who will determine whether it meets their interests and addresses their problems.

This is not to argue, however, that feminism should set the agenda for men's studies. Men have to take responsibility for the questions that emerge in their explanations of men and masculinity (Seidler, 1994: 112). While I would agree that some form of accountability by men to women is essential in researching masculinity, this does not involve the relinquishing of responsibility for determining the direction of the research. Making those to whom we are accountable arbiters of practice and research would, yet again, take away responsibility from men. This process of accountability must involve dialogue with women.

Developing a Collective Politics Among Profeminist Men

The strategic concerns of the research – how to inform a profeminist politics among men – invited a collaborative mode of inquiry. It is my view that questions of political strategy are best formulated collectively. Thus, to address the formulated research aims, I invited a number of self-defining, profeminist men to participate in a collaborative inquiry that would take the form of an anti-patriarchal men's consciousness-raising group.

From my involvement in profeminist politics, I drew up a list of 20 men whom I knew personally and who I believed would identify with a profeminist stance. Ten of these men were, at the time of the research, active in MASA; the others were from a range of activist backgrounds including the non-violence movement, perpetrator counselling, 'left' politics, an alternative community and non-sexist educational programmes for boys in schools. Because my focus was on both personal change and political strategy, I believed that it was important to choose men who were in some way taking a public stance with their profeminism. Of the 20 men who attended the initial meeting, 11 men committed themselves to the full project over a period of 15 months and 22 meetings.

The empirical focus of this research was not to present detailed profiles of the participants as individual men. Rather, following Connell (1996: 172), the aim was to elucidate the shared historical situation the participants found themselves in as a group of self-defining profeminist men and to articulate the social logic of their response to that situation.

The early stages of the research involved us in exploring what Pheterson calls our 'internalized domination'. Internalized domination is 'the incorporation and acceptance by individuals within a dominant group of prejudices against others' (Pheterson, 1986). How do we theorize our position as white, heterosexual men? What dilemmas and issues do we face as profeminist men? Is it in men's interests to change? How and why do we develop a progressive anti-patriarchal politics?

What happens when white heterosexual profeminist men reflect upon themselves? To explore our subjectivities we used processes of anti-patriarchal consciousness-raising and collective memory-work (Haug, 1987). Both of these methods encourage participants to reflect upon the ways in which they have accommodated to or resisted hegemonic forms of masculinity.

Many feminists have identified appropriate deconstructive projects for men, including an examination of men's sexuality (Cicoux cited in Jardine, 1987: 60), why men like pornography (Rich, 1983: 66) and men's relationships with their mothers (Jardine, 1987: 61). An examination of these topics and others are reported in Chapters 5 and 6 of the book.

As we began these discussions, more particular questions of strategies and alliances emerged. How can we relate to feminism and what kind of alliances can be formed with the women's movement? How does homophobia relate to heterosexual masculinity and what kind of alliances can be formed with the gay men's movement? How do we engage critically with the men's movement? Other questions about alliances were also developed in relation to anti-racist groups, trade unions and the labour movement and the peace and environment movements. To address these issues, we adapted Touraine's (1977) sociological intervention method for studying social movements. This method involved us in dialogues with both allies and opponents of profeminism. A detailed discussion of these methodologies is undertaken in the Appendix.

Deconstructing Men, Masculinity and Power

It seems appropriate to alert the reader to the different uses that are made of the concepts of men, masculinity and power in this book.

I problematize the use of 'men' as a generic category because it implies homogeneity. I argue for the importance of identifying differences among men and of specifying *which* men we are talking about. However, I am suggesting that, while acknowledging the differences, it is still relevant to talk of men, in some instances, as a collectivity or at least as an overarching category of human beings. Thus, while avoiding the term as a global category, I continue to use it at times, albeit reservedly, to refer to men as an identifiable aggregation, recognizing that it embraces a multiplicity of experiences, representations and projections.

 In relation to masculinity, I reject its singular and normative use as an expression of 'what men are' generically. There are a range of masculinities in society reflecting the differences amongst men fluctuating over time and space and expressing men's ways of living and acting differently.

Masculinity and patriarchy are sometimes fused together, or their semantic fields tend to overlap, because the dominant mode of masculinity is patriarchal and the enactment of this mode reproduces patriarchal structures. By contrast, a premise of this book is that men can enact non-patriarchal masculine subjectivities and thus break the real and implied nexus between men, a normative model of masculinity and patriarchal dominance.

It is frequently proclaimed that one cannot understand men and masculinity without understanding power (Hearn, 1992: 21; Kaufman, 1994: 146). There are, however, many different ways of describing and conceptualizing power. Most writers distinguish between various forms of organizational, institutional and social power on the one hand and the subjective experience of powerfulness on the other. These distinctions have been articulated in a variety of ways including 'threat power' and 'integrative power' (Boulding, 1990), 'power-over' and 'power-to' (Yoder and Kahn, 1992) and 'outer power' and 'inner power' (Crespi, 1992).

It is said that men tend to conceptualize power as the first set of categories, 'the capacity to impose control on others' (Kaufman, 1993: 146). This form of power is the ability to force opponents to give in for fear of unpleasant consequences. While men may rely more on threat power than integrative power, it is not uniquely masculine, for women can also use power in this way, as evidenced in white women's control over women of colour (Griscom, 1992: 407).

These distinctions help us to understand what Kaufman (1994) refers to as 'men's contradictory experiences of power'. On the one hand, it is widely acknowledged that men dominate most forms of organizational, institutional and social power, thus constituting men's gender power. On the other hand, many men experience feelings of personal disempowerment. While for some men this may be a reflection of their position in class or race hierarchies, for others it is a recognition that their social or institutionalized power may not always correlate with their experience as individual men and their *feelings* of powerfulness.

Many men lack integrative power because they have focused so much on the exercise of threat power (Kupers, 1993: 179). Furthermore, the more inner power a man has the less he will feel the need to control others (Crespi, 1992: 104). These contrasting views of power suggest that men's capacity to impose control on women, albeit exercised differently in different places and in different classes, is not the only form of power. Women's capacity for integrative power, and the capacity to develop 'power-against' (Onyx, 1993: 1) through resistance, means that women are not completely powerless.

This challenge to the notion that men are all-powerful in all aspects of their lives does not lead me to the conclusion reached by Farrell (1993) and others that 'male power is a myth'. In recognizing the importance of other forms of power, I do not deny the phenomenon of institutionalized gender power, nor of class and state power. Rather I suggest that gender power relations can be transformed by both women *and* men in local struggles against the different forms of power exercised at the everyday level of social interactions.

An Outline of the Chapters

In Chapter 2, I critically review debates 'about men' within modernist feminism and theories of masculinity in the new men's studies literature, focusing specifically on men's agency in maintaining or challenging patriarchal social relations. Chapter 3 examines the implications of the current debates within and between postmodernism, critical theory and feminism for the study of men. Chapter 4 describes processes of anti-patriarchal consciousness-raising with men and illustrates the dilemmas and contradictions facing profeminist men.

The next two chapters draw upon memory-work to explore men's subjectivities and practices. Chapter 5 examines aspects of father–son and mother–son relationships in the context of the current debates on father absence, the father 'wound' and boys' separation from their mothers. In Chapter 6, I examine two social practices that reinforce hierarchical heterosexuality – homophobia and sexual objectification – and explore the potential for heterosexual men to reconstruct their gender and sexual identities in ways that do not involve domination over other sexualities and over women.

Chapters 7–9 outline accounts of dialogues with allies and opponents of profeminism to explore the potential of a collective politics among profeminist men. Chapter 7 examines the political dimensions of the men's movement and the appropriateness of locating profeminist men's politics within it. Chapter 8 explores the potential for alliances between profeminist men, feminist women and gay men. In Chapter 9, I explore the extent to which it is in men's interests to change towards gender equality and consider whether it is possible for men to formulate non-patriarchal interests.

The final chapter draws together the various arguments of the book. I consider the implications for theorizing and changing men's subjectivities and outline methods for working with men towards gender equality.

PART I

THEORIZING MEN
AND PATRIARCHY

2   The 'Man Question' in Feminism and the New Men's Studies

How should I, as a man, approach the feminist debate about men? How should men read feminist theory? Of course these are not questions that many men consider because most men, including academic men and members of men's groups, do not read feminist theory at all. While female scholars have to read what both men and women write, academic men feel the need only to read each other (Hanmer, 1990: 24). Many men writing on gender do not acknowledge feminist theory and some writers argue that feminism is about women and has little to say about men (Brod, 1987: 61).

A man who reads feminist theory must respond to the feminist arguments but the question is: How can he respond? Male writers, sympathetic to feminism, and who comment on feminist theory, acknowledge that they confront a series of issues. Men cannot pretend to be impartial. It is questioned whether men can understand the position of women in feminist theory and hence whether they can be of any use to feminism (Smith, 1987: 35). As the writings are mostly intended for women, this introduces subtleties with which most men are unable to cope (Marine, 1972: 11). It is also recognized that men's view of feminist theory must be a view of the surface because they are unable to access the complexities available only to participants (Bouchier, 1983: 90).

Some feminist critics are even more sceptical of the value of men's reading of feminism. Over 25 years ago, Daly (1973: 32) argued that when men study feminism, they do so to gain 'easily exploitable knowledge about women's situation'. Ten years later, Klein (1983: 414) reiterated this view by suggesting that the presence of men in women's studies is a contradiction in terms. More contemporary feminists echo these views. Men are said to study feminism in order to co-opt it and turn it towards their own interests (Marcus, 1988: 100) or to approach it as a topic to 'get on top of' or as a terrain to be 'conquered' and not as a process to which to commit oneself (Sofia, 1993: 36).

Others argue that men try to split feminist academics by accepting some and rejecting others (Canaan and Griffin, 1990: 37). Certainly, men can use feminist theory against feminism by constructing 'good' and 'bad' feminisms (Ross, 1987: 87). There is a tendency for men to acknowledge only some female scholars. Feminist object-relations theorists, such as Chodorow (1978) and Dinnerstein (1976), have been the most popular among men whereas radical feminists, such as Dworkin (1981), Griffin (1981) and Daly (1975), and materialist feminists, such as Delphy (1984) and O'Brien (1981), tend to be either ignored or heavily criticized.

Male criticism of feminist theory is indeed problematic. How do I as a man engage intellectually and politically with feminist theory without misappropriating it? As a scholar, I can endeavour to engage in a dialogue from a self-conscious standpoint, whilst recognizing that a total awareness of my historically conditioned stance may be impossible. As an activist in anti-sexist men's politics for over 20 years, I have grappled with these issues.

I believe that men's study of men needs to draw upon the early writings of feminism as a starting point for their research. I do not believe that commentary on feminist theory should be exclusively a female discourse. Men have an important position in relation to feminism because one of its objectives is to change men as well as women.

Following Spivak (1987: 24), I argue against a determinist position which maintains that, since I am a man, I cannot speak. She describes as 'genitalism' the view that posits that depending upon which genitals one has one can or cannot speak in certain situations. Acknowledging that when speaking as a man, I speak with a different voice from women, I need to develop a biographical critique of my own position and self-interest in the existing relations of gender dominance. From this position, I can seek to continue dialogue with feminism as a basis for critical self-reflection.

Men and Patriarchy

My starting point for this book is the patriarchal structure of Western societies. The concept of patriarchy has been used as an 'umbrella' term for describing men's systemic dominance of women. Millet (1972: 23–58) was one of the first feminists to use the term to describe the unequal relations of power between women and men. Walby (1990: 20) defines patriarchy as 'a system of social structures and practices through which men dominate, oppress and exploit women' and Ramazanoglu (1989: 34) similarly calls it 'a concept used to attempt to grasp the mechanisms by which men in general manage to dominate women in general'.

All feminist politics are based upon some explicit or implicit theoretical understanding of patriarchy which influences feminist views about prospects for change. Whilst the historical development of the political and general debates about patriarchy will not be discussed here, a brief summary is necessary to provide a context for the main concern of this chapter, the feminist and anti-sexist debates about the agency of men in the reproduction of patriarchy.

For Marxist feminists, patriarchy is a reflection of the structures governing economic production. Family and gender relations are seen as sites where the relations of production are reproduced. Thus, Marxist feminists focus on the ways in which male dominance benefits capitalism as 'the material base upon which patriarchy rests lies most fundamentally in men's control over women's labour' (Hartmann, 1981: 15).

Radical feminists, in contrast, point out that Marxists ignore the centrality of male power in the oppression of women. Rather than seeing gender dominance as arising from economically unequal relations, it is considered the primary source of oppression and men's power over women is regarded as the most basic and important organizing principle of social life (Firestone, 1971: 20–1).

Feminists also engage in heated debates about the extent to which capitalism and patriarchy are two interacting systems, as in dual systems theory, where they are regarded as parallel and autonomous systems of social relations which sometimes meet and intersect or whether they form a unity in terms of patriarchal capitalism (Hartmann, 1981) or capitalist patriarchy (Eisenstein, 1979).

The concept of patriarchy itself has equally been criticized for being ahistorical. Rowbotham (1981: 365) rejected it because of its biological connotations and the suggestion that male dominance was unitary and unchanging. Barrett (1980: 14) criticized it as apparently fixed and unchanging, suggesting 'a universal and transhistorical oppression'. Similarly, Connell (1987) believes that the concept of patriarchy oversimplifies the structures of gender. Thus, there is ongoing debate about the universal status of the concept of patriarchy as the primary cause of women's oppression.

Since patriarchy has some currency as an acceptable term for describing systemic male domination, I will continue to use it here, avoiding its biologically determinist connotations. By patriarchy I simply mean institutionalized male power. I argue that patriarchy is best understood as an historical structure with changing dynamics, allowing, as I will try to show later, opportunities for intervention. By contrast, some feminist versions of the concept of patriarchy allow no place for intervention and offer no position from which men can challenge the gender order.

On the one hand, radical change in gender relations of course depends on changing the material and structural conditions on which patriarchy rests; obviously, the structures of patriarchy exist beyond the individual actions of particular men. I fully accept the feminist notion that men's subjectivities and practices are produced and reproduced within patriarchal structures. I also recognize that patriarchal relations are structural and embedded in the institutions and social practices of our society and cannot be explained by the intentions of good or bad individual men, notwithstanding that individual men continue to be the agents of women's oppression.

On the other hand, implicit in many theories of patriarchy is the notion that male dominance and masculinity are reflections of each other. In some radical feminist theories of patriarchy, all men are seen as a coherent 'gender class' with the same vested interests in controlling women. Such analyses are biologically or structurally determinist and the political prognosis is pessimistic. If all men are the enemy, then it is difficult to envisage the possibility of men and women working together against patriarchy (Edley and Wetherell, 1995: 196). If all men are innately violent and controlling there can be little optimism for change, let alone there ever being any future in which men and women can live their lives together in some form of justice and harmony.

The critical issue here then is the extent to which men, masculinities and forms of male dominance *are* reflections of each other. To what extent can we separate the psychologies of men from the social structures and ideologies of male dominance? To what extent will a focus on men's subjectivities and practices as opposed to institutionalized male dominance yield different interpretations of men's power and ways to change it? These are questions that I intended to develop further in undertaking this research.

Mederos (1987: 25) usefully distinguishes between the institutionalized patriarchal system in which men gain benefits through their structural advantages in 'employment and control over social institutions' and the personal patriarchal system in which men actively 'make various types of claims upon women at home or elsewhere'. This book is concerned more with the personal patriarchal system and with the question of men's agency in the oppression of women. To what extent can men *decide* not to exploit women's domestic work? To what extent can men *choose* not to degrade women sexually? What is required for men to *opt for* alternative practices and behaviours?

Men changing their personal lives to become more equal with their female partners will thus, in and of itself, not challenge structured patriarchy, but it is argued that men have *choices* as to whether they accept patriarchy or work collectively against it. Before men can organize collectively, though, they must transform their subjectivities and practices. Following Hearn (1992: 19), I believe that there are spaces in patriarchy for men 'to appreciate the possibilities of being different and being against sexism and against patriarchy'.

Furthermore, if men's subjective experiences are left unexplored, they could be seen as being naturally inclined towards domination. So it is important to research their experiences as 'oppressors' to understand how patterns of internalized domination become part of men's subjectivity.

The Potential for Men to Change

The potential for men to change and the reasons why they might do so have been the subject of considerable debate within feminism. It has been said that one belief a feminist needs for working with men in progressive movements is that 'men are capable of change, indeed that men are demonstrating change in their individual relations to women and to each other' (Cockburn, 1988: 304).

Some feminists have pointed out that men will not change simply because women want them to and that they will not relinquish power and privilege on request (Segal, 1989: 12; Phillips, 1993: 16). On the other hand, a total withdrawal from men, as advocated by some feminists, is likely to lead to a lessening of demands upon men. The more women pressure men to change, the more men will be forced to examine the presumptions and prerogatives of masculinity.

Men must do more than just change their personal behaviour with women some of the time, and not oppose other men's attitudes and values when in a group of men. Many men will turn on men who form an alliance with women and this is why so many anti-sexist men will try to change the way they are with women but not with men (Arcana, 1983: 283). It is important, however, that supportive men challenge other men's anti-feminism even if this means forfeiting their regard (Cockburn, 1991: 226). In this way, women do not have to use all of their energy trying to change men.

hooks (1992: 111) challenges profeminist men to put a priority on educating the masses of men in feminist thought. Men should stand up to other men and say 'no more rape', to change the consensus reality that condones violence against women (Noble, 1992: 106). Some feminists demand that men analyse and tell women why so many of them use pornography (Segal, 1990: 113) but the overriding and most repeated demand is for men to 'listen' to women (Carlin, 1992: 123).

How are men expected to respond to these demands? Three feminist readings of men and change can be identified. These are material self-interest, enlightened self-interest and responsibility/justice views.

Men's Material Self-Interests

The early radical feminist view identified men as the oppressors and as intrinsically violent and women-hating. They were seen as having too much to lose to be reliable allies with women in challenging patriarchy. Some radical feminists believe that men will never change and that their dominance is inevitable (Segal, 1987: 17). In this view, men oppress women because they are biologically programmed to do so. Within this perspective, there is no basis for men to change.

Furthermore, it is argued that men have the ability to undermine the threat of feminism by incorporating their critique and adjusting their ideology. In this view, it is in men's interests to co-opt feminism and femininity. If female qualities become more highly valued, then they can simply be incorporated into men's power base. In support of this view, Leonard (1982: 159–60) argues that men use feminist analysis to exonerate themselves and to deflect attention from male privilege and men's behaviour towards women.

At one level it can be seen as logical for men to oppose women's liberation because, in the short term, men will lose out as women compete with them for status and money. But is this a sufficient explanation for men's resistance to change? Many other levels of resistance have been noted including: men's fear that women's equality will emasculate them (Marine, 1972: 264); that those who dominate cannot conceive of any other alternative other than being dominated themselves (Figes, 1972: 52); fear of the all-powerful mother (Bouchier, 1983: 152–3); and men not being accustomed to being held responsible for anything negative about themselves (Hanmer, 1990: 27).

Whatever the reasons, one has to acknowledge that most men seem particularly resistant to the idea of adapting to the changing role of women. While some individual men have changed and there have been some shifts in the dominant ideology and practices of the state, there is little evidence of any overall change in men's dominance. In this context, it is understandable that men who are genuinely trying to change themselves and challenge other men will be accused of collectively seeking ways to preserve old privileges. When such men befriend feminism they will discover that 'they can do no right' (Wilson, 1983: 234).

While I understand the basis of this pessimism, I reject the premises underlying this view and I endeavour to demonstrate, in this book, theoretical and practical support for the view that men can change in the direction of feminism. Two contrasting feminist perspectives support this position.

Men's Enlightened Self-Interests

While men's position carries with it more power and status, it also brings the burden of responsibility that could lead men towards their liberation. According to Adair (1992: 62), to oppress others, it is necessary to suppress oneself and systemic male dominance not only oppresses women, it deforms men themselves; for example, men die more frequently from stress-related illness and violence and have a shorter life expectancy (Cockburn, 1991: 222). In this view, the reason for men to change themselves is 'to save their lives' (Ehrenreich, 1983: 140). Steinem (1975: xiv), in an introduction to a book by an early male writer on masculinity, praised 'the enlightened self-interest' of the author, making 'him a more trustworthy feminist ally than any mere supporter or sympathizer could ever be'. Men can thus be trusted if they admit that their own self-interest can be served by feminism.

It is true that patriarchy distorts men's lives as well as women's lives. Many men feel grief and may have been victimized as boys. One has to ask, though, in what ways would a men's movement, organized around men's enlightened self-interests, advance women's struggles? Starhawk (1992: 28–9) fears that men in the men's movement will blame women for their problems and defend their own privileges. Brown (1992: 97–8) is also angry at the tendency of the men's movement to portray men as victims, arguing that the newly developed ability to cry needs to be combined with a commitment to listen to the pain of others. Thus, the risk in arguing that it is in men's interests to change is that men may adopt a strategy that benefits them, rather than focusing on over-coming the oppression of women.

Furthermore, the issue of personal exploration as opposed to activism is a contentious one. Does changing oneself as a man help to challenge patriarchy at the structural level? Does personal change in particular men's practices undermine patriarchal relations? I share Segal's (1990: 283) rejection of rely-ing on the psychological to explain the social and her criticism of the tendency to reduce politics to individual struggles in personal life.

Men's Responsibility for Gender Justice

Starhawk (1992: 28–9) reminds us that if men want to liberate themselves from 'the male malaise' they will have to let go of male privilege, rather than engaging in intrapsychic self-affirmation in ways that avoid awareness of sexism, heterosexism and other forms of social injustice. Men must 'come to understand the injustice that has been done to women [and] the way it distorts all social relations' (Ruether, 1992: 14–15). The struggle to overthrow patri-archy must be a movement of both men and women, in which men must acknowledge the injustice of their historical privilege as men.

hooks's (1992: 13–14) discussion of anti-racist work is relevant here, as she is critical of the view that it is only when those in power understand how they too have been victimized that they will rebel against the structures of domi-nation. She says that 'individuals of great privilege who are in no way victimized are capable via political choices of working on behalf of the oppressed'. Thus, one can reject domination through ethical and political understanding.

Men are extremely sensitive to ethical and moral issues especially when expressed as a belief that they should take care of women. However, if men are inclined to be fair minded, they should look at the overall system and con-struct a notion of what an ethical relationship between men and women would look like (Hite, 1987: 702). The most compelling ethical basis for a rec-onciliation between men and women is the feminist principle 'that women are also persons' (Ehrenreich, 1983: 182). If a man adopts ethical principles regarding dignity and a just society, he is concerned not only about his own partner but also about women in general (Gondolf, 1987: 347). It is important to acknowledge that, throughout history, men have taken principled stands on women's rights.

The Site of Profeminist Men's Politics

Identifying the most appropriate arena for men to engage in this struggle is a major dilemma. The men's movement has been the major arena in which the process of men's change has been discussed, but many feminists have criti-cized that movement. In the early 1980s, some feminists were critical of attempts to unite components of men's liberation and anti-sexism within the one movement. They criticized the view of some anti-sexist men that men's liberationists have 'to start somewhere' and they were doubtful about their belief that the latter would be slowly radicalized. They suggested that this openness to the men's liberationists may – in part – be an expression of their own contradictions. Bradshaw (1982: 188) asserted that anti-sexist men will have problems if they do not dissociate themselves from other men's groups and, as a minimum requirement, they have been asked to make anti-sexist commitments to differentiate themselves from the other groups (Sebestyen, 1982: 232).

Some feminists have contemplated the possibility of a role for men in the feminist struggle. Friedan (1981: 40) argues that women have gone about as far as they can go without alliances in changing men. Wolf (1993: 26) takes a similar position, differentiating between egalitarian and patriarchal men, and argues that 'the civil war of gender does not involve men against women in two distinct sides'. Thus, she sees the fundamental conflict as being between the patriarchs and the egalitarians.

Delphy (1984: 109), on the other hand, criticizes the view that the dividing line is not between men and women but between feminists and anti-feminists. She argues that anti-feminist women are not separated by objective interests the way men are and, while she acknowledges that the support of some men will be useful at times, their support is not seen as an indispensable condition for the success of the women's movement.

Following hooks (1993: 37), however, I believe that men should be part of the feminist movement and that they have a major role to play in the elimination of sexism. Cockburn (1991: 233) supports the view that feminists need to develop practical alliances with supportive men and to work consistently with those who support 'the equality project'. While it may be debatable whether feminists *need* men's political co-operation, I believe that feminism can benefit from the advocacy and alliance of men.

From Feminism to the New Men's Studies

This critical review of feminist theories of men's agency in the reproduction of patriarchal relations demonstrates the extent to which 'the man question' is a source of conflict within feminism itself. The oppressiveness of heterosexual instrumentalism, the use of power and control tactics by men, the prevalence of sexual and physical violence against women, the exploitation of women's labour in the home and the disadvantaged position of women in the paid labour force are all testimony to the validity of feminist analyses. However, unless one is positing a separatist vision of a world without men, women's prospects for liberation require the capacity of men to change.

Whilst feminist analyses have made significant contributions towards understanding men and have articulated positions on the limitations and potential of men to change, they have not theorized or suggested strategic ways forward for men. This is a task that profeminist men can undertake. In challenging men's dominance and hegemonic masculinity, feminism has created the space for men to critically re-evaluate our position. Because of our location in patriarchy, profeminist men can contribute something different in the analysis of how men's dominance is maintained and, consequently, how it can be changed.

While this book departs from those feminist analyses that are pessimistic about men's capacity to change, I locate myself within the feminist tradition. Men have a necessary relationship to feminist theory because it has a purpose in changing us too. Men's sexuality can be loving, caring and nurturing and a non-oppressive heterosexuality is possible for men. I believe that it is also possible for men to work towards an equalization of the authority/power structure in the family and assume equal responsibility for child care and housework. I further believe that men can foster a process of change in workplaces that will support women's struggles for better working conditions. It is important for women to continue to make demands on men and men should respond to these demands for both ethical and enlightened self-interest reasons.

To sustain this argument, however, I must demonstrate that men's subjectivities and practices can break away from the ideologies of male dominance and that changes in men's subjectivities and practices can contribute to the transformation of gender relations.

Whilst I have been inspired and influenced by feminist theorizing about men, this did not in itself provide a theoretical framework for this project, as the subject of 'men' has not been a central priority in feminist theorizing. Furthermore, there are many feminisms and, as I have demonstrated, many feminist theorists who are divided on 'the man question'.

In the context of the feminist debate about men, it is thus necessary to review the dominant theoretical approaches in the masculinity literature, including sex-role theory, Jungian psychology, psychoanalytic theory and materialist theory, and examine their answers as to why men oppress women and whether and how they can change. My purpose here is not to give a comprehensive review of these theories – that has been done elsewhere – but to critically appraise them in terms of what they offer regarding strategies for changing men's subjectivities and the structured gender relations they are enacting.

Sex-Role Theory

The sex-role approach to masculinity utilizes the theoretical ideas underlying liberal feminism, wherein women's disadvantages are said to result from stereotyped customary expectations, internalized by both men and women. Inequalities between men and women are said to be eliminated by giving girls better training and more varied role models (Connell, 1987: 33–4). Furthermore, it is argued that 'just as women are socialized into being submissive, men are socialized into being dominant' (Clatterbaugh, 1990: 43).

Sex-role theory informed the early men's liberation movement of the 1970s, whose theorists maintained that freeing sex-role conventions might also be good for men. Thus, men were encouraged to 'break . . . out of the straight-jacket of sex roles' (Farrell, 1975: 8) and 'to free themselves of the sex-role stereotypes that limit their ability to be human' (Sawyer, 1974: 170). The implication was that men could transform themselves without reference to wider social processes, the male role being something we could dispose of, allowing the human being in the man to emerge.

One of the major limitations of sex-role theory is that it under-emphasizes the economic and political power that men exercise over women. Male and female roles are seen to be equal, thus enabling men and women to engage in a common cause against sex-role oppression. Furthermore, men's resistance to change in both the distribution of power and in the sexual division of labour is ignored. Because of its inability to theorize power and interests, its often implicit dependence on a normative standard case and its lack of historical analysis, I support Connell's (1987: 50) view that sex-role theory should be abandoned as an adequate way of exploring masculinity.

Jungian Theory

Jungian perspectives on masculinity have, in recent years, replaced sex-role theories as the dominant framework informing the men's liberation component of the men's movement. Jung argued that, in addition to the personal unconscious, there is also a collective or universal unconscious, the contents of which are the same for all individuals everywhere (cited in O'Connor, 1985: 21). The patterns lodged in the collective unconscious are called archetypes.

The most central archetype relevant to understanding masculinity is the anima, the archetypal image of the feminine at work in a man's unconscious psyche (McBride, 1980: 27). In Jungian terms, men's feminine traits such as feeling, compassion and intuition become repressed in the interests of the masculine ego, where they are deeply buried in the personal unconscious and are often only able to be expressed as projections on to women.

To change, men are encouraged to reclaim their feminine traits so that they can relate to real women and allow women the space to be themselves (O'Connor, 1985: 133–4). A man must analyse the anima figures of his dreams and fantasies and reflect on his relationships with the women in his life in order to integrate his feminine qualities (McBride, 1980: 33). The re-emergence of the feminine is seen as a necessary compensatory response to the oppressive domination by masculine archetypes (Tacey, 1990: 780).

The premise is that if one has come to terms with both the masculine and feminine qualities within oneself, the problems associated with being a man or a woman in the social world will handle themselves. Some writers have argued that if men express their feminine side and allow themselves to be more vulnerable, they will bring their personal lives into a public domain and relinquish power.

The focus on the integration of the masculine and the feminine assumes that what goes on inside the human mind is of more importance than what goes on in the world (Pratt, 1985: 98). There is no demonstrable link, however, between being vulnerable and soft and giving up power. Jungian theory minimizes the importance of the relationship between the individual and society and has little to say about male social power and patriarchy (Weir, 1987: 36).

Individual personal change will not address the problems of exploitation and power inequality. By focusing on personal change, there seems to be no need to change economic and social structures and men thus settle for individualistic solutions (Kaufman, 1993: 271–2). This seems inevitable when most personal growth and spiritual paths promise individual liberation and fulfilment with not enough attention to, or irrespective of, social and economic conditions. There is no acknowledgement that most of the individual suffering in the world is an experience of oppressions that are related to class, race, sex or sexuality. Thus, I maintain that Jungian theory is also inadequate for theorizing change in gender relations.

Psychoanalytic Theory

Orthodox psychoanalytic theory has had much to answer for in relation to the reinforcement of women's subordination. In the early 1970s it was subjected to numerous feminist critiques, but in 1975 Mitchell (1975: 301–2) wrote a qualified defence of psychoanalytic theory arguing that it was important for feminist struggles because sociological solutions alone would not end women's oppression. For her, dominant ideologies were deeply buried within women's unconscious and psychoanalytic theory was essential in understanding the ways in which these ideologies were internalized.

The most significant development in feminist psychoanalytic theory for understanding masculinity since Mitchell is the work of Chodorow (1978: 106), who argues that father absence creates difficulties for boys to develop their sense of masculinity. In her view, the more the father is absent from the family, the more severe will be his son's conflicts about masculinity and fear of women. She asserts that the experience of being mothered by women leads to a psychology of male dominance and the desire to be superior to women. As men are mothered by women, it reduces their capacity to parent and thus reproduces the sexual division of labour. The implication is that if men become more involved in child rearing, the male personality structure would change leading to the elimination of male dominance in the larger society (1978: 213–19).

A number of male writers have taken up Chodorow's feminist object-relations theory. Most notable are the essays contained in an anthology edited by Humphries and Metcalf (1985). Object-relations theory is used to explore men's anxiety about their gender and sexuality and to offer an explanation about how men's gender-based dominance is reproduced. This anthology represented the culmination of the theoretical position of the Men Against Sexism movement in the UK in the 1970s and 1980s.

Some male writers have used object-relations theory to explain men's violence and sexually aggressive behaviour. Lisak (1991: 260) proposes that there is a relationship between father absence and the prevalence of 'macho' behaviour and violence against women, whilst Frosh (1994: 113) similarly posits that men sexually abuse women because of their abhorrence of the feminine within.

Chodorow and object-relations theory, however, have been criticized on numerous grounds that are relevant to the concerns of this book. For Segal (1987: 151–2), infantile attachment to the mother is only one aspect of the formation of masculinity and the theory ignores the multiplicity of social practices which separate boys from girls. Kellner (1989: 131) similarly argues that Chodorow under-emphasizes the importance of social and ideological structures outside the family, whilst Rutherford (1992: 37) notes that her model of masculine personality fails to take class and race differences into account in the formation of masculinities.

Brittan (1989: 195), in turn, suggests that object-relations theory can be interpreted as blaming women and mothering for reproducing the gender system, thus letting men 'off the hook', and for McMahon (1994: 240) the theory does not adequately take into account men's agency in the maintenance of patriarchy and fails to recognize the extent to which the division of labour is in men's interests.

Even if men engaged in more child care and allowed the 'feminine' side of their personalities more prominence, I question whether this would necessarily lead to a greater level of equality between men and women. Furthermore, according to Segal (1987: 153), violence and discrimination against women are more a result of the inequalities of power between men and women than of intra-psychic dynamics in men.

Whilst it is important to understand men's psyches and their interconnectedness with material factors, I reject Chodorow's view that there is a linear, if not causal, relationship between the male personality structure, with its genesis in parent–son interaction and male dominance. It is thus important that we continue to explore the relationship between men's psyches and the social and material context, enabling us to more adequately address the relationship between personal and social change.

Materialist Theory

In response to the inadequate analyses of men's institutionalized power, a number of writers have emphasized how masculinity is socially reproduced within an historical context of gender relations. Here, masculinity arises from contextualized social activities and is 'the sum of men's characteristic practices at work, with their families, in their communities, in the groups and institutions to which they belong' (Edley and Wetherell, 1995: 96). These writers draw upon Marxist and feminist materialist analyses to understand masculinity.

For Winter and Robert (1980: 252–72), as masculinity and men's roles are more strongly identified with the public or instrumental sphere than femininity and women's roles, they will be more likely to reflect the social–psychological changes brought about by advanced capitalism. Because men are concentrated in the highly rationalized sectors of the labour force, masculinity can be understood as a result of the development of technical reason in advanced industrial societies. As technical rationality in the workplace requires the ability to subjugate one's emotional life to the interests of efficient co-operation, it is necessary for men to find emotional support in the nuclear family.

Such a perspective thus emphasizes the impact of changes in the division of labour and class location on the development of masculinity. Male dominance is explained in socio-economic and structural terms: a consequence of the structure of the current mode of economic production (Edley and Wetherell, 1995: 99). This would suggest that to understand men in patriarchy more completely we must also look at the effects of differing class locations and distinguish between working-class and middle-class masculinities.

In contrast to Marxist perspectives, feminist materialists point out that the sexual division of labour within the home 'is just as pervasive and important for defining masculinity and men's experiences as class divisions in paid work' (Edley and Wetherell, 1995: 115). Hearn (1987: 59–71), for example, argues the importance of sexuality, child rearing, nurturance and care for others as significant practices in the production of masculinity and thus posits a materialist account of reproduction.

Both Marxist and feminist materialist theories share the view that to understand men we have to understand their material and economic position and their social practices both at home and at work.

If masculinity is socially constructed, men have the possibility to change, but in order to change we would have to reconstruct the social relations of gender in both the private and public arenas. It is not enough to bring some sort of 'new man' into existence; we would have to reconstruct the whole gender order by developing new laws, values and organizational forms (Cockburn, 1988: 323). This includes challenging the masculinism of trade unions, political parties and social movements. It also involves openly supporting campaigns against sexual harassment and sexual assault and anti-discrimination policies as well as acting against patriarchy through the creation of anti-sexist groups and networks (Hearn, 1987: 168–70).

What is, however, not elucidated by materialist perspectives is the process by which masculinity 'gets into' men and how men might come to work for these changes; missing in these perspectives are the mechanisms through which men's personality and masculinity come to reflect the socio-economic structure of capitalism and the gender relations of patriarchy. We need to understand the ways in which dominant ideology is internalized in the psyches of men and how this ideology interacts with material conditions to shape men's experience.

Without a conceptual framework encompassing and reflecting the relationship between the lived experience of men and the institutional structures in which they are embedded, the possibilities for transforming men's lives and the social relations of gender are doubtful. One either ends up in despair, immobilized by an overly socially determined self or one posits a voluntarist and idealist view of how men can change ignoring the material and social basis of patriarchy.

This dualism between voluntarism and structural determinism or between agency and structure is perhaps the most pervasive dichotomy in social theory. A significant attempt to address this dualism is Giddens's theory of structuration (1976, 1977, 1984) which rejects both structural determinism and voluntarism.

Structuration refers to 'the dynamic process whereby structures come into being' (Giddens, 1977: 121). Giddens (1976: 161) shows how structures are constituted by human agency and are thus not to be regarded 'as simply placing constraints on human agency, but as enabling'. As people are never governed completely by social forces, they can intervene and make a difference in their social practices. In Giddens's (1984: 70) view, social agents always have the potential to act otherwise than they do.

Giddens's theory of structuration is useful at the conceptual level in demonstrating how structure is constituted by practice and in emphasizing the *capacity* of agents to break the rules and routines which reproduce those structures. It does not, however, address the processes by which agents can break with these structure producing social practices.

Feminism as Postmodern Critical Theory

Dissatisfied with existing theories, I began to read feminist and critical theorist interrogations of postmodernism and poststructuralism. There are many forms of postmodernism reflecting the extent to which they break with notions of modernity and the extent to which they retreat from an emancipatory politics. These distinctions have been variously articulated as 'weak' and 'strong' postmodernism (Benhabib, 1992: 213–25), 'a postmodernism of resistance' and 'a postmodernism of reaction' (Foster, 1983: xi) and 'progressive versus reactionary appropriations' (Giroux, 1990: 16).

In this book, I side with those expressions of postmodern thinking that do not totally abandon the values of modernity and the Enlightenment project of human emancipation. Only 'strong' or 'extreme' forms of postmodern theory reject normative criticism and the usefulness of any forms of commonality underlying diversity. I believe that a 'weak' form of postmodernism informed by critical theory can contribute effectively to the construction of an emancipatory politics concerned with political action and social justice.

I thus began to explore the implications of postmodern feminist and critical theories for the study of men and masculinities. A detailed discussion of these issues is undertaken in Chapter 3. It is appropriate, however, to mention here the way in which this theoretical approach enabled me to rename the issues under investigation.

From a postmodern critical perspective, masculinity is not an inherent property of individuals. Rather, we learn the discursive frameworks and work out how to position ourselves 'correctly' as male (Davies, 1989: 13). Within these frameworks we are invited to take up or turn down different subject positions and a sense of masculine identity that goes with them. That is, each framework enables men to think of themselves as men in particular ways (Jackson, 1990: 286). Such a perspective enables us to identify that the supposedly fixed position between anatomical sexuality and gender stereotypes can be broken. We are thus more able to legitimate behaviours that do not seem to derive from one's biological sex.

Through the recognition of a possible multiplicity of identities for men we are able to challenge the view that it is not in men's interests to change. Men's interests can be reconstructed by men repositioning themselves in the patriarchal discourse and by men constructing alternative profeminist subject positions. The research focus on men and change is thus reframed as a concern with the discursive production of profeminist subject positions for men.

3 Postmodern Feminism and the Critical Study of Men

In recent years feminist theories have all been interrogated by postmodern and poststructural perspectives. There has been considerable debate about the implications of these interrogations for the feminist project of the emancipation of women. Little attention, however, has been given to the implication of these debates for the critical investigation of men.

Early feminist theory assumed that a distinct identity was being denoted through the category of women. This premise informed the political project of radical feminism to re-value the feminine, which patriarchy has devalued, as an alternative basis for social organization (Weedon, 1987: 31). These feminists thus asserted an essential feminine that is repressed by male domination, but within which it would be possible to develop a different and better society. This 'essentialist difference' emphasized the differences between women and men (Barrett, 1987: 37).

Essentialism is usually understood as a belief in fixed properties that allegedly define the nature of things, leading to the idea that women and men can be identified on the basis of eternal, transhistorical, immutable essences (Fuss, 1987: xi). Postmodern feminists, by contrast, challenge the central humanist assumption that men and women have essential natures. They criticize those feminists who attempt to identify distinctly female traits, for example women being more peace-loving and closer to nature than men.

Modernist feminists assume that the term 'woman' denotes a common identity. Postmodern feminists, by contrast, have challenged the notion that there is some essential commonality or bond among women. Spelman (1988: 136) says that, unless she knows more about two women other than the fact that they are women, she cannot really say anything about what they might have in common. Instead, we should only speak of particular women and particular men constructed by historically specific sets of social relations.

Western feminist thought has been charged with taking the experiences of white, middle-class women as normative and representative of all women. Postmodernism provides a basis for avoiding this danger (Nicholson, 1990: 13). The term 'women' is no longer allowed to stand for all women, any more than 'men' is allowed to stand for all members of the human race (Soper, 1990: 13). The generalized opposition of male/female obscures the differences amongst women in behaviour, character, desires, gender identification, sexuality and historical experience; when everything within each category is assumed to be the same, differences within each category are suppressed (Scott, 1988: 40, 45).

While all women may currently occupy the position 'woman', they do not occupy it in the same way. Consolidating all women into a falsely unified 'women' has helped to mask the power that divides women's interests. Women have been and are oppressed, but we need to be ready to abandon the binary thinking that has established women as a group that could be collectively oppressed in a uniform way (Poovey, 1988: 59, 62).

Feminist Postmodernism or Postmodern Feminism?

In response to this critique a number of feminist writers have come forward to defend the category of 'women'. Fuss (1987: xiii, 40) has offered a qualified defence of a particular version of essentialism, arguing that it can be used in the service of both progressive and reactionary discourses. Thus she talks of essentialism*s* and rejects the essentialist/constructivist binarism, acknowledging that hegemonic groups have used essentialism as a political tool against oppressed groups but arguing that in the hands of the oppressed, essentialism can constitute a powerful strategic weapon.

A further critical view contends that postmodernism 'depoliticize(s) the collective struggle against domination' because it undermines 'the political strategy by which the binary dualisms of capital–labour, centre–periphery, male–female and assimilation–ethnic purity are converted into an either/or logic' (Smith, 1992: 505). In rejecting generic categories it is said that all attempts to speak in general for a particular group give way to individualism, thus denying the validity of any political community (Soper, 1990: 13–14). Thus it is claimed that postmodernism makes 'feminist political action impossible' (Mouffe, 1992: 371).

Evans (1990: 462) argues that in spite of the differences between women which often lead women to oppress and exploit one another, there remains an understanding of women that is in the interests of all women to challenge and this challenge is best maintained by the continued focus on sexual difference. While the category 'woman' embraces a multiplicity of experiences, it is still identifiable. Postmodern approaches may prevent discussion between women and prevent them from creating theories that articulate their experience. Rather than assuming that the category 'women' submerges any actual differences, this should be investigated empirically. Hirschmann (1992: 300) distinguishes between feminist postmodernism and postmodern feminism. She agrees with those who argue that the tenets of postmodern theory make the concept of unitary women and feminism impossible, but maintains, I think correctly, that there can be a postmodern feminism that uses deconstruction and other postmodern methods to deconstruct patriarchy and allow the marginalized voices to be heard.

Postmodern Feminism and the Study of Men

While being mindful of the dangers identified in the feminist debates about essentialism and difference in relation to the category of 'women', I am interested in what we can learn from these debates about the category 'men'. If we question the constituency of 'women', then we must equally question the constituency of 'men'. If there is progressive potential in unpacking the term 'women', why not unpack 'men' too? More work needs to be done on the whole category of 'men' and its relation to humanity. The men of white feminism have too often been white, middle-class men, for women who wanted equality with men did not seek equality with non-white men (Phelan, 1991: 128). Thus we should avoid lumping all men together in a uniform category and, when discussing men, we should remember *which* men we are talking about.

To deconstruct men as a category enables us to break down the supposedly fixed position between anatomical sexuality and gender stereotypes. We may be more able to legitimate behaviours that do not seem to derive from one's sex (Poovey, 1988: 59). Thus the progressive potential of a postmodern perspective would be to reveal alternative modes for the construction of masculinities not yet realized (Saco, 1992: 39). Ironically, some feminists suggest that the progressive possibilities for deconstruction may be greater for men than for women. Weedon (1987: 173) argues that it is important for men to deconstruct masculinity and the role that it plays in the reproduction of patriarchal power. She claims that this is politically more important for men who have claimed an objective rationality than it is for women, whose voices have been by this discourse.

Kristeva (1981) argues that only men can put in jeopardy their symbolic position, because only they are subjects with a position to subvert. As men have had their 'Enlightenment' they can more easily afford a sense of decentred self and a humbleness regarding the truth of their claims but for women to adopt such a position would weaken further what has never been strong (Di Stefano, 1990: 75). Indeed, one cannot deconstruct something that has never been fully granted, whereas men have not been denied the status of subject (Braidotti, 1987: 237). Thus some forms of postmodern theory can be used to deconstruct ideologies of male domination.

Deconstructing Men

As demonstrated in Chapter 2, how to theorize men has been a major source of disagreement among women, with much of the early feminist critique resting on a categorical model of gender that regards men as a monolithic identity.

How meaningful is it to talk about men as a homogeneous category? How relevant is it to refer to men as a collectivity with a unitary set of interests? What are the implications of a categorical approach to men? For example, talking about men's interests suggests that all men can be taken as a group in which most or all men are essentially the same. So when it is said that it is in men's interests to maintain gender inequality, does this refer to *all* men or only a specific group of men? When it is said that men control the mode of reproduction, are all men being referred to? What about gay or anti-sexist men? When it is said that men dominate the public sphere, are all men or a particular circle of powerful men with exclusive interests being identified (Brittan, 1989: 108, 198)?

Are all men violent and are all men potential rapists? As previously discussed, answering this affirmatively can produce a sense of guilt, despair and paralysing self-hatred in men. It leaves little room for men to change. Men are even able to accept this view of themselves as a justification for doing nothing since it appears to be a facet of their nature.

One of the difficulties with the statement: 'Men oppress women' is that it makes oppression definitional of men. It implies that men oppress women by virtue of being men. If, instead, we say things like 'Men oppress women because they control the institutions of the state', or 'because they exploit their labour in the home', or 'because they use power and control tactics with them', it seems to imply a possibility for change. If we define men solely as oppressors, all that men can do is to will their own demise as men (Middleton, 1989: 9, 13).

Furthermore, can we assume that all behaviour that takes place between men and women is determined by that one, general gender-based group relation? To talk about gender relations between men and women distracts our attention from issues such as race and class. We should always keep in focus *which* men and *which* women we are talking about.

Diversity and Difference in Men's Lives

We are now entering a new stage in which variations among men are seen as central to the understanding of men's lives. Thus we cannot speak of masculinity as a singular term, but rather should explore masculinities. Men are as socially diverse as women and this diversity entails differences between men in relation to class, ethnicity, age, sexuality, bodily facility, religion, world views, parental/marital status, occupation and propensity for violence.

Differences are also found across cultures and through historical time. Connell (1991: 3) has pointed out that the discourse about 'masculinity' is constructed out of 5 per cent of the world's population of men, in one region of the world, at one moment in history. We know from ethnographic work in different cultures how non-Western masculinities can be very different from the Western norm.

This is not the place for a detailed analysis of difference and diversity issues for men. What is relevant for my purpose here are the implications of a focus on difference for understanding men's oppression of women because these different positions provide differential access to personal and societal power.

Most of the literature on men and masculinity focuses on middle-class professionals and managers and the lives of these men are often taken as representative of masculinity *per se*. Power is not shared equally among men and men's class locations influence the nature of their dominance over women.

In addition to the class bias in the men and masculinity literature, there is also a presumption of whiteness in discussions of men's lives. To address this imbalance, we have seen in recent years, in North America and the UK, accounts of masculinity written from the perspective of black men and men of colour (Mercia and Julien, 1988; Staples, 1989; Gordon, 1993). The writings of black men emphasize the role of racism in the development of white masculinity.

Furthermore, very few books written by heterosexual men have seriously attempted to come to grips with gay liberation arguments. Moreover, most do not acknowledge that mainstream masculinity is heterosexual masculinity. From the gay viewpoint, heterosexual masculinity is a privileged masculinity that is created and maintained by homophobia at the expense of homosexual men and women (Nierenberg, 1987: 132).

Research suggests that men undergo changes throughout the life cycle in relation to their experience of their bodies and in relation to aggression and dominance, as well as shifts in value orientations (Thompson, 1994). These changes have implications for how men position themselves in relation to women.

Men also differ markedly in terms of how they position themselves in relation to feminism. Connell (1991: 15) notes from the men he has interviewed that responses range from 'essentialist rejection' to 'wary endorsement' to 'full blown acceptance'. Clearly men vary in their level of awareness of their oppressive role in relation to women. Organized responses range from men's rights groups which deny that men have power in society, men's liberation groups, where women's issues disappear completely as men search for the 'deep masculine', to profeminist responses, where men embrace the feminist analysis and publicly support women's struggles (Kimmel, 1987: 272–80).

Diversity, Difference and Gender Power

The feminist movement, even as a white, middle-class movement, began to come to terms with debates about race, class and sexuality from the 1970s onwards, while men's leftist movements and men in business and the state have been much slower to respond to issues of difference. Women have more easily managed to reach across class, age and cultural differences than men because as an oppressed group they need to form alliances that strengthen their struggle. Hollway (1989: 129) suggests that women are more easily able to incorporate greater multiplicity than men because of women's relations of otherness to humankind.

Because white, middle-class heterosexual men have had no clearly identifiable common enemy to organize against, they have had less incentive to explore diversity and differences (Orkin, 1993: 22–3). Furthermore, as the more powerful group, these men have no power-maintenance reasons to explore differences amongst themselves. White, middle-class, heterosexual men are the ones who have created various 'others' on to whom their own repressed parts can be projected. This group of men has most difficulty in acknowledging their multiplicity and so identifying with others (Hollway, 1989: 130).

There is a connection between marginalized and oppressed people and 'marginalized and oppressed parts of ourselves' (Ingamells, 1994: 3). The more people acknowledge multiple parts of themselves, the more they will be able to identify with different positions. So when men come to appreciate difference between and within us, we are likely to be more open to the shifts involved in attending to, for example, feminist and anti-racist claims and the categories of 'men' and 'white' and all that they represent are more likely to be challenged (Ferguson, 1993: 179–80).

Where else does this acknowledgement of diversity and difference in men's lives lead us? It could be said that there are problems when we extend a deconstructive analysis from feminism to the politics of masculinity (Middleton, 1989: 14). When criticized by women, men have been very quick to say that one cannot generalize and that all men are different. A common defence among men has been that if all of what women say about men is not true for *them*, then none of it is true. This extreme inductivism is the opposite danger to essentialist deductivism.

The question is whether the recognition of differences between men means that we lose sight of men as a gender. Some would argue that it is not relevant to consider differences in men's experiences, as we may distract attention from *all* men's culpability in the oppression of women (Orkin, 1993: 23). Segal (1990: 205) points out that recognizing a plurality of masculinities does not in itself address the social and political domination of men over women. I am aware of the danger of multiple masculinities becoming a new means of ignoring women.

However, to critique the notion of a homogeneous category of men is not to deny the reality of systematic gender inequality. The fact that men are divided among themselves along ethnic and class lines and enact competing versions of masculinity within the same class or ethnic group only makes the task of analysis more difficult (Brittan, 1989: 141). Indeed, 'the power and domination of men over women persist in many diverse ways, partly through these differences' (Hearn and Collinson, 1994: 115).

Thus emphasis on diversity and difference 'ought not to degenerate into a diversified pluralism that gives insufficient attention to structured patterns of gendered power, control and inequality' (Collinson and Hearn, 1994: 10). Differences among men can only be understood with reference to the structure of the gender order and the recognition of multiple masculinities does not reduce the sociology of masculinity to a postmodern kaleidoscope of lifestyles (Connell, 1992a: 736). Clearly we must avoid the danger of losing sight of patriarchy.

One way to avoid this danger is to theorize men simultaneously 'along two axes, the male–female axis of men's power over women within the marginalized groups, and the male–male axis of non-hegemonic men's relative lack of power *vis-a-vis* hegemonic men' (Brod, 1994: 89). This is consistent with Collinson and Hearn's (1994: 11) exhortation that 'both the unities and differences between men and masculinities as well as their interrelations' should be examined.

The implications of the preceding analysis demonstrate the extent to which the study of masculinities is a study of power relations. Many of these different masculinities stand in different relations to power. Hearn (1987: 90) describes this in terms of 'hierarchic heterosexuality', to acknowledge that some men are more powerful than others. Connell (1987: 92) distinguishes between hegemonic masculinity and various subordinate masculinities. Some men are in positions where they can impose their particular definitions of masculinity on others in order to legitimate and reproduce the social relations that generate their dominance.

Thus, although large numbers of men benefit from patriarchy, they do not all benefit equally. Middle-class, white, heterosexual masculinity is used as the marker against which other masculinities are measured. When Hearn (1992: 3) set out to investigate the ways in which men maintained and reproduced their power in the public sphere, he made it clear that he was referring especially to able-bodied, heterosexual, middle-aged, middle/upper-class, white men. Such men not only dominate women but also dominate different types of men; for example, heterosexual men dominate gay men, upper-class men dominate working-class men, white men dominate men of colour. This domination does not necessarily involve a conscious process of exploitation (although, of course, it may); it exists because of the relative privileges to which heterosexual, upper-class, white men have access.

Clearly, forms of bonding *across* class, race and ethnic lines operate at the expense of women (Kimmel, 1987: 61). Men in general are advantaged through the subordination of women, although, ethnographically speaking, different men are advantaged in different ways. This does not, however, deny the existence of 'anomalies' consistent with the global subordination of women. There are sites, as identified earlier, where women hold power over men or are at least their equals. The intersection of gender with class, sexuality and race relations produces sites where dominant–subordinate relations are more complex; for example, where white heterosexual women are employers of working-class men, patrons of homosexual men or politically dominant over men of colour (Carrigan et al., 1987: 90). Thus, while not all men have power in relation to all women, all men are embedded in power relations, as are all women, since power is ubiquitous.

Trying to understand the complexities of power relations, I have turned to Foucault (1978), who maintains that the traditional dichotomous understanding of power is insufficient. He challenges the polarization of such categories as 'ruler', 'ruled', 'oppressor' and 'oppressed' because they fail to untangle the way in which power is manifested and constituted subjectively.

In his view, power is not a thing or a commodity; it is not something that some groups have and use to control others who are powerless.

Thus, power is not something that is centralized in the state or power elites. Wherever there is power there is resistance (Foucault, 1978: 95). This resistance to power would not necessarily manifest itself as a frontal assault on state institutions. For Foucault, there is no one place where society can be transformed.

Foucault's concept of power has been criticized by numerous feminists. Eisenstein (1988: 18) argues that Foucault's notion of power 'privileges diversity, discontinuity and difference while it silences unity, continuity and similarity'. Lloyd (1993: 439) argues that Foucault's theory is inadequate to an understanding of the continuities between dispersed manifestations of power. Hartsock (1990: 169) also challenges Foucault's concept of power for implying that everyone participates in the operation of power thus inferring that the victims of power are in some way to blame for their oppression. Ramazanoglu (1993: 10) says that by arguing that power is everywhere and available to everyone 'it can encourage us to overlook women's systematic domination by men'. Foucault's analysis is seen as undermining feminist politics because if power is widely diffused through networks of social relations it appears to dissolve the feminist claim that men possess power over women (Ramazanoglu and Holland, 1993: 239).

By contrast, along with Sawicki (1988: 186–90), I argue that Foucault's concept of power is compatible with some feminist perspectives. Although his analysis of power undermines earlier feminist analyses of patriarchy as a monolithic power structure, Foucault's theory can be understood to acknowledge the possibility of gender relations as serving men's interests. While rejecting the idea that power is centralized within a single system (let alone a single position), Foucault (1980: 99) does acknowledge that forms of global domination exist. However, he is concerned with the ways in which decentralized and localized forms of power are shaped by the more global manifestations of power. Such an analysis of power has implications for understanding patriarchy.

The implications of this analysis centres on the importance of studying the multiplicity of discourses and practices that oppress women. Thus, to acknowledge that power is diffused does not mean that men's and women's powers are equal. Materialist insights illustrate how men accrue powers over women from a range of other discourses and practices (Hollway, 1982: 484).

Discourse and Masculine Subjectivities

Foucault (1980: 93) defined discourses as 'historically variable ways of specifying knowledge and truth – what it is possible to speak at a given moment'. They specify sets of rules and the function of these rules is to define what is or is not the case. Thus, the vocabulary of discourses allows choices to be made only within its own rules.

Discourse analysis examines the assumptions, language and myths that underpin particular positions in order to show that discursive practices are ordered according to underlying codes and rules which govern what may be thought or said at any time (Tilley, 1990: 290). For example, socio-biology as a discourse shapes notions of what constitutes normal masculinity and femininity by arguing that certain meanings are the true ones. Often, the prevailing view is only able to prevail because people are unaware that it is only one of several possible alternative views. Certainly in this way the dominant discourse of science has silenced the experiences of women and ethnic groups. Dominant discourses involve processes of domination whereby the oppressed often collude with the oppressor taking for granted their discourse and their definition of the situation (Gitlin, 1989: 106).

Marxists and feminist materialists argue that discourses are not autonomous from social relations (Callinicos, 1985: 87). They maintain that there are real institutional bases to the processes, for example the economy and patriarchal social relations. Capitalist relations of production continue to be the central organizing features of Western society. Commodity production and wage labour for capital still exist and workers are still dominated and exploited (Kellner, 1989: 177). Also, women's oppression is not purely ideological or discursive; it also constitutes a specific material oppression (Moi, 1985: 147). Thus, from a materialist perspective, discourses can be understood as part of the ideological apparatus which operates to legitimate the social order.

Such arguments are often used to discredit discourse analysis (Callinicos, 1985; Sarup, 1992), but many postmodernists would acknowledge that discourses represent political interests and that the most powerful discourses in our society have institutional bases in law (Weedon, 1987: 41, 109). The recognition of discourse as a dimension of the real does not lead to abandoning attempts of understanding an extra-discursive reality.

Extra-discursive factors are those 'which cannot be grasped in the analysis of discourses; it is literally what is outside discourse' (Bailey, 1993: 72). There are extra-discursive phenomena in the form of powerful social forces that have their own logic and cannot be encompassed by discourse theory (Henriques et al., 1984: 109). However, I am concerned here with the way material conditions have effects through discourses.

Discourses make positions available for individuals and these positions are taken up in relation to other people. When taken up, the world is seen from the standpoint of that position and this process involves, among other things, positioning oneself in relation to categories and story-lines. It also involves locating oneself as a member of various sub-classes of categories as distinct from others. So one develops a sense of oneself 'as belonging to the world in certain ways and thus seeing the world from the perspective of one so positioned' (Davies and Harre, 1990: 46–7). Through this process, people can become *fixed* in a position as they are shaped by 'the range of linguistic practices available to them to make sense' of the world (Potter and Wetherall, 1987: 109).

The individual is thus constituted and reconstituted through a variety of discursive practices and changing material circumstances. The relevance of this notion for my argument is that men can reconstitute themselves through a self-conscious and critically reflective practice.

It is within discourses that we are offered subject positions, which convey notions of what it is to be a man or a woman and which constitute our masculinity and femininity (Weedon, 1987: 100). Thus masculinity is not an inherent property of individuals. Rather, we learn the discursive practices of society and work out how to position ourselves as 'male' of a certain type (Davies, 1989: 13). Our masculine sense of ourselves is historically provided in a series of social practices within different discursive frameworks. Within these frameworks we are invited to take up or turn down different subject positions and a sense of masculine identity that goes with them. That is, each framework enables men to think of themselves as men in particular ways (Jackson, 1990: 268).

There is no single patriarchal discourse of masculinity, and a number of contradictory ones are currently available to men. Furthermore, discourses are not all equal in relation to what men '*as subjects* may have invested in them; some subject positions are more compelling for men than others' (Saco, 1992: 24). In this context, hegemonic masculinity may be considered as a dominant discourse.

As discourses compete with each other for the allegiance of individual subjects, however, the accommodation of subjects to particular discourses is never final and is open to challenge and change. Thus the nature of masculinity is one of the key sites of discursive struggle for men (Weedon, 1987: 97–8). As people *choose* positions in discourses, I am interested in why men choose to position themselves as patriarchal subjects in the gender discourses in which they participate. Why is it that some men take certain positions in a discourse rather than others? Under what conditions will men choose to position themselves as non-patriarchal subjects in their discourses? What accounts for the difference between men?

One answer to these questions is that it is a combination of emotional investment and vested interests in the relative power the position offers (Saco, 1992: 35). Hollway (1982: 237) acknowledges that it is in part a result of investments and returns resulting from such discourses, but she also argues that it is a result of the available positions offered by discourses. The relevant implication is that increasing the range of subject positions in a discourse will open up more opportunities for change in men's lives.

Thus, to sum up, masculine subjectivity is understood as a process involving constant negotiation of multiple subjectivities, or fragments thereof, in which men have unequal investments. For example, a man's social identity may comprise being a white, upper-class, heterosexual man. Some identities will be prioritized over others, since 'in a divided society it is very difficult to hold on to numerous composite identities equally at the same time' (Hearn and Collinson, 1994: 111).

Postmodernism, then, decentres the self and promotes the notion of multiple selves, which are fragmented and contradictory (Jackson, 1990: 40). Multiple subject positions resulting from involvement in different discourses lead to individual men being composed of a set of contradictory positionings or subjectivities. This multiplicity of discourses leads to internal conflict and contradiction.

Reforming Masculine Subjectivities

In acknowledging the power of dominant discourses, it is necessary to avoid discourse determinism, whereby individuals are mechanically positioned in discourses, leaving no room to explicate the possibilities for resistance and change. While subjectivity is constructed within discourse, subject positions cannot be predicted as the outcome of specific discourses and dominant discourses can be resisted and challenged, and this resistance is an important stage in the development of alternative subject positions.

Thus we need to develop ways of encouraging resistance. One way of doing this is to study the experiences of men who do resist, for such men demonstrate that they have not accommodated to the dominant discourse and have refused the positionings placed upon them, and this refusal constitutes an important element of human agency. The possibility of agency is opened up to the subject by 'the very act of making visible the discursive threads through which their experience of themselves as specific beings is woven' (Davies, 1993: 12). Some resources must be available, though, for the individual to have agency. These include: a definition of oneself as one who makes sense of the meanings within discourses; access to alternative discursive practices; access to means of bringing about alternative positionings; a belief in one's capacity to reposition oneself; and access to others who will support alternative positionings (Davies, 1990: 359–60).

Thus, while individuals may, under certain circumstances, resist their particular positioning in dominant discourses, these opportunities are shaped by the availability of alternative discourses. One needs then to have knowledge of more than one discourse and to recognize that meaning is plural. This enables some degree of choice on the part of the individual, but 'in order to have a social effect, a discourse must at least be in circulation' (Weedon, 1987: 106, 110).

In this view, one brings about social change through 'the production of new discourses and so new forms of power and new forms of self' (Ramazanoglu, 1993: 24). Even if the possibility of generating new discourses does not exist and a choice of alternative discourses is not available, it is still possible to resist dominant discourses (Weedon, 1987: 106). One is able to do this by working on the contradictions between old and new discourses.

Thus resistances are expressions of contradictions resulting from the exercise of power. The implications for women of the contradictions in patriarchal discourses have been previously acknowledged. Feminism is regarded as a counter-discourse that resists 'the hegemony of male domination [and] utilizes the contradictions in these hegemonic discourses in order to effect their transformation' (Hekman, 1990: 190).

The contradictions in patriarchal discourses equally provide the starting point *for men* to generate counter-discourses. Men's subjectivity is equally contradictory and while men may have a lot to lose by responding to feminism, they also have much to gain, because of the limitations imposed by hegemonic masculinity on their own lives. Furthermore, as women change their positions in patriarchal discourses, the repercussions will interrupt men's positioning as well (Hollway, 1982: 502–3).

The postmodern concept of the decentred subject, then, has greater critical potential for provoking inner change in men than the humanist notion of an innate self. The aim is to decentre the dominating self of traditional masculinity and allow the possibility of fragmented and contradictory multiple selves (Jackson, 1990: 268–9). Thus the task is to destabilize and denaturalize 'the scripts in place and create the space for a variety of different masculinities to be performed' (Gutterman, 1994: 234). The progressive potential of this analysis would be to reveal alternative possibilities for the construction of masculinities not yet realized (Saco, 1992: 39). Profeminism is one such masculinity that has yet to be fully realized.

Changing Men, Changing Gender Relations

Many women have questioned the genuineness of some men's apparent support for feminism. They have argued that there is frequently a large gulf between commitment to egalitarianism in principle and in practice (Thomas, 1990: 153). Feminists can only judge men's words and actions but, as previously discussed, some feminists regard all male praise of feminism as a takeover bid in disguise (Moi, 1989: 184).

Given that men have for centuries denied women the opportunity to have their own space and time to build solidarity, they cannot expect that, all of a sudden, women will appreciate some men's willingness to examine their own experience. Like Burghardt (1982: 111), who confronted this dilemma as a white man working to end racism, I believe that the resolution of this conflict resides in praxis. As a man, I can be involved in fighting sexism and still be viewed as sexist by women, which is an understandable perception for women to have about men. The dilemma can be resolved as profeminist men's activities reveal that they are not as sexist as some women thought and, through their anti-sexist practice, they discover elements of sexism still with them that need attention.

Of course, because of our dominant subject position within patriarchy, forming an alliance with feminism(s) will never be a simple matter. Men's practices in acting against patriarchy will always be problematic as we do not occupy the same position in relation to the dominant power structures as women. On the other hand, there are men who have endeavoured to live according to egalitarian and non-sexist principles. Such men stand in contrast to other men who have not made the slightest concession to feminism (Brittan, 1989: 182). I would argue that these men do not have the same interests as other men, nor do they share the same identity. There is more to us than categories. We have an integrity that cannot be captured in those terms. While men cannot not be oppressors at present, we can do things differently. It is thus important to analyse men both in terms of their individual and their collective practices.

Many of men's positive responses to feminism have been personal and private matters. Men have been able to develop a less oppressive sexuality, become more nurturing in their relationships, abandon violence, take responsibility for child care and housework, and confront power and control issues in their personal relationships. They are able to make significant changes when they begin to recognize the limitations and potential destructiveness of traditional masculinity. Men can change to make their lives more satisfying and longer when they learn how their gender socialization contributes to stress, relationship difficulties and health problems.

Of course, men are also criticized for over-emphasizing this area of change. Most of the current literature about men has a psychological focus. The orientation is on therapy and the use of the healing metaphor to address issues such as the father 'wound' and crises of emotions and personal meaning (Osherson, 1986; Farmer, 1991; Biddulph, 1994). Men's anti-sexist politics have been overshadowed by the more personalized and depoliticized concern with men's emotions and men's roles. The focus on men's problems in their relationships with women and other men and with themselves potentially deflects responsibility from their oppressive behaviours and consequently men can find a way to do nothing (Stoltenberg, 1991: 8–9).

The structural dimension and strategy, however, should not ignore altogether that there will be emotional consequences for men which need to be addressed. Where men's self-esteem is built on a disproportionate access to resources, establishing relations of equality will of necessity initially result in feelings of loss of self-esteem which is something men will need to come to terms with.

Only a few heterosexual men have moved beyond personal change processes to search for a collective politics of gender among men and have recognized that they need to speak out against men's violence against women. Promoting collective responsibility among men to end men's violence is a central principle of many profeminist men's public practice. Profeminist men have been involved in the prevention of rape, speaking out against pornography, working to end men's violence in the home, and organizing in support of women's reproductive freedom. These attempts to develop a counter-sexist politics of heterosexual masculinity have been largely confined to middle-class men and there is much to be done to relate profeminism to the experiences of working-class men. Nevertheless, profeminism for men is one of the major forms of resistance to dominant masculinity.

Conclusion

The most significant implication of the application of critical, postmodern ideas to the study of men is that it enables us to think critically about change in men's subjectivities and practices. It enables us to break from considering men as a homogeneous category and it helps us to understand the multiplicity of ways in which particular men dominate particular women in specific contexts. Establishing a theoretical basis for discerning these different masculinities and their different implications for the oppression of women allows for a more realistic base for the political strategy of recreating men.

Furthermore, by conceiving of these masculinities as discursive phenomena which compete with other discourses for the allegiance of individual men, there is greater potential for provoking inner change in men than the humanist notion of masculinity as an essence. The multiplicity of discourses lead to internal conflicts and contradictions for men, opening up the possibilities for change.

Postmodern feminism also provides us with a way of understanding those men who do depart from patriarchal subject positions. Self-identifying profeminist men are one such group of men. A profeminist commitment among men represents a major form of resistance to dominant masculinity. Profeminist practices by men challenge the standards of identity that give men status in patriarchal discourse and allow identification of alternative subject positions for men to take up. Progressive, straight, white men are one group of men who are rejecting hegemonic masculinity and whose lives and experiences may contribute to our understanding of the process of forming profeminist subjectivities and practices.

PART II

RECREATING MASCULINE SUBJECTIVITIES

4 Constructing Profeminist Subjectivities

An initial response by men to the 'second wave' of the women's movement was to form consciousness-raising groups. Men's consciousness-raising groups have existed in Western countries since the early 1970s, but these first groups had virtually disappeared by the early 1980s. Thus, when men began to return to the processes of consciousness-raising, they knew little of the existence of the earlier groups nor of what they had achieved or why they had failed.

In the 1970s, men's consciousness-raising groups were of two types: men's liberationist and anti-sexist. Men's liberation argued that sexism oppresses both men and women by prescribing stereotyped sex-role behaviours that are dehumanizing and which cause great emotional suffering. They saw consciousness-raising groups as vehicles by which men could get in touch with their feelings, free themselves from sex-role stereotyping, learn to be more caring for other men and struggle together against the imposition of the socially oppressive male role (Hornacek, 1977: 123–4). Men's liberation writers accentuated the negative aspects of the male role, affirming the 'oppressed' rather than the 'oppressor' qualities of being a man. They denied a hierarchical structure of oppression between men and women and gave little attention to the role of men in the oppression of women (Snodgrass, 1977: 138).

In contrast to the above, anti-sexist consciousness-raising groups regarded sexism as an institutionalized way of life in which women were systematically oppressed by men. They pointed out that those who gain considerable material, psychic and other benefits by the subordination of another group ought to be recognized as the oppressors, not as the oppressed. Men's liberationist consciousness-raising was said to support male domination by reinforcing men's sexist consciousness; anti-sexist men's consciousness-raising, by contrast, was designed to support the women's movement by changing men's male supremacist consciousness (Hornacek, 1977: 124).

Schein (1977: 132–4) suggested that, even when there is some level of commitment to feminism, there are dangers in men's consciousness-raising groups. These dangers included collusion against women, misdirecting anger towards women, avoiding challenging other men's sexism and containing the experience within the group.

Anti-sexist consciousness-raising groups came under criticism from many progressive quarters. Some straight leftist men criticized men's groups for their middle-class composition and for what they saw as their preoccupation with personal life. Some gay men criticized men's groups for their reluctance to confront the oppression of women and gay men and, as a consequence, their homophobia. Some feminists criticized men's groups as simply a new form of male bonding that would reproduce patriarchy (Gilding, 1982: 38–9).

Women were thus often suspicious of men getting together in consciousness-raising groups, because they feared that this would be a reassertion of male power in the face of feminism. Such groups could avoid confronting power over women by hiding with men. Anti-sexist men's groups were also accused of uncritically and undifferentially accepting feminist ideas and perceiving women as the sources of political correctness (Intervente, 1981: 148).

In spite of these dilemmas and challenges, though, anti-sexist consciousness-raising was seen by profeminist men as a way to understand their own sexist behaviour, to develop emotional support in other men and to encourage their anti-sexism. As such, these groups had and continue to have the potential to become an important part of profeminist practice by men.

Uncovering Themes Through Consciousness-Raising

Giddens (1992: 117) has observed that men have been 'unable to construct a narrative of self that allows them to come to terms with an increasingly democratized and reordered sphere of personal life'. The stories that the men in the collaborative inquiry group tell here are stories in which they are attempting to do just this. As such, these stories also provide new narratives which in turn have the potential to influence future stories and future lives. These men are self-consciously living the changes in gender relations.

The aim of this phase in the research process was for the men in the group to analyse our position as profeminist men and develop a strategy for how our awareness of the difficult and contradictory position in relation to feminism can be made explicit in theory and practice. This necessarily involved an interrogation of our masculinity and a questioning of the privileges that are afforded to us by our gender.

Thus, during this exploratory phase in the process, we used consciousness-raising as a method to deal collectively with what it means to identify oneself as a profeminist man. We started by generating a series of questions. What are the basic problems that profeminist men face? What are the dilemmas and issues we grapple with as profeminist men? What accounts for these problems and dilemmas, given the gendered structure of society? Why is it that some men take up a profeminist subject position? What kind of subjectivities will support profeminist men's politics?

For many men who support feminism, there is confusion about how they are supposed to act. So, we began the process of identifying dilemmas associated with attempts at living out a profeminist commitment and arising within our own psyches, in personal relationships, in workplaces or connected to our political activism. No attempt was made to resolve the dilemmas we identified; rather, this chapter sets the scene for the more indepth exploration of the issues through memory-work and the further explication of them through dialogues with allies and opponents of profeminism.

The main themes that emerged from these discussions are linked by the logic of the group process which encouraged a critical self-questioning. Thus, while the participants move between issues of sexuality, violence, needs, work, intimacy, identity and change, they are voicing their experience of the associated dilemmas and the contradictions.

Feminist Conscience and Men's Needs

The starting point for discussion was the question of how profeminist men deal with the internal conflicts that evolve if their motivation for change comes primarily from a political and moral stance. It is often said that some of men's behaviours should change, if for no other reason than those behaviours are oppressive to women. Men are thus encouraged to relinquish some of their privileges for ethical reasons, irrespective of whether or not it is in their long-term interests to do so. But what are the consequences of changing only for ethical reasons? Do we repress our needs and desires? Do we become involved in a continual struggle between our needs and our preferred non-patriarchal behaviour?

A number of participants addressed this issue by talking about internal conflicts between profeminist ideals and patriarchally constructed experience. Pat described how this process occurs for him:

> I have a propensity to be lustable and practices that go back to youth. Despair about being driven by this stuff, still realizing the power of it. I walk past a news stand and see a naked woman. Part of me wants to kick the window in and another part of me says 'wow'. I have a very clear understanding of the feminist catch-cry that rape is at the end of every wolf whistle. I understand exactly what they mean. I understand it from my own convoluted experience of that continuum of lusting and fantasizing. What drives it? I started to realise the power, wanting the 'power over', the power hit. It's a big issue for me. I have a clear understanding of that connection between sex, lust and 'power over'.

Here Pat struggled to understand what drove his desire for power over women. Most of the time he is aware of it and he manages it. He has learnt how to interrupt it when it is happening, but it continues to be a struggle in his life. He continued:

> So if this is something a supposedly good bloke like me struggles with, then what about all these other people, people in factories, people who have got poor resources to feel personally centred and empowered? No wonder they go home and beat the wife . . . There's a big issue about being personally centred.

Being 'personally centred' is for Pat a way of resolving this internal conflict. What does he mean by this? He says that he sees a direct correlation between his lack of personal centredness and his desire to take power over women or to lust after them. 'Having power over' and 'lusting after' seem to be the same for Pat. When he is not feeling good about himself he is more likely to want to have sexual power over women.

Biddulph (1994: 55–7) refers to this as 'the creepification' (sic) of men's sexuality, 'the temptation to choose power over women rather than the risky and vulnerable path of meeting them as equals'. For many men, sexuality is so closely identified with power, that it is almost inseparable from it; men learn to experience their sexuality in terms of conquest and power (Seidler, 1989: 39). Profeminist men know this, but this knowledge is often projected on to *other* men.

Doing something about the 'other men' who rape is often a motivating factor for men to get involved in groups like Men Against Sexual Assult. Sometimes this obscures one's own complicity in sexually abusive behaviours, as Graham reflected:

> My dilemma is that three years ago I saw anybody who was a perpetrator as bad and wrong . . . I put a lot of energy into how wrong that was. It's like I threw a boomerang out and it's come back and hit me. Because I have to own the perpetrator that's in me. I've actually connected with that part of me. So my dilemma is how do I stay in a group called Men Against Sexual Assault, where our whole philosophy is against men who do that sort of thing. Yet part of me is connected to that . . . I'd rather not have found that in me . . . But I don't know how that fits with where MASA is.

Graham was realizing that it is important to confront 'the rapist within', to help men understand their complicity in the rape culture (Biernbaum and Weinberg, 1991: 23). Otherwise, by focusing on other 'bad' men, we project the problem and fail to acknowledge our own complicity.

Part of the process of change for men, therefore, is for them to acknowledge their oppressive thoughts and feelings and admit to the ways in which they have been brought up to hate and despise women (Seidler, 1991a: 37). For men to change their experience of sexuality requires a re-educating of their minds and their bodies. Consciousness-raising is one way to do this by 'coming to understand the dynamics of our own experience through which our sexuality has become tied at such a deep level to our need to control other people and particular facets of ourselves' (Seidler, 1989: 43).

There is, therefore, a conflict between changing men's behaviour on the basis of a moral and ethical stance and dealing with their needs and desires. Many men responded to feminism by feeling guilty about themselves as if the only course open to them were to renounce their masculinity. This involved, for some men, a false identification with feminism and a further estrangement from their experience as men (Seidler, 1991b: 6). As a consequence, the only valid political role for men in sexual politics was seen as servicing the women's movement.

A men's consciousness-raising group does not make sense simply as a place to feel guilty about being a male. The group has to work for the men themselves and not be simply an adjunct to women's liberation (Benson, 1981: 153). This is one of the ongoing issues with which many anti-sexist men's groups struggle. How are we to maintain a balance between anti-sexist activities focused on the oppression of women and more self-oriented activities? The aim is to achieve an anti-sexist practice that does not become a rigid moralism and to attain a vision of men's liberation that does not dis-solve a recognition of the larger relationships of power and subordination (Seidler, 1991c: xii–xiii).

There are problems associated with the anti-sexist strategy of promoting a moral position which stresses the necessity for men to change. Whilst the assumption is that men have a moral propensity to undermine the relations that privilege them, such an anti-sexist practice is based neither on our terms nor on men's interests, but on women's terms. It depends upon men negating their own interests and demands a high degree of self-denial (Rutherford, 1992: 47, 57–9).

As many writers have pointed out, we cannot wish away angry and violent impulses or tendencies to dominate and control, but it is necessary to expose and critically analyse them (Seidler, 1991a: 132). We have to acknowledge that we cannot create a progressive sexual politics solely out of our ideals; we have to be able to live the changes out in our lives.

Men can be consciously profeminist and still have partially unconscious patriarchal desires. As discussed earlier, these splits can be understood as men being caught between profeminist and patriarchal discourses which demand contradictory things from them. In addition, as men begin to change their subject positions and live out a profeminist commitment, both with women and with other men, they often feel that they are 'not doing enough'.

'Not Doing Enough'

A recurring theme running through the discussions with the participants can be encapsulated by the question: 'am I doing enough'? Ray, for example, described a situation at his work where he had taken on additional responsi-bilities to enable a female colleague to free up time to complete a higher degree, but she had not used this time to pursue her study as planned:

So I'm caught in this dilemma about where my boundaries are. How do I work out when to say 'I'm going to give you the opportunity to do things', and on the other hand saying 'I'm finding this really difficult'. I've said that to her gently on a couple of occasions. How do I negotiate those situations? How do I say with women who I'm trying to support and develop a feminist relationship with: 'This is it. I can't do any more.' And how do I handle the feelings that come up when that gets stuffed up? It comes up in my relationship with my partner. To what extent do I stand up for myself in the relationship and to what extent do I give over in terms of knowing her circumstances and her issues?

Adam identified closely with Ray's dilemma, especially in terms of his intimate relationship. How much does he sacrifice to have his partner's needs met? How much does he see to ensuring that his own needs are met? This was an issue with which many of the men identified.

For profeminist men who are in intimate relationships with women, we carry in addition to our own oppressive behaviours, projections of our partners' experiences with other men, whether they be fathers, previous lovers or workplace colleagues. Should we accept some level of projection from our partners? In addition to responsibility for our own individual behaviour, should we also carry an element of responsibility for the negative impact that other men have had or continue to have on our partners? I posed the question of how you untangle these issues. Alan commented:

Herein lays the difficulty of relationships. I mean that's part of what's going on. For me, one part of it is gradually getting to know myself and my own stuff that I want to put on to her as separate and then hopefully over time knowing her and letting her know me. So we can see what belongs to her and I together and what belongs with other things that we need to deal with separately. But there's no doubt, it's a mess.

A number of questions arose from this issue. How much should individual profeminist men compensate women's structural disadvantage and their experience with other men? How much privilege do individual men give up? How much do they cast their own needs aside? Do they have to respond selflessly to women's needs all the time? What do they do if women do not make use of the 'gift' or what if it is not appreciated?

As men take their fair share of responsibility for both domestic work and equitable relations in the workplace, it will often feel like carrying an extra burden. This is one of the costs of relinquishing privilege. On the other hand, the extent to which profeminist men should take 'more' than their share to compensate for previous ongoing structural disadvantages poses a different set of considerations to be addressed.

Working with and relating to men is the other side of the dilemma about whether men are doing enough. In the following extract, Phillip talked about dilemmas in dealing with the problem of denial in men who are violent:

I'm doing groups with perpetrators. They spend the first five to ten weeks in denial stage. They might have a lot of ideas about equality and respect in relations and how they might do that but they always come around to saying: 'Oh yes but women are this or that.'

The issue is, am I doing enough? . . . How much do I let it go? You can't pick up everything. You'll get out there and say: 'Hey get a few things straight.' You'll get some particular bloke who thinks he's been hard done by in the separation, who'll just go on and on and on about it. You can take all the group time to confront him . . . and get nowhere. But then you're worried about the other guys picking up on him and you hear him getting some followers. The personal dilemma is: am I doing enough? Because I'm hearing these things that I disagree with that I'm letting go.

Phillip identified a political problem in men's violence counselling which feminist women have observed as a collusion between counsellors and perpetrators in men's groups. Bathrick and Kaufman (1990: 113), who work with violent men, audiotaped group sessions for their female supervisors who challenged the way in which they did not confront assumptions of privilege and dominance. If we do not confront men's abusive and sexist behaviour, are we colluding with that behaviour? This is a problem for relations between men more generally, especially when being confronted with the ubiquitous challenge of just being 'politically correct'.

How confronting should we be with other men? Tony spoke of the tension of saying to men that they should get in touch with their part in the patriarchal world, while at the same time wanting to bring men together in a way that doesn't frighten them off. How do we invite men to examine their behaviour without increasing their resistance? We acknowledged that this was a problem for us as well. How do we deal with the various levels of our denial about our oppressive behaviours?

Part of the resolution of this issue is to begin to recognize and articulate the various levels of resistance and change. We were attempting to grapple here with the unconscious level of resistance. In doing this work, a question was raised about the validity of men's experience.

Personal Experience and Male Dominance

A crucial element of feminist methodology has always been to validate the experience of women. But what about the experience of men? To what extent can profeminist men trust their experience of the world, given that many of us occupy positions of dominance in relation to women? Can we accept our account of our own experience?

This issue became a central focus of discussion in the group. In response to Michael's comment that he did not always trust his experience, Pat asked: 'So the question that begs there is: what do you trust?' Michael said that it often came down to his motivation:

Why am I doing what I'm doing? Am I doing it for reasons that feel grounded and true or am I doing it for dubious reasons? Sometimes I like the answers I get to the questions and sometimes I do not.

Those of us who struggle against our positions of dominance in social relations sometimes try hard to 'get it right', to act in ways that the subordinated group finds acceptable. If, however, we focus on 'getting it right' for them, we may do so for the wrong reasons and there are times when we might 'get it wrong' but act out of motivations that are grounded in our own sense of integrity.

Ray said 'OK. I can say I'm following my trust and my intuition but can I trust my trust?' There was laughter in response. 'I'm in a dominant position in a patriarchal system.' Pat interrupted with 'If you can't trust your trust, what can you trust?' There was more laughter at this point, although Pat's question was serious. Ben then brought the conversation back to my original question: 'Do we have to set moral standards to move forwards? Can we hope that there's something inside here that we can hopefully go back to to connect with?' Ben was immediately supported by Peter:

> This is a very interesting question for me too. One of the most dangerous things patriarchy does is deny people's experience. We learn to deny our own experience and pick up this role we're supposed to do. To be able to trust your own experience is absolutely essential in my opinion.

Peter went on to qualify his comment: we need to look at our experience critically but we have to start with our experience first. He believed that trust is essential for men if they are committed to change but did not believe that a moral commitment will sustain men. Pat asked: 'If you don't trust your own trust, how are you going to trust anyone else? How are you going to build life nurturing bridges with our brothers and our sisters?'

Tony said that he often found it easier to trust others than he did himself, leading into a discussion of whether we should trust the oppressed, that is, women and their experience, more than we trust our own, as we are the oppressors. Do women understand men's experience better than men do? Peter was quick to comment: 'A woman can't connect with my experience. You can paint a broad brush. Women have painted us as a blue. But what shade of blue are we? How do we feel being that blue colour?'

Graham argued that men have a better understanding of where they are because women cannot know their experiences but they 'understand better where men could be'. He believed that some women have a better vision of how gender relations could be different and how men could be with them. There was a rather unqualified privileging of men's experience, in Graham's earlier comment, that some in the group expressed discomfort with.

Ray asked whether the recognition of an experience he has necessarily involves its interpretation; if that was so, he had problems with trusting his experience because his interpretation is patriarchally constructed. When questioned, he acknowledged that his moral frameworks for understanding experience are not only shaped by patriarchy. Common explanations for what his experience means are likely to be patriarchal, but if he reflects critically and looks at alternative interpretations, he may be able to posit a non-patriarchal stance.

The notion of what constituted experience was problematic in the discussion. Phillip challenged Ray for separating his experience from moral understanding. For him, understanding was a part of his experience. He argued that many men denied their experience and they maintained patriarchy 'by not seeing what's happening'. In his view, before you could trust your experience, you would have to acknowledge it and there was support in the group for this view. Graham argued that it was important 'to own what is before we go to where it should be'. Ben agreed, saying that 'there's a need to start with ourselves before we go out there with the programme'. He talked about the importance of asking himself: 'When do I find I'm being dominating? When do I find I'm not listening to women?'

There was a sense of excitement in this discussion as participants felt that new questions were being asked and new interpretations were attempted. The nature of our experience seemed central to our dilemmas. Where do interpretative frameworks fit within the context of our experience? What does acknowledging or owning our experience mean? What does it mean to problematize our experience?

This discussion evoked the central dilemma as to whether men's accounts must always be suspect. Seidler (1994: 107–11) argues against the radical feminist view that men's accounts of their own experience should never be trusted as that could imply that men do not have to learn to take responsibility for themselves. We should, thus, not automatically discount men's accounts of their experience. On the other hand, how do we subject this experience to critical scrutiny?

Consciousness-raising can help men to reclaim a connection to the aspects of our experience which our culture marginalizes and compels us to negate, but this involves challenging those men for whom direct experience is thought to speak for itself. There is a tendency to privilege 'raw authentic experience' over an understanding of the role played by socially and culturally specific interpretation. No experience is unmediated and it can never guarantee the truth because it is always open to contradictory and conflicting interpretations (McLaren and da Silva, 1993: 60–2). Furthermore, individuals do not always have adequate knowledge to explain everything that is relevant to understanding their lives.

Alary (1990: 227) usefully distinguishes between four stages in experience: lived experience, described experience, pondered experience and conceptualized experience. The latter stage constitutes a form of critical knowledge which enables us to determine what is right and just. It is the construction of critical knowledge, through the process just described, that contributes to the construction of a profeminist men's standpoint elaborated in Chapter 1. This

notion of critical knowledge also helped the group answer another recurring
question.

Motivating Men to Change

Connell (1987: 266–7) makes the point that it is difficult to construct a social
movement that is based on the attempt to dismantle men's own interests, and
Morgan (1992: 39) adds that, while the awareness of being oppressed can
often lead to effective change, the process is quite different for the oppressor.
He suggests that the motivation for men to change is more likely to be from
an ethical rather than an experiential position.

Thus, men's consciousness-raising cannot proceed along the same path as
women's liberation. Because of the hegemony of masculinity, men are
unlikely to share the excitement of self-expression which women discovered.
For men, it is often a process of gaining some self-distance from within patriarchal culture.

We grappled with this issue in the group: it involved a commitment to
challenge 'internalized domination' or 'the incorporation and acceptance by
individuals within a dominant group of prejudices against others' (Pheterson,
1986: 148). On the other hand, the very decision to participate in an anti-
sexist group already reflects a degree of readiness to do this. All of the men
who joined this group assumed that they occupied some degree of privilege
relative to women. Participants already understood something about 'how
interactive dynamics and cultural imagery perpetuate oppression and [were]
committed to social justice enough to want to change them' (Young, 1990:
255). *How* to do this, however, is problematical, as Adam identified:

> I've been thinking how interesting it is that all of us represented here are all repre-
> sentative of the dominant culture. We're all white males in a white supremacist
> patriarchy, trying in some form or another to identify as profeminist men, as dif-
> ferent to representatives of the oppressors. Where's our standpoint in that process
> of identification? We're shifting our standpoint from saying: 'Well I don't want to
> represent the patriarchy. I don't want to represent white, male domination. I want
> to shift that to something else' . . . I've read lots of testimonies of people being
> oppressed. But it's very interesting to read some really personal stuff of being put
> in the opposite situation . . . wanting to have power over women.

Of course, this is not only a dilemma for men; it is an issue that white,
heterosexual women also face in relation to women of colour and lesbian
women. How do you establish a standpoint when you occupy a position of
dominance? If you experience an oppression, the process of sorting out your
position involves a clearer process.

If you are a black, lesbian woman, you can identify with those three con-
stituencies and organize against a racist, homophobic and sexist society and
thus set out to achieve the interests of the group with which you identify. If,

on the other hand, you are one of the 'oppressors', but support the interests of the oppressed, your source of identity is not clear at all. Nevertheless, the position of dominance has its costs, as Tony pointed out: 'An oppressor constituency seems to be loaded with contradictions itself . . . I don't feel like we were born oppressors. We were trained to be. Part of the ways of learning to be oppressors are oppressive in themselves.'

Peter argued that the main questions were: 'Why are we discontented? Why are we seeking to shift ourselves? What's wrong with being an oppressor?' What he found most difficult about being the oppressor was the experience of separation it caused. He felt separated from people in relationships and estranged from himself: 'For example, a woman who doesn't want to have anything to do with me because I'm a man. If I talk over somebody, it instantly creates resentment which creates separation. What motivates me to do things is my desire to connect with people.'

Tony's and Peter's comments challenged the notion that change will *always* be resisted by those who are privileged. Peter identified the contradiction between the benefits of patriarchy and the costs for men and he demonstrated that men can also desire to break with distorted human relations. They can desire to do this for both ethical and enlightened self-interest reasons, as illustrated by the following responses to the question raised in the group: 'Why are we profeminist?'

Peter commented that being profeminist for him is 'supporting the process of women's empowerment, supporting women in the right to choose how they define themselves', and he added that his involvement with feminism has been empowering for him as well.

Tony said that feminism had helped him to understand the values that are embraced by men, like competition, domination and control over our feelings. Seeing himself as profeminist was a way of expressing that he did not value those things. He also felt empowered through being profeminist.

Harry reflected upon being trained in male-dominated beliefs and how for many years he acted accordingly. By participating in the group he was 'making a certain declaration that I wish to be an agent of change'. He did not want his daughters to have to operate in the sort of world that he was a part of: 'It was very competitive, very dominating, very controlling and homophobic and so on.' As he grew older, he discovered that his assumptions and his actions were inadequate:

> They lead to more and more difficulty in as much as other people weren't able to have a place in the sun and that my own place in the sun became more and more obscure. It didn't become lighter. It became darker. This was counter-productive.

Through his involvement with feminist women, Harry saw that there were other ways of looking at the world and other ways of acting and he was forced to re-appraise what had happened to him and to the women around him.

Bruce indicated that the main motivation for him to be profeminist was a sense of compassion: 'Feminist analysis gives me a way of understanding women's experience in the world, in a way that I would not normally come across.' Feminism had helped him to understand: 'what is going on in terms of personal relationships, in terms of the power behind it, and how men can become close to women and have more fulfilling relationships'. It had also enabled him to understand the structural level of power relations where men control and make decisions about how society operates.

Michael responded by saying that for him feminism had been important at two different levels. It had helped him to develop a greater clarity of how he related to women and how it had given him a lens through which to make sense of his relationships with women: 'It enabled me to develop a clearer vision about how relationships with women could be different.' He also acknowledged that it had been painful too, as it meant giving up some forms of social power: 'In relinquishing that social power it has been painful because I had previously constructed my identity around having it. But in place of it, I felt more empowered at another level.' In addition, he said that feminism had helped him to understand his relationships with men more clearly and how he wanted them to be different.

As articulated here, profeminism derived from a compassion and empathy with women and a desire to be supportive of their efforts to achieve equality. It has provided insight into relations with women and how they can be improved and it was felt to be empowering for men.

It is obvious that although men enjoy privileges as a result of their domi-nance over women, 'they also typically owe their profoundest experiences of love to women – through their mothers, sisters, lovers, wives and daugh-ters . . . the victims of male dominance are also the object of filial, heterosexual and paternal love' (Brenkman, 1993: 190). Thus, heterosexual men may be encouraged to change because they want better lives for the women in their lives.

It is not *only* ethical reasons that lead men to challenge patriarchy. Some men do recognize that non-patriarchal subjectivities and practices can be in men's interests as well, but this requires us to problematize the nature of these interests as examined in discussion of the following theme.

Why Men Resist Change

In spite of the potential gains, many men resist the process of change advo-cated here. I thus raised the question of *why* do these men resist change? In what ways is it *not* in their interests to be profeminist?

Peter argued that most men have not heard what feminism is saying yet; in his view, these men do not understand feminism. Alan believed that most men lack opportunities to talk with women and men about the issues we grapple with and that many men would not know the first step to take to have these discussions. Ben thought that men are socialized and pressured to reject fem-inism, especially by other men who want them 'to get back into line'.

Most men lack consciousness of their dominant position and those of us who have it can easily slip back. Phillip noted that 'every now and then I get a jolt, because I realize I'm assuming things as a patriarchal male oppressor' and it happened typically with women he was close to.

Gary also talked about the difficulty of sustaining his profeminism and how easy it was for him to drop back out of it. He knew many men who would say, 'Yes I used to do that', as though it was a phase that they went through. But how do you get men to stay with it? He reflected 'I don't often feel I get a great sense of support from other men, being profeminist', and further noted that most social movements are motivated and sustained by self-interest. He talked about our difficulty in trying to come up with something different, when 'we are men who are basically at the top of the heap'. In his observation, sustaining the commitment does not last, at which point Michael commented: 'Some men seem to want to have it both ways. They want to continue to be at the top of the heap, but they want to feel better about being at the top of the heap.' This comment generated quite a lot of laughter in the group. Michael went on to talk about how men want to improve the quality of their relationships, but want to do it in a way that does not involve relinquishing their social power, which, he acknowledged, is painful.

Phillip reiterated that most groups were based on self-interest but Ben argued that it depended on how we identified our 'true needs'. In his view, a lot of men were unable to identify the advantages of equal relations and they thus found it hard 'to understand the benefits of being true to yourself'. Ben thus grappled with the idea of conceiving self-interest differently which would involve a reconstruction of men's subjectivity. Peter suggested that we should see our oppressor role as a weakness, to which Adam agreed, adding that moving away from the oppressor role is a strength which involves a process of redefining weakness and strength. Recognizing one's weakness is a necessary first step, as Peter commented: 'When I'm not feeling good about myself, images of women come to me much more strongly. I have more needs and a much stronger desire to be with women.' This is a comment that would be reiterated at different times by other participants as well. It is as though men lose a sense of strength within themselves and that their dependency on and desire for women is in some way connected to this loss.

While the oppressor may be within us, we have the capacity to challenge the dominant definitions of truth and to point towards an analysis that can lead to an alternative vision (Lorde, 1984: 58). The process of change for men is emotionally painful as there are losses for them and because change is in conflict with men's interests as they have been constituted. In the process of this change, however, men come to reconstitute their interests and they come to redefine what it is to be a man.

Redeeming Manhood?

At the beginning of one of the early meetings, I raised the question about whether we always thought of ourselves as men. Were there times when we were *more* conscious of being a man?

Bruce said that it was an interesting question, 'When do I most feel like a man?' What came to mind for him was being with other men and talking about mechanics and cars, but he said that he was often conscious of 'playing along with them'. He talked about observing himself being a man. This is almost like 'performing' as a man, consciously enacting a notion of manhood that he knew is a mask.

Phillip's notion of manhood was connected to doing 'manly' things, like fixing his car and spending time with his son who is interested in traditional male activities. Manuel, the only gay member of the group, talked about how, when younger, he tried to display behaviour that was deemed to be masculine. He no longer felt the need to do that: 'Sometimes I'll go in the opposite direction for shock value and I love getting responses.' He believed that it depended on how comfortable you were with yourself.

Michael talked about his experience of leaving school at 14 and working in factories until he was 20. During that time, he worked with much older men and had no peer culture. He talked about his estrangement from the masculinity of the workplace and yet how he also sought to affirm his masculinity through the hard physical labour: 'I was affirming my masculinity by demonstrating that I could hack this alienating work and I was proving I was a man.' The reality was that, the more he felt the need to prove himself as a man, the more alienated he felt from that culture of manhood.

Phillip related strongly to the sense of being enveloped in a male culture as a teenager: 'I think it is a common experience to feel that we are in this culture, but not part of it.' Peter also remembered growing up and how, when you got to a certain age, you were supposed to turn from a boy into a man, but that never happened to him. 'I never felt like a man. I could never feel comfortable being referred to as a man.' Even when he had passed that age of transition he still felt like a boy, and it is only in the last few years that he has been able to say, 'Yes, I am a man'.

In each of these comments, there was an ambivalence and negative connotation in identifying with 'being a man'. Does profeminism necessarily entail a dis-identification with manhood? Stoltenberg (1993: xiv) argues that manhood cannot co-exist with 'authentic and passionate and integrated selfhood'. He maintains that men should refuse to believe in manhood as an ethical position to resist the injustice that is done in its name (1993: 304).

Can manhood then be redeemed or reconstructed? This question led us to reconsider notions of the self and subjectivity in the context of the participants' experiences.

Multiple Subjectivities, Multiple Masculinities

Towards the end of one of the early meetings, a number of us began to talk about dialogues within ourselves. I came to understand this discussion through the notion of multiple subjectivities and the way in which individual men's contradictory subjectivities can lead to internal conflict (Gutterman, 1994: 220).

Phillip talked of having 'this inner person inside me', whilst Peter commented that he had lots of inner voices. This was greeted by laughter, but it was a laughter of recognition. Michael talked about his experience of moving in and out of different voices; in some of the voices he felt more 'grounded' than others. Sometimes, he felt a conflict between a 'grounded' voice and a voice that would lead him to feeling awful about himself. He was grappling with the internal split between what he desired and what he judged to be developmental for him as a person. Peter related closely to this experience:

> The way that my particular behaviour comes out is where one of those things just comes up and grabs me and just goes for it. One of those voices goes straight and I just go with it. It's not a considered thing. It's not a choice at all. But other times when I'm feeling quite grounded and quite good and clear about where I am, this voice comes up and says something and another one will come up and I can choose out of all that. And I still might be wrong, but it has more chance of creating something better.

When in a more reflective mood, Ben was aware of the different voices inside him – voices that come from social expectations, put-downs, patriarchal norms and physical desires – but when out in the public world 'there are a few that tend to dominate. And I suppose I see the challenge for me is to be able to re-balance those so that the ones which I feel are morally favourable are the dominant ones.' In Ben's view, a lot of men listen to the voices that lead them to dominate, as domination is, for them, the process to get their needs met. But how do you get men like that to look at another way? Most men, he said, are not used to 'unpacking the fact that these tensions exist'. This process requires some level of critical reflection, a capacity to step back and question one's experience within a supportive context.

Stoltenberg (1993: 141) conceptualizes this internal conflict as being between a selfhood 'I' and a manhood 'I'. 'You decide moment to moment whether to favour your selfhood or whether to favour your manhood.' Whilst this may sound overly simplistic, there are parts of men that are committed, on the one hand, to feminist goals and visions and, on the other hand, there are parts of men that are influenced by traditional norms and privileges. How can we encourage men to affirm the former and dis-identify with the latter?

Conclusion

The men in this study are involved in a process of re-forming their subjectivities and their practices in the wake of feminist critique and challenge. Through the conversations reported here, these men reveal what it means for them to be profeminist. They tell us something about the personal and political implications of being a profeminist man at this historical moment, thus demonstrating that non-patriarchal subjectivities are available to men. These subjectivities, however, involve dilemmas and contradictions, for they are formed out of conflicting discourses and practices.

I believe that through the process of anti-patriarchal consciousness-raising of the kind described here, men can work on these contradictions even without being able to finally resolve them, given their external/internal dialectic. Thus, although consciousness-raising is concerned with personal change, such a process is a necessary part of the struggle for social transformation. The social dimensions and historical shifts of masculinities can be clarified through anti-patriarchal consciousness-raising. Consciousness-raising groups provide a link between personal experience and the wider social context of men's lives. It is through consciousness-raising that we have been able to formulate new questions and it should therefore not be seen as outdated and of less relevance to men today.

The process of inquiry described in this chapter is but one step in the process of social change. Consciousness-raising groups on their own are not enough. There is the danger of becoming preoccupied with personal change at the expense of challenging social structures. Men's profeminist politics has been overshadowed by men's concern with emotions and personal life. The question is: how do men move beyond personal change to articulate a collective politics of gender among men? Anti-patriarchal consciousness-raising is an important step in that process. If we want to disrupt old cultural patterns and create new ones, we must deal with individual psyches and discursive practices as well as with social structures (Davies, 1993: 198).

Our vision of the world would alter if we believed in the possibility of more men becoming profeminist, but the very idea of profeminist positioning is ignored and denied by the dominant culture (Vorlicky, 1990: 276, 288). Profeminism, as a subject position, has yet to be fully realized, and to fully realize it will require the promotion and extension of profeminist discourses and this will be the subject of both psychological transformation and political struggle.

Profeminism should not be seen as an end point in men's journey towards partnership with women. In the context of men's patriarchal positionings, profeminism provides, at least, a 'counter-narrative' for men to position themselves against hegemonic masculinity and thus provide a starting-point for men to constitute non-patriarchal subjectivities and practices.

5 Recreating Sonhood

The reproduction of patriarchal gender relations is not inevitable in families. Sometimes sons will break with patriarchal traditions because they recognize the destructive consequences for their lives and the lives of women. Sons can construct their masculine subjectivity through dis-identification with patriarchal fatherhood and through empathy with the experiences of their mothers. This chapter is based on memory-work amongst participants exploring these issues by examining tensions in father–son and mother–son relationships. It is especially concerned with theorizing how these experiences can contribute to profeminist subjectivities and practices.

The first part of the chapter examines how memories associated with discontent in father–son relationships and the ensuing group discussions enabled the research group to identify the construction of some of the ways in which patriarchy is transmitted from father to son. It focuses on how men make sense of their experiences of abuse in their relationships with their fathers. In the second part of the chapter, I explore how memories associated with ambivalence in mother–son relationships led us to re-examine our feelings towards our mothers and how they have influenced our relationships with women.

Sons and Fathers

How important is a boy's identification with his father? There is a widespread assumption that boys need to identify with their fathers to acquire their masculinity and, if they do not, it is assumed that they will have personality and gender problems (Brittan, 1989: 33). Numerous writers on men and masculinity claim that there is a relationship between fathers' physical and emotional absence from their sons and boys' personal and social behaviour. In the 1970s, there was a strongly held view by some theorists that children in fatherless families were more likely to become juvenile delinquents and that the psychological effects of father absence and the lack of a male role-model were likely to impair a boy's sense of his masculinity (Herzog and Sudia, 1971: 13–16). In addition, too much mothering and 'inadequate fathering' was thought to lead to overt aggression (Hamilton, 1977: 28) and homosexuality (Pleck, 1987: 92).

The Father Wound

In more recent writing on men, the major emphasis has been on the significance of the father 'wound' or father 'hunger', suggesting that most men
carry deep wounds as a result of their relationships with their fathers. The
most damaging of these wounds is said to be caused by fathers' remoteness
and absence (Farmer, 1991: 24–5). Corneau (1991: 13) argues that lack of
fatherly attention leads to the son's inability 'to identify with his father as a
means of establishing his own masculine identity' and, consequently, such a
son 'is unable to advance to adulthood'.

Some feminist writers have also argued that greater involvement of men in
child care would lead to a decrease in men's violence against women. Horsfall
(1991: 98) argues that fathers' physical and emotional distance from their sons
creates difficulties with gender identity for the sons. In her view, the greater
the emotional distance, the lower the male self-esteem and the greater the
insecurity about masculinity, hence rendering it more likely that men will be
violent towards women. Miedzian (1992: 82) adopts a similar position arguing that 'high levels of violent behaviour are frequently linked to a boy's
having had inadequate fathering'. These views are supported by Lisak's (1991:
249) research into rapists' relationships with their fathers, which were marked
by physical abusiveness, physical and emotional distance and unavailability.

What is it about the fathers' role that is seen as significant in shaping the
gender identity of sons? The research of Emihovich et al. (1984: 867) in the
1980s revealed that fathers held very traditional sex-role beliefs and expectations
and that these clearly influenced their sons' beliefs. Their findings are consistent
with the research cited by Miedzian (1992: 85) that reveals that fathers are dis-
turbed by any of their sons' behaviour that is not typically masculine.

Furthermore, whilst this literature advocates greater involvement of
fathers with their children, it also encourages clear distinctions between men's
and women's roles: fathers are expected to be the main transmitters of culturally approved forms of masculinity to their sons. Thus, it is not clear
whether greater involvement of men in child care would break down traditional sex-roles or reinforce them (Pleck, 1987: 92–4).

Taubman (1986: 16–17) argues that men's attitudes towards women will
become less patriarchal and more egalitarian as a result of men becoming
more involved in parenting, but Wilson's (1990: 135) research challenges this
view. His study of single fathers showed that the men's relatively high level of
involvement with their children did not influence their patriarchal attitudes
towards women. Many men, interviewed by White, whose fathers had not
deserted their families would have preferred that their fathers had not been
present (cited in Silverstein and Rashbaum, 1994: 238). Some boys may be
better off if their fathers are not available.

Children learn relations of power and domination by observing the relationship of their parents. The majority of respondents to Hite's (1994: 369)
survey report second-class treatment of the mother by the father. As children
observe the father being able to make unreciprocated claims upon the mother,

the boys may come to regard a man 'as someone able to get certain services from a woman', leading to 'a sense of male entitlement'. Men can come to believe that they deserve something from women 'and this sense may even be experienced as a "right"' (Mederos, 1987: 34).

Many writers postulate a direct correlation between the behaviour of the father and the subsequent behaviour of the son. Farmer (1991: 26), for example, suggests that a boy whose father is a tyrant will learn to be a tyrant himself, and Lee (1991: 43) argues that if a boy perceives his father to be competitive or an abuser, he will take it upon himself to be the same. For this to occur, however, boys need to identify with their fathers.

Boys' identification with traditional fathers is the prevailing social practice, but why should this necessarily be so? It is clearly not always desirable, because, in this case, the norm is one of male domination. Identification with traditional fathers is one mechanism that reproduces hegemonic masculinity, male dominance and patriarchy (Christian, 1994: 190). The father–son relationship thus replicates the sexual and political values of the wider culture.

I believe that fatherhood should be ideally conceived in terms of nurturance. Boys want fathers who are 'warm, receptive, physically affectionate and comforting, open and honest about their feelings and approving and accepting of their sons despite their sons' failures' (Arcana, 1983: 142). Furthermore, men should take greater responsibility for the numerous instrumental tasks involved in child care to relieve the burdens on women.

On the other hand, until most fathers are non-patriarchal, nurturing fathers, the father–son relationship is likely to continue to reproduce the norms of misogyny and male violence (Christian, 1994: 191). While it is important for sons to identify with nurturing, egalitarian fathers, it is equally important to dis-identify with patriarchal fathers. This is consistent with Christian's (1994: 192) findings on the family background of anti-sexist men, that 'men who do not identify with traditional fathers or who do identify with non-traditional fathers are more likely to have sympathetic attitudes towards women and feminist ideals'.

According to Pleck (1983: 115), the main problem does not seem to be the absence of the father so much as the imposition of rigid sex-roles; if our ideas about male and female roles were less rigid, he says, boys raised by their mothers would not have to act 'hypermasculine' to prove that they are 'real men'. It would be more acceptable for 'real men' to be caring and empathic. This is consistent with research cited by Lisak (1991: 259) which suggests that boys' identification with women is only a problem in a society that emphasizes sex differences and values men above women. In the language of this book, the main issues are positional identification and the valuing of non-patriarchal subjectivities.

Patriarchal Expectations in Father–Son Relationships

What understanding do profeminist men have of father absence and the father 'wound'? Are their experiences different from those of other men?

After some discussion, the group decided to use memory-work to explore experiences during times when we had wanted or needed a nurturing or supportive response from our fathers and we did not get such a response. (See Appendix for an outline of collective memory-work.)

The premise of the memory-work experience was not to deny that we may have had nurturing fathers, nor was it to suggest that incidents of 'wounding' were not balanced by occasions of support and affirmation by our fathers. Rather, these memories were to provoke discussion on discontent in father–son relationships. We wanted to understand more fully the way in which such discontent is constructed, as it seemed to be such a powerful element in both masculinity therapy and the mythopoetic men's movement. We were also curious to see what sort of memories a cue of discontent with fathers would evoke for us.

Five memories of such experiences were produced by the group in response to this cue. The memories were written in the third person to encourage a description of particular events rather than a justification or explanation of the events. The aim was to uncover elements of the workings of dominant forms of masculinity as expressed in father–son relationships.

The first three memories elicited accounts of failed expectations between fathers and sons. The following memory from Michael relates to his need to talk to his father about his distress associated with work:

Michael (aged 16) was distressed. He had been a manual worker for two years now and he hated the work. He hated the noise and the dust and the physical demands of the job along with the boredom associated with much of it. He felt isolated and lonely in the job, even though his father worked there. All the men were older and he had no close friends his own age. He also felt troubled on an emotional level about his experience of himself as a male and he began to wonder about his sexuality.

He approached his father in the lounge room after work one night. He said 'Dad, there are a couple of things I want to talk to you about.' His father acknowledged the statement, but he did not put the paper down. 'Firstly Dad, I'm unhappy at work. I don't get any enjoyment out of it. I want to do something different.'

His father put the paper down. 'Listen, you've only been working for two years. I've been working for over 30 years. You can't expect work to be enjoyable. You just have to get used to it. All jobs have their good and bad aspects. You won't find any job that you'll like all the time. You just have to get used to it.' Michael began to talk further about his feelings about work, but it seemingly fell on deaf ears.

'Dad there's something else I'm feeling troubled about, some other stuff that's not only to do with work. I want to talk to someone about it.' 'What is it to do with?' 'It's not easy to explain, but I'm very unhappy with myself at the moment,' Michael said, trying to find a way to open it up. 'Don't worry about it,' his father said. 'You'll grow out of it. It's just a phase. You'll be OK.' There didn't seem to be anything further to say. Michael withdrew and went to his room.

In this memory, Michael was struggling with both sexual identity issues arising from his sense of marginalization from dominant masculinities and his alienation from a masculinist workplace culture. He had constructed himself as possibly gay because he had not conformed in a range of ways to expected male behaviour. This memory demonstrates the power that homophobia has in the making of masculinities.

There was a strong sense of despair evoked by the memory. Michael was trying to talk about his unhappiness and was rejected by the many clichés in his father's response: 'You can't expect work to be enjoyable . . . You'll grow out of it. It's just a phase.' His father was dismissive and unable to give him the time that he wanted.

In discussing the episode, Michael said that he blamed his father for the lack of choices and opportunities in his life. He felt resentful about the years he spent doing manual process work: 'It was the conditions of your life. You didn't expect to be happy . . . Work was pretty shitty and hard. That's the way work was. That's the way the world was . . . You just accepted the reality of it.' Dominant ideologies about work are translated through fathers to sons, shaping the expectations and satisfactions in the world of work. In this memory, Michael is given the message by his father that there is no way out; there is nothing that he can do to alter his life. However, Michael resisted this pressure; he did not accept 'the reality of it'. He made dramatic changes in his life, breaking away from his class location and his positioning as a particular kind of male.

Furthermore, as Michael became more politically active, he came to see his father in the context of the material conditions of his life, within a point in history, within a class and doing the best he could. He came to acknowledge that we live in a class-divided society where people did not make changes. By seeing his father in the culture of his time, he became more forgiving of him, which seems very common, particularly among working-class sons. Many sons come to forgive their fathers for their failings because they come to see their fathers' neglect and abusive behaviour as a result of their sacrifices for them and the family (Nordstrom, 1992: 4).

Peter said that he identified with Michael's memory: 'I could feel the thickness of it.' There are certainly similarities in Peter's memory, also involving a work related experience:

He was about 15 at his first full-time job in a cabinet-making workshop in Collingwood. He had been at this job for about six months, not liking it much. He found it boring and repetitive and grossly underpaid at $1.66 an hour. There was quite a lot of pressure for him to stay at this job. In his father's words: 'If you're not going to stay at school then you'll damn well work, if you think you're going to stay at home.' He was 15. He smoked too much dope. He was disillusioned with the state of the world. School didn't connect with him. This job didn't connect with him. He did not really know what he was doing there or what he wanted to do or that he may even have a choice. He started being late for work, daydreaming rather than sanding the 4,000th chair leg with complete attention and enthusiasm. He was there in body and every day less and less in spirit. Eventually the inevitable happened. He was sacked. What a relief. But what about the old man? He told his father that it was nothing he did. They just didn't need him any more. His father had already talked to the boss and knew that he was not what you would call the *most enthusiastic workman. His father knew about his arriving late and that if he tried harder he'd still have a job. His father started yelling, abusing: 'worthless failure, lazy and useless'. He'd confirmed by his actions what his father had been telling him for years. He didn't want to know anything about where he was or who he was. The boy did not meet the required standard. There was a job to be done. He had failed to do it.*

As Peter read the memory, there was strong emotion in his voice. He began the discussion of his memory by stating that there is a lot about his father that he finds very painful and difficult and he felt scared to share it with people.

Tony was immediately struck by Peter not meeting the criteria he was supposed to meet to be worthwhile in his father's eyes. In both of these memories the fathers are conveying to their sons that what they feel about a job is irrelevant; it is having the right attitude about the job that is important. As in the first memory though, in spite of Tony's experience that he had no choice, he expressed his agency by turning up for work late, until 'the inevitable happened; he was sacked'.

All of the men in the group easily identified with these two memories as they elicited recollections of a judgemental or angry father. Many men feel that their fathers are disappointed in them as they struggle to live up to their fathers' expectations. They come to learn, though, that they can never fulfil those expectations and are unable to gain the approval, respect and acceptance they want from their fathers.

The following memory from Bruce also illustrates a son's failure to live up to his father's expectations:

Bruce had a request for his father. He was in financial difficulty and needed a small amount of money to tide him over for a couple of weeks. Bruce's father's response was: 'No I'm not willing to give you that money. I am willing to give you a very large sum of money that you can use towards the purchase of a house.' And Bruce said: 'That's not what I need.'

Discussing the memory, Bruce said that his father believed that he had betrayed his class by not becoming a professional. He remembered his father saying: 'It sounds to me like you're doing really well in your work with children. What about lecturing in Early Childhood Development Studies?' Bruce was able to articulate to his father why he valued his work intrinsically but there was this idea that he had failed by not pursuing a professional career. Fathers become disillusioned when sons fail to become the men they envisage.

Some men knew that there was something missing in their relationships with their fathers but several of them showed that they had no sense at the time of how it could have been any different. Here is an excerpt from the discussion following Peter's memory:

Peter: It's like we didn't have a personal relationship. We had a father–son relationship . . . I couldn't think about an experience where I hadn't been fathered because my whole experience was of . . .

Michael: Not being fathered?

Peter: Or of being fathered. That's all there was.

Harry: Your experience of being fathered was so negative that when you think of being fathered, you think of that negative list of things.

Peter: In my mind it wasn't negative. That's just how it was.

Harry: What now might be seen as negative just was.

Peter: Later on I met other people's fathers and I was struck by the contrast. In some ways my father's death made me grieve that I didn't have a father. I never really had a father. I never really knew who he was. I was quite amazed in what you wrote Michael, that it could ever come into your mind to go and ask him something. That would never have entered my mind.

Harry: Yes, you guys, you believed a relationship could exist. I'm intrigued that there was something you wanted. I couldn't figure out what it was I was supposed to have. It wasn't there.

Michael said that he did not know what he wanted from his father at the time, but now he was able to say:

> I would have wanted someone who would have listened and acknowledged what was going on for me and being open to talking about it and working out what I might do about it and affirming my desire to make a change.

The semantic field covered by 'fathering' in English is the act of impregnating, whilst the concept of 'mothering' conveys nurturing and care-giving. In the excerpt from our discussion on fathering, Michael and Peter convey these different meanings of 'fathering'. Why did some of us have expectations of our fathers, while others had no sense that it could have been different? Or more widely, why is it that some people recognize what is missing in their lives and some do not? The answers to these questions are related to issues of access to alternative ways of being, a capacity to critically appraise experience and a sense of one's agency to address the discontent.

Violence and Fear in Father–Son Relationships

Violence and fear of violence are other themes that run through men's stories of their fathers. The following memory is one in which Tony describes an early childhood experience of his father's rage:

> Tony [aged 7] was fighting his little brother in the backyard of his house. He saw his father rushing towards them obviously to intervene. 'Dad'll fix him up': Tony clearly thought that he'd been wronged and that his brother was the guilty party in the dispute. His father looked annoyed and flustered as he approached. His father didn't act to plan. Instead of admonishing his brother, his father grabbed him, turned around and picked up a stick from a pile of sticks that was handy and hit him on the backside. Tony was stunned. He wanted to yell out: 'It's not fair.' But he didn't. It all happened so quickly.

In discussing the memory later, Tony said:

It's something like getting caught up in a rage. It's like getting caught up in a whirlpool. It's like 'what the hell is going on here'? My father's approaching me. He would often be in this rage. He was quite volatile at times. He would be quite unpredictable, when it would come out. What I remember mostly was that it just wasn't fair. It was one of quite a few instances of injustice. The main thing I remember was being scared of him, scared it would be like that in the end. When I typed it out on the computer this afternoon, I typed 'It's not fair' in capital letters. I wanted to yell it out.

Tony's memory conveys his powerful sense of injustice and writing it brought the feelings associated with it to the surface, including the feeling of fear. The memory elicited a painful experience from Harry: 'I can remember my father beating the shit out of my mother in the kitchen and I used to hide under the bed.'

Many boys fear their father's anger and punishment. In Hite's (1994: 335) research, 41 per cent of boys report that their father had an explosive temper that they had to watch out for. Furthermore, many of the men interviewed remembered being physically punished by their fathers. Townsend's (1994: 37–8) Australian study demonstrates similar trends and even when there was no physical violence, many men reported being afraid of their fathers.

The following memory from Alan tells a story of a different kind of fear:

It was Christmas Eve. The 12-year-old boy named Alan and his brother Anthony, 10 years old, went to work with their father, Bernie. Bernie was a plumber and his current work involved laying sewage pipes for residential properties in a small town about 21 miles from where the boys lived. They finished the work they had to do for the day and Bernie and the boys and the labourer went off to the pub. The boys wanted to get home because it was Christmas. And Bernie stayed and drank more and Alan had observed how his father's behaviour had changed and that his father was getting drunk and tired. And he started to get really concerned about driving home. Alan spent that half-hour or so terrified in the car as his father veered back and forth across the road; terrified that he wouldn't make it home and terrified that they would hit another car. Each time a car came towards them, his father veered back to the right side of the road. Very luckily they made it home. And he thanked his lucky stars.

Alan began the discussion of his memory with:

It was terrifying. A real let down, a real disappointment. Because I think it was the first time I had felt put in a situation that was really unsafe by him and totally out of my control. I really desperately wanted to get home. There was no way I could challenge my father and say you can't drive. You've been drinking too much. It was really at that time that my relationship changed with him and I didn't respect him from that point.

There was sadness in Alan's voice when he recalled this memory. He reported that he had never confronted his father about the incident but since that time, he has never allowed himself to be put in a similar situation again and he has generally tried to extract himself from all situations of vulnerability. While his survival may have been threatened in that situation as a 12-year-old boy, situations of vulnerability he encounters as an adult male are unlikely to be as life threatening.

Oppression in Father–Son Relationships

After examining each individual memory of our fathers, we then considered the memories as a whole, looking for common patterns and recurring themes. A common theme informing all of the memories was betrayal. Emotional abandonment, violence, fear and pressure to conform to fathers' expectations can all be equated to forms of betrayal. All of the men were disappointed in or betrayed by their fathers because of the father's lack of power in changing the situation. The father is either not listening or demonstrates his inability to change which is in turn perhaps linked to the growing awareness of the son's own future lack of power. Tony expected his father to solve his problem with his younger brother but the father does not, while in Alan's memory, drunk fathers can do little. The sons are also disappointed in their fathers' unjust and oppressive use of power.

These men's experiences with their fathers are not atypical; they are the ones who together construct the notion of the father 'wound'. By contrast, another way of theorizing these memories is to argue that, as boys, the men have been *oppressed* by their fathers. The concept of oppression has not generally been used to characterize boys' relationships with their fathers, but the extent to which they have suffered violence, abuse and rejection at the hands of their fathers may invite us to understand their experiences in these terms.

In his interviews with anti-sexist men, Christian (1994: 189) conceptualizes boys' experiences as suffering from the generational dimension of patriarchy. The meaning of patriarchy is 'rule by fathers', which implies that, as well as men dominating women, older men can dominate younger men. The men in his study saw links between their oppression as boys and women's oppression and the perceived similarity in these experiences may provide the potential for dialogue and alliances.

What is significant in the reflected memories of their fathers is that framing their experiences as 'oppression' enabled the men to identify with women's experiences of men. This is evident in discussions following a number of the memories. For example, after Peter's memory, Harry asked:

> Would it be the lack of fathering that would make feminism that much more important?

> *Peter*: I think feminism just made sense to me because I had the experience of oppression, basically, his oppression and the all-pervasiveness of it. It was thick and present when he was home. So I think I was quite feminist before I even met a feminist. I think feminism articulated a lot of things for me.

In discussing his memory of requesting a loan from his father, Bruce saw a connection between his father's arrogance about wanting him to have a certain attitude towards money and experiences that his mother had:

> When I'd learnt some stories about the conditions under which she had to raise me, a whole lot of things began to click and I began to have more empathy for my mother and my relationship with her changed. I've become quite angry with my father and quite sympathetic to my mother.

Following Tony's memory of feeling unfairly treated by his father, Bruce asked:

> I wonder if there's any connection between that line of feeling and your interest in feminist theory.

> *Tony*: Yeah, there could be. I always felt I was on the outside of a lot of things. In some ways I have often felt like I wanted to side with victims and getting in touch with everything being unjust and unfair. In some ways, it was like I was on side with my mum in a way because she was also scared of my father.

Thus, the experiences of sons with their fathers may have parallels with their mother's experiences with the same man. Many boys have the same struggle that women have with men, trying to get them to 'open up' and communicate more. The men in this study had already begun to reframe their experiences with their fathers and this may have contributed to their ability to connect with women's demands for respect and equality and for an end to sexual violence. Such men were more likely to be drawn to feminism because it expressed their concerns about morality and justice. The memory-work contributed further to this reframing, allowing the men to reposition themselves in relation to their fathers.

Beyond the Father Wound

In most of the literature on father–son relationships, there is a focus on forgiveness and reconciliation. Biddulph (1994: 22) believes that father-hunger is perhaps the most important concept in male psychology and, seeing it as the starting-point in men's journey to health, he encourages them to develop respect for their fathers. Similarly, Farmer (1991: 32–4) encourages men to see their fathers as 'wounded' as well and to understand that much of their fathers' remoteness and violence was their means of coping with their wounds. Such an understanding is seen as a first step towards healing the father wound. Blaming one's father is seen as preventing one from moving beyond anger to the hurt and sadness. Bly (1990: 92–122) argues that all fathers, even those who are unsupportive, emotionally remote and alcoholic, are to be forgiven.

For men who feel the loss of their fathers, however, forgiveness and reconciliation may not always be the best way forward. Many men conclude that
to love their fathers they must excuse them, but this could require accepting
behaviour that is inexcusable. Men may also want to excuse their fathers so
that they too can be excused (Arcana, 1983: 181). It may be premature for
men to forgive their fathers, if they have not acknowledged their anger and
disappointment towards them.

Horsfield (1994: 45–7) argues that the powerful ought to be called to
account for the abuse of their power before forgiveness and reconciliation can
occur. Thus, in this view, forgiveness is not the means towards recovery but is
something that 'may happen at the end of the long hard process of recovery
and then only if the conditions of forgiveness have been fulfilled'. Further, a
reconciliation between father and son may 'strengthen forms of male bonding that reinforce patriarchal expressions of power' (Hite, 1994: 341).

In some situations, it may be more appropriate to discourage identification
with the father and to reject some aspects of his behaviour. Consciously sorting out those lessons from our fathers that reinforce patriarchal manhood
from those that encourage justice is a difficult process but an uncritical reconciliation between father and son, that does not address the father's
controlling or abusive behaviour, should be challenged.

Furthermore, I question whether there is some sort of universal need for
men to have a particular kind of relationship with their fathers. The presumption underlying most of the work on father absence is the view that a
son raised by a mother necessarily lacks something that can only be acquired
from the father. Biddulph (1994: 99–100), for example, claims that 'boys have
a biological need for several hours of one to one male contact per day'. In his
view, boys cannot learn how to be a man from their mothers, 'no matter how
good they are'. While there may be some lessons that men can better teach
their sons, I question the assertion that there is a biological need to which
only fathers can respond. Research demonstrates that boys who are without
a father or closer to their mother are psychologically and emotionally health-
ier, adhere less to patriarchal stereotypes and are more responsive to change
(Hite, 1994: 341–2).

The construction of gender identity, however, is not only determined by
family relations; it is more fluid and negotiable than that. I believe that we can
reverse the things that are done to children by parents and other socialization
agents but this reversal requires access to other discourses through which
gender identity can be formed. The mass movements of the 1960s provided a
political rationale for rejecting the ways of the father; such movements provided an alternative discourse in which young men could position themselves.
Profeminism potentially provides young men with an equivalent alternative
discourse to form their gender identity against that of patriarchal fatherhood. Mothers (as well as profeminist fathers) can provide boys with
pathways to access this discourse.

Sons and Mothers

The Mother Wound

There is a widespread view that mothers are a problem for men in Western societies. Men's distancing patterns are said to connect to unresolved issues involving mothers (Gurian, 1994: 49). Similarly, Osherson (1992: 175) maintains that men's struggles with women in relationships are often based on 'unfinished attachment struggles with mother – their simultaneous desire to be close and separate.'

The tension between a desire for intimacy and connectedness with women and a desire to withdraw and shut them out was evident in a comment by Tony, which was instrumental in our decision to explore the connection between our relationships with our mothers and our partners:

> I was thinking of how I relate to women and my sexuality . . . even how I define what being in a relationship is all about. One of the things I've been thinking lately is wanting to be intimate and relate to Pam and then wanting to withdraw from her, shut her out of my life. It seems like a real roller coaster. Sometimes I'm in it really deeply. Other times I start tuning out. I start removing myself . . . Sometimes I want it all my own way. Sort of like wanting to feel safe and secure at the same time.

Tony's dilemma goes to the heart of many issues between men and women. A number of writers have commented on the tension men feel between their desire for intimacy with women and their fear of dependency, associated with their unresolved experiences with their mothers. Men fear dependency and commitment and are terrified of their own vulnerability (Jukes, 1993: 92). They associate dependency with their mothers and the resultant feelings this generates hinders their ability to form intimate relationships with women.

The questions are: What is the source of this problem? Is it too much of mother or not enough? A number of writers posit that separation from the mother is necessary and healthy for men and Farmer (1991: 175–6) argues that it is one of the main tasks in moving to manhood. He acknowledges that the wound of separation may hurt but maintains that it is a healthy wound. Similarly, for Keen (1991: 19–21), 'mother is a problem that needs to be solved and we find it difficult to break the symbiotic bond'. Separating from mother is seen as the only way to manhood.

Thus, mothers are seen by some writers as getting in the way of masculinity and are regarded as inevitably emasculating boys. Masculine identity is reproduced by repressing the feminine, and when boys separate from their mothers they reject feminine qualities within themselves (Silverstein and Rashbaum, 1994: 233).

Whilst the men and masculinity literature admits that the boy's separation from the mother is a wounding experience, one has to ask whether boys *need* to separate from their mothers? Do boys need to repress closeness with their mothers to become masculine? Defining the issue in such terms portrays mothers as the problem. By contrast, I suggest that healthy development incorporates the learning of *interdependence* whereby attachment and separation complement one another.

One consequence of separation without attachment is that men are often unable to develop a sense of empathic identity with women and if we spend our lives separating from our mothers will we be able to reclaim the feminine parts of ourselves? As some men distance themselves from their mothers and do not get enough nurturing, they later feel needy of women. On the other hand, while many men recognize their need for mother, they are often unable to openly express it (Osherson, 1992: 176).

Men yearn for the mother and fear being trapped by her and these feelings of love and fear remain with them, so that when they meet women, they exhibit ambivalence and fear as well as attraction. Such feelings obviously have implications for men's capacity for loving and accepting women's love and, consequently, men keep their emotional distance from women for fear of both 'entrapment' and abandonment (O'Connor, 1993: 178). Benjamin (1988: 52) even goes so far as to argue that domination 'begins with the attempt to deny dependency'.

Although the preceding discussion draws upon a range of sources in the men and masculinity literature, it is underpinned by the wider theoretical debates within psychoanalytic theory in general and feminist object relations theory in particular. The limitations of psychoanalytic perspectives on masculinity have already been articulated and will not be repeated here. However, while departing from the general premises of these perspectives, it is nevertheless important to examine some aspects of the terrain that these theories address, in this case mother–son relationships.

We were curious about the links between our relationship with our mothers and with women partners and wondered whether resolving issues with mothers would result in improved relations with women. Consequently, the second memory-work project we developed was on mother–son relationships. I am mindful of Jardine's (1987: 61) comment that 'men have not even begun to think about their mothers'. While men's relationships with their fathers have received considerable attention in writing about men and masculinity, there has been a resounding silence by men on their relationships with their mothers. It is certainly rare to see any examination of men's experience of the ambivalence and pain associated with distancing and separation.

The cue we used to evoke the memories was to recall a situation with our mothers in which we felt a sense of discomfort. The aim was to analyse memories in which there was a sense of distancing ourselves from our mothers, in order to explore the meanings we gave to those processes of distancing. What would memories of distancing from mothers tell us about our relationships with women?

Distancing Mothers

The following memory from Tony demonstrates the theme of distancing:

> *The boy was about 13 and he was walking down the main street of Frankston with his mother. He didn't want to be there. He was annoyed with his mother that he was there. He was going shopping with her to buy clothes for him, which he didn't want to do. He didn't want to have new school clothes because he didn't like new clothes. He didn't want to be seen by his school mates. So he physically distanced himself from his mother. He was walking a few steps back in a similar way to which he had seen a schoolfriend of his do the previous year, but he could tell by the way the boy was walking that he was with his mother.*

In discussing the memory later, Tony said that he lapped up his mother's company when he was at home. He talked about how much he appreciated her cooking and ironing and cleaning clothes but why did he have to go shopping with her? Why couldn't she go out and buy the clothes without him? In an attempt to explain his experience he says: 'I was meant to be a boy and I was meant to have some sort of power. And my mother still seemed to have control over me and I hated that.'

Tony's comment is an insightful reflection. It helps us to understand boys' emotional and psychological domination of their mothers: to accept his mother's authority is to lose his self-respect. He was asked whether there were any similarities in that experience and his experience of shopping with his partner:

> I just cringe like anything. It bugs me. I can really feel myself well up and think: 'Oh hell.'

Harry: What's that about?

Tony: I suppose it is something about smothering or something. Wanting to be grown up, feeling self-sufficient and feeling like I can look after myself.

Michael: Does it feel like it is about control? If a partner says: 'Let's go shopping. I will get you a new shirt.'

Tony: Yes it does.

Harry: What about when you go shopping with your partner for food?

Tony: In a previous relationship I felt there was a lot of that stuff. At times, I felt like she was just waiting to find that there was something there that she disapproved of in some way. To me that felt really controlling. I felt like this is really putting the pressure on.

Harry: I feel really uncomfortable when you talk about that because I experience that. The tomatoes were wrong. The spuds were wrong. The sauce was the wrong brand. In the end you just give up. You say: 'OK, I will push the trolley.' And that didn't suit me at all. Your description of that period in your life just brings up heaps for me. I am very uncomfortable and distressed.

The issue of women's power in the domestic sphere brings up a number of issues for men. Michael commented that one of the biggest issues in his relationships with women was when they either tell or ask him to do something. There was much laughter in the group, as the participants easily identified with the experience. Some of men's responses to doing their share of domestic work may be related to not accommodating to what they perceive as women's control. As Tony pointed out, they are meant to be men and to have some sort of power.

In the following memory, Michael recalls a similar experience:

> *He was about 13. He was living in a country town in New South Wales, going to a state secondary school. His parents lived on the fringe of the town. It was too far to walk. Although there was an irregular bus service that passed near the school, his mother insisted on driving him to and from the school. It seemed as though he was the only boy in his grade who was driven to and from school by his mother and his classmates commented negatively upon this on various occasions. 'Your mother drives you to school. Are you a mummy's boy?' After a while he went to his mother and said 'Mum I would like to take the bus to and from school.' His mother said 'Don't be silly Michael. I don't mind driving you.' Michael said 'But mum I would prefer to go on the bus.' And his mother asked him why. 'Well I would just rather go on by bus that's all', he said. And she said 'No I'll drive you. It is quicker and safer.' His mother was adamant about it. There was nothing more to be said. The next afternoon the school bell went and he walked out of the school building and saw his mother's car parked near the school entrance. He ran more quickly than usual and got in the front seat beside his mother, but as he sat down he slid slightly forward so that he was not riding so high in the car. Over time, he would gradually slide more and more forward, so that eventually his head was about level with the dashboard. If he had to be driven by his mother, he would decrease the likelihood of being seen.*

Following Michael's memory, the group explored the significance of him being called a mummy's boy:

> *Tony*: So you didn't like being called a mummy's boy?
> *Michael*: No.
> *Harry*: Was it true?
> *Michael*: Well I guess it must have been true. If it was true, it wasn't something that I was wanting to embrace.
> *Harry*: More importantly, what does it mean? Does it mean that mum loved you and cared for you and was close to you and wanted a close relationship, and that this was inconceivable given the peer pressure? Was there comfort in your relationship with her?
> *Michael*: Well, it is a bit similar to what Tony was saying. I saw all sorts of parallels between my story and yours . . . Yes, there were comforts that were provided by my mother at home. And while those comforts were provided in the context of the home that was fine. But I didn't like those comforts to be seen more publicly outside the home.

Harry identified the issue clearly. Michael was torn between enjoyment of his mother's nurturance and the stigma of being referred to as a 'mummy's boy'. To be called a 'mummy's boy' can be experienced as being one of 'the worst things in the world' (Osherson, 1992: 175). 'Mummy's boys' are taunted by other boys and, consequently, boys are forced to separate from their mothers by the threat of humiliation when they would not otherwise choose to make the separation (Kreiner, 1991: 6). There is thus a split between the private and the public manifested in the tension between the experience of the mother and the experience of peer group culture.

Devaluing Mothers

As stated earlier, most boys observe their fathers' attitude of superiority towards their mother. This is the context in which boys have to decide whether to identify with their mother or with their father. A boy learns that if he wants to be accepted into male society, he has to turn his back on his mother. The following memory from Alan demonstrates this process:

> *Alan was about 12 or 13 years old. It was teatime and he was sitting around the kitchen table with some of his siblings and his father. His mother was cooking dinner. They were discussing an issue that was not of particular importance. However, his mother said something that might have been construed as silly, that she didn't understand. So Alan and the others started hassling her, implying that she was stupid. Then to his surprise, his mother ran out of the room in tears.*

In discussing the memory later, Alan described a strong sense of collusion in the incident, of men ganging up on the woman. He said: 'I recollect having a very close relationship and it really struck me of being so insensitive to her, being cruel. I feel like I was so cruel. I felt very ashamed, even now.' In Alan's memory, the mother was constructed as stupid based on an assumption about 'male knowledge' being superior or 'right'. Michael related closely to this memory. His mother was a full-time housewife and, while both his mother and father were poorly educated, his father read widely and was informed about the state of the world. His mother did not read as widely: she was only semi-literate. The story Alan told about his mother being seen as stupid occurred in Michael's house, as well; his father would be very condescending towards her. Before becoming critical of what was happening, he perceived his mother as being not very intelligent. There was pain in his voice as he recalled this experience and his inability then to feel proud of his mother, because of the way in which women and the feminine were devalued.

Depending on Mothers

How do sons address their dependency needs in relation to their mothers? We explored this question in discussing issues arising from other memories. Phillip's memory reveals his fear of having lost his mother's love:

Phillip was fighting with his brother, while the dining room at his house was being painted. He was 9 or 10. The crockery from the dining room was stored in his brother's bedroom. During the fight, Phillip threw a book at his brother. He remembers, in slow motion, the arch the book made as it slithered through a line of plates and cups. These plates and cups were special because his mum had saved up for them during the war, when her husband was away. So Phillip was a very sorry boy and was sent to bed that night without any tea.

About 9.00 at night he came downstairs and saw his mum was sitting at the kitchen table crying. He hopped on her knee and they had a big cry together. Then he understood that it was alright. He was not going to be persecuted for this.

In commenting on the memory afterwards, Phillip remembered crying in distress because he thought: 'I have really blown it this time.' He has felt that feeling many times since then: 'Feeling like a chastised little boy can be a big thing for me.' When that happens, he feels defensive and wants to fight.

The reference to feeling like a 'little boy' was a recurrent theme throughout the discussion about mothers. Phillip's memory elicited a recent experience from Michael. He had accidentally broken a special vase his partner had owned for several years. When he told her about the breakage, she was upset but he did not want to take responsibility for breaking it and emphasized that it was not his fault. In that situation, he described how he felt like a little boy who needed to be told that it was alright.

Phillip says that, in his view, most men have not got over their reliance upon their mothers; they have shifted the focus to partners for emotional support and emotional security. When he has left or been left by a partner, feelings 'of losing mum' come back to him. Michael reflected how some of the ways in which he cuddles with a woman were to do with his 'unresolved dependency needs'. Whilst many men are unable to accept their dependency needs, describing them as 'unresolved' suggests a psychological weakness, whereas the notion of interdependence tends to affirm that in some situations we will be dependent and that is acceptable.

The following memory from Peter illustrates the tension between being depended upon and having one's own dependency needs:

He was about 20. He had a really good relationship with his mother. They had become quite close since his father died about 3 years earlier. He had been quite supportive providing some stability in an otherwise difficult few years for his mum. But she didn't have to worry about him. He was fine. Not so fine were a few of his siblings who for various reasons were having difficulties of one sort or another. His mother took an active interest in checking in with them, arranging dinners with them to offer an ear and to get to know how they were going. Peter had his own problems and it was at this time that he became aware that he needed support as well. He found it quite difficult to ask. This would go against the normal pattern of events, the normal way they related. He was too busy listening and supporting his mum. It was hard to change the dynamics of this relationship. She was a very busy and very giving woman and he knew that she needed to have this space. But he couldn't help feeling a bit resentful. He was supportive, stable, calm and had things under control.

In discussing the memory later, Peter connected this experience with his mother to his current relationship, where it is much easier for him to be supportive and to listen than to be supported. He says that the hardest thing for him is to acknowledge 'that I am not in control, that I am in need and it is not all stable and calm'.

The other group members could identify with this experience. Tony related his experience of working with partners of women who had been sexually abused as children. These men were able to be supportive with their partners, but at the expense of acknowledging their own needs and feelings and at times this became destructive in their relationships: 'Of course I can't relate to that at all,' he said sarcastically.

Michael recalled instances where in relationships with women he had put his own needs aside to be supportive to his partner's needs but his own neediness would 'erupt' and he would then want her to put her needs aside. This would not always happen and he would experience himself saying 'It is not fair. What about my needs?' This experience elicits an immediate response from Phillip:

> That is exactly what happens to me too. Unfortunately I am less conscious of it than I want to be, so it sort of comes up. I really enjoy that steadiness, you know. And then it comes up. It is totally demanding and the way I do it is very little boy demanding.

As men we are often unable to accept that at different times and in different contexts we need what women are able to offer us. To acknowledge our dependency at these times does not mean that we are weak men. However, because dependence on others, particularly women, is seen as a sign of weakness, men frequently are unable to develop genuinely interdependent relationships with women and often end up expressing their needs in a demanding rather than interactive way.

Blaming Mothers

Mothers are often accused of dangerously enmeshing their own identity with that of their sons and of over-protecting them whereby they 'indulge for their own gratification, in compensation for an unsatisfactory marriage' (Gomez, 1991: 49). Bly (1990: 18) posits that mothers typically exercise possessiveness over their sons.

A number of writers attribute the estrangement of sons from their fathers to the involvement of mothers. Biddulph (1994: 35) argues that a mother will often turn her son against his father and Bly blames mothers for getting in the way of boys' relationships with their fathers. In his view, this constitutes a conspiracy between mother and son. Tony responds to Bly's charge of conspiracy:

> To me it was about safety. It wasn't a conspiracy. It was more like a necessity, my relationship with my mother. I just saw my father for ten minutes a day and sometimes

that ten minutes was something to dread. What's dad going to do when he gets home tonight? Is he going to be volatile? Is he going to be friendly? Sure I had a closer bond with my mother than my father, but I wouldn't call that a conspiracy.

As discussed previously, the major consequence of such 'over-mothering' is seen to be the creation of 'mothers' boys'. Men who become 'mummy's boys' are said to be 'dominated by the desire to perform well to gain approval and to avoid female anger or rejection' (Keen, 1991: 21). Bly (1990: 2–3) argues that 'mummy's boys' were 'too tied to women as children, and then as adults are too tender, too empathic, too interested in women's issues'.

Profeminist men are often criticized by other men as mothers' boys. Corneau (1991: 75–6) questions his profeminist client's reasons for embracing feminism. He argues that his client used feminism to ingratiate himself with women and the reason for this involvement with feminism was based on his desire to be rewarded with maternal affection.

Similarly, Forrester (1992: 106) suggests that the desire of one of his clients to be a feminist man was 'really a desire to be underneath, to be dominated sexually and politically by the feminist women he admires'. His profeminism was regarded as 'a kind of masochism, or a kind of fascination with the all-powerful woman figure'.

It is important to challenge the framework within which these comments are made and to shift the terms of the debate about profeminism. It is likely that profeminist men will be closer to their mothers than their fathers and it is important for these men to acknowledge the strong influence of women, rather than to dis-identify with them. Such men can perhaps contribute the most to changing gender relations.

Honouring Mothers

In response to the cue of discomfort with mothers, the men produced memories of distancing, devaluing and dependence. In all of the memories there were connections between dependency issues with mothers and these men's relationships with women. The reference to feeling like a 'little boy' was a recurrent theme throughout the discussions. Through the memory-work, it was evident that there was a lot of ambivalence in these men's relationships with mothers. They, like most males, had received strong messages that they should distance themselves from their mothers or else risk ridicule as mothers' boys. Unlike most males though, who want to suppress the ways that they are like their mothers, these men had struggled to own the positive influences their mothers had upon their lives, although they were denied a framework within which they could easily do that.

In contrast to the memory-work with fathers, the mothers do not betray or disappoint the men, perhaps because there are few expectations to be lived up to. Here the sons want control over their mothers, whereas they do not want control over their fathers. Furthermore, in contrast to some memories of fathers, where it is the *inaction* of the fathers that is the problem for the men, it is the *action* of the mothers that is identified as problematic.

Given that the majority of men are pressured to distance themselves from their mothers, what can be done? Men can reflect on 'how they would be different if they did not have to separate' (Carey, 1992: 68). Considering that, in losing touch with their mothers, men may have lost touch with parts of themselves could itself be a powerful force in provoking change.

It is also important that men endeavour to understand their mothers as women with their own life-histories, expectations and needs. Such analysis can enrich their perception of women as a whole. Men can get to know their mothers better, to ask them about their experiences before they became mothers, especially in relation to experiences such as discrimination and harassment (Pasick, 1992: 212). A lot of men have difficulty seeing their mothers as women with separate lives before and apart from motherhood. To acknowledge the truth of our mothers' lives requires us to recognize their oppression and our institutional power over women and, to the extent to which we are able to do this, we will enhance the potential for partnership with women.

Conclusion

Memory-work enables men to reflect upon and shape their own experiences and, in so doing, it contributes to the formation of non-patriarchal subjectivities and practices. The memory-work recorded here reflects sons' experiences of family life and, following Hearn (1987: 187), I believe that to reclaim our experience as sons, 'through the self recognition of sonhood' is to challenge patriarchal constructions of fatherhood and manhood. Naming ourselves as sons, as threatening as it may be to some men, provides the basis for the formation of alternative non-patriarchal subjectivities by repositioning ourselves against the dominant mode of identity reproduction.

Reframing our childhood memories enables us to reconnect with our emotional histories and enables a critical stocktaking. Remembering is not only an attempt 'to understand the past better but to understand it differently' and it enables us to challenge dominant social relations (McLaren and da Silvar, 1993: 75–6). Memory-work enabled us to examine the emotional and psychological basis of our relationships with women and other men, including our unconscious feelings about them.

The family is, however, only one of the sites that form men's subjectivities and practices; we learn how to become men from a wide range of social practices. Two of these social practices are homophobia and the sexual objectification of women, which will be examined in the next chapter.

6 Recreating Heterosexualities

Many writers have noted that most heterosexual men project their identities by defining gay men and women as the 'other'. It thus seemed pertinent in the context of this project to explore the potential for heterosexual men to reconstruct their gender and sexual identities in ways that do not imply their domination over other sexualities and over women. Two social practices that reinforce oppressive, discriminatory forms of heterosexuality are homophobia and the sexual objectification of women.

In the first part of this chapter, I demonstrate how consciousness-raising about homophobia is an important strategy in transforming masculinity. If one accepts the possibility that one's sexuality may be different from the norm, it may redress the exclusion of others defined as different from oneself (Young, 1990: 155). Thus, confronting homophobia may enable men to address other issues of difference in their own lives and the lives of others.

The second part of this chapter explores the construction of male heterosexual desire as it is manifested in sexual objectification. I propose that, through the analysis of memories of objectification, men can heighten their awareness of the ways in which their heterosexual desire is socially constructed and that, from this understanding, they can strengthen the alternative construction of non-patriarchal sexualities.

Homophobia

The Gay Liberation Movement formulated the term 'homophobia' to identify the irrational fear of homosexuality. According to Kirk and Madsen (1989: 26–7), heterosexual men dislike gays because they believe that homosexuality is caused by sinfulness, mental illness or recruitment. Jung and Smith (1993: 90) identify the fears linked with homosexuality as undermining the family, destabilizing society, weakening procreativity, confusing youth and preying on the vulnerable. An underlying premise is that homosexuality is a perversion: gay men are misidentified as corrupt, diseased and evil. These alleged causes and consequences are imaginary. Most heterosexual men have a distorted image of the gay world and thus homophobia is irrational because it generally embodies misconceptions and false stereotypes of male homosexuals.

Homophobia also involves the suppression of homoerotic desire and men's attempts to purify relationships with other men of sexual connotations (Kimmel, 1994: 130). Sedgwick (1985: 1) used the term 'homosocial' to describe the non-sexual social bonds between men and to analyse how these social bonds keep men in power.

Some writers argue that this 'inability to recognize any homosexual impulses in oneself causes men to project all homosexual desires outward on to gay men' (Kupers, 1993: 49). Hence, latent homosexuality is seen as causing homophobia. Many men are unable to admit that their own heterosexuality is suspect and flawed. Homosexuality must then stay abnormal if heterosexual men are to be able to regard themselves as normal.

There is currently some debate about the merits of the term homophobia to describe discrimination against gay men and lesbians. Roberts (1989: 5), for example, is concerned about the effects of using the psychological construct of phobia, fearing that it may divert attention from social and institutional arrangements. There is the danger that it may overly psychologize prejudice against gay men and lesbians. Kitzinger (1987: 61) points out that the concept of homophobia encourages individualistic explanations of a phenomenon that is socio-political: 'classifying homophobics as sick is far less threatening than any attempt to look at the issue in political terms.' In this sense, homophobia is part of a 'reverse discourse, where once it was the homosexual who was viewed as sick, now it might be the heterosexual who is charged with pathology' (Dollimore, 1991: 233–4).

While I recognize the importance of these criticisms, I believe that the term should be retained because it has now gained some currency among both the gay and heterosexual communities and it seems to provide an acceptable concept denoting anti-gay bias. It is, however, important to locate discussions about homophobia within a wider debate about heterosexual dominance or heterosexism. Heterosexism is an ideology that denigrates and stigmatizes all non-heterosexual behaviours and relationships. Heterosexism creates the climate for homophobia by assuming that the world must be heterosexual and it is the ideological underpinning of homophobia.

Heterosexism and homophobia, together, represent one of the main patterns in gender relations (Connell, 1987: 60). Institutionalized heterosexuality has become an important social norm that is enforced by social policies, schools, the family, the media and the police (Kinsman, 1987: 104). Thus, in this context, homophobia pressures men to maintain hegemonic forms of masculinity.

Male heterosexual identity is thus reproduced by fear and hatred of gay men. Furthermore, it is important for heterosexual men to acknowledge that homophobia and patriarchy are inextricably linked with the former serving an important function in reproducing the latter and in promoting misogyny and sexism among men (Kaufman, 1993: 20). Research demonstrates that homophobic attitudes towards gay men and lesbians coincides with support for traditional family and gender roles (Herek, 1987: 70). Thus, by conforming to hegemonic masculinity, heterosexual men tend towards homophobic attitudes.

Homophobia also constrains heterosexual men as it is widely recognized as one of the major barriers preventing more intimate relationships between men. The fear of homosexuality inhibits men from touching each other out-side certain socially acceptable situations (Garfinkel, 1985: 163). Heterosexual men try to avoid doing anything that other men might interpret as effeminate or unmanly. Men fear that any intimacy between men may sully their sexual identity.

Overcoming homophobia thus seems very important if a greater degree of intimacy between men is to be developed. In addition, homophobia can also interfere with men's capacity to be intimate with women because they are gen-erally afraid to feel close and continue to feel that they have to act 'the man' (Stoltenberg, 1992: 17). It is thus in men's self-interest to end homophobia, because it expands our options as men and expands the types of relations we can have with other men.

Being conscious about homophobia and having a desire to confront it within ourselves, we decided to explore memories of what might be regarded as homophobic episodes in our lives. The cue for these memories was to recall a situation in which we felt discomfort in a situation of intimacy with another man.

We approached this topic with trepidation and apprehension with all of us holding back from the initial reading of the memories. There was nervous laughter and restless movement as we prepared ourselves for the disclosures that were to follow.

Pleasure and Danger in Adolescent Male Sexuality

The following memory from Tony describes an early adolescent sexual expe-rience with another male:

Tony was about 14 and he was with Greg, a friend he played cricket with. Greg was two years older than him. They were at Tony's parents' place and they had the house to themselves, as Tony's parents had gone out. Late that night, Greg suggested that they sleep in the same bed together and Tony went along with it. He put his pyjamas on and got into bed. They were lying there and Tony could feel Greg's hand on his penis. Tony's penis had already been erect. He started playing with his penis and Tony let this happen for a while, pretending he was asleep. Finally, he decided to get out of bed because he felt he needed to go to the toilet. He understood later that he was about to ejaculate, which he'd never experienced before.

Greg and Tony had similar encounters over the next couple of years. Greg was always the initiator of this unspoken thing. They'd never talked about it. It was always this unspoken thing that nobody else was to know. That was Tony's main fear. Nobody else was to know. Tony was horrified and disgusted at the same time. He had questions about what this was going to mean for his sexuality. He was really petrified of being found out.

One time he and Greg had taken more of a risk. They were stimulating each other's penises in Tony's mother's bedroom, when they heard somebody walking down the corridor. They managed to get their trousers up in time and lie on the bed. Tony never ever forgot how close that was. After his mother had come into her room, got what she wanted and walked out again he was still shaking, shaking like a leaf.

The emotional tone of the episode was conveyed by the faltering way in which Tony read the story, as the experience still held some power for him. Asked about how he felt about telling the story he said: 'There was certainly some fear about it. There was this story that just kept on hanging around in the back of my head. I just felt like I had to tell it.'

Secrecy is a strong theme in the memory: 'Nobody else was to know.' In discussing the episode later, Tony reported that he and Greg never discussed the incidents, even after they stopped. Tony simply made up his mind to make sure that he would not end up in a private space with Greg again. It would be eight years later before Tony would tell the story for the first time to an intimate woman friend.

It is interesting that this memory was elicited as a response to the cue of discomfort with another man. It could also be read as a response to feeling desire for another male, although there is no sense of Tony's sexual responsiveness to Greg's advances. He talked about 'going along with it' and 'letting it happen'. We are left to presume that there was no desire or agency on his part. He is unable to construct himself as being active in the process or acknowledge any pleasure in the experiences. He does not want to take any responsibility for this sexual liaison.

It is not uncommon for boys of Tony's age to engage in mutual stimulation. Interviews with 21 young Australian men all reported patterns of adolescent sexuality in which mutual stimulation between boys was a common experience and, as in Tony's experience, this sexual contact was most likely not to be spoken about (Connell et al., 1993: 117–18).

The story was very familiar to the group. How many other similar untold stories are there? Why do young men feel so unable to tell their stories? Why do such experiences remain unspoken between boys? What would the effect be if such stories were discussed at the time and later told to other men and boys? When these stories are not told, boys learn that it is not acceptable for males to be close to each other.

Another memory of an adolescent sexual experience with a male is recounted by Harry, though this memory raises more explicit issues of power and desire:

In 1950 Harry, aged 13, was a virgin and really interested in the girls around him. There was a man living on the corner who was in his middle 40s–early 50s and this man witnessed this gang of young people going about together. It was clear that all the young people were excited by the adolescence of growing up.

The older man decided that he would share a group of photos with the young boys in the group. He said: 'I have a set of photographs to share with you.' Harry was intensely interested in these photographs, which were heterosexual photographs, a group of men and women together. This was the first explicit information that Harry had ever seen. So the bloke invited him back to see the photos by himself. Then the man played with Harry, whilst Harry was looking at the photographs, and he experienced his first ejaculation, which was just extraordinary, quite an experience.

Some days later the older man invited one of the boys of the gang and Harry to go out into the bush. They went out into the bush with him and once again there was a very strong obligation in the association. There had been a strong obligation in the past few days and it continued on. Harry and the other young man and the older fellow went out into the bush in this fellow's car and once again the photos were viewed. There was mutual sexual stimulation going on. Then the older man said he wanted Harry to have sex with him. Harry felt that he had to do that. So Harry made love with this older man. Immediately afterwards Harry was alarmed on a number of grounds. It appeared to be dirty. It seemed to be morally wrong. And Harry felt ashamed, deeply ashamed.

There is a sense of 'pleasure and danger' in this memory and, in discussing it, the group questioned Harry about the extent of his self-determination in this experience. While he spoke of 'a strong obligation in the association', he also spoke of having 'made love with this older man'. In spite of the obligation Harry felt, there is a stronger sense of agency here. It was suggested that what occurred could be interpreted as sexual abuse and Tony also questioned the degree of willingness on Harry's part. Harry, on reflection, said that the memory was a story of sexual abuse and that he still carries scars from it, but he also made it clear that, although he felt overwhelmed by the nature of the circumstances, he wanted it to happen: 'The obligation was very great. But I was excited also. The obligation was there and I reacted with excitement to the obligation.'

Harry's account is consistent with Leahy's (1991: 9) description of male adolescent sexuality as 'spontaneous, adventurous, sexual pleasure is guaranteed and casual contact is exciting'. Subjects in Leahy's study all validated their involvement in intergenerational sex with men by 'viewing these relationships as a growing independence from the confinement of parental authority and influence. The adult was sometimes seen as a mentor or at least a loved friend' (1991: 18). All boys had either encouraged or been pro-actively involved in having sex with older males. Leahy argued that issues of power could be adequately negotiated in such a way that boys and men could have sex together in a non-exploitative and non-abusive way.

The main issue here is whether boys of Harry's age are fully able to consent, given their relative powerlessness vis-à-vis adult partners. An article by Beane (1992), which described his experience as a 17-year-old having sex with a 12-year-old boy, generated a major controversy for both Beane and the editors of the profeminist magazine in which it appeared. Craft (1993: 18), in a trenchant critique of Beane and the editors, argued that this first-person narrative was all about trying to pressure several boys into sex and that the author's 'fond memories' were about what many would interpret as child sexual abuse. Are there lines separating intergenerational sex from child sexual abuse and are the lines about what is 'acceptable' different for heterosexuality and homosexuality? Will what constitutes abuse in a heterosexual context necessarily be so in a gay context? These were questions left unresolved in our discussions. We were conscious that initial gay sexual encounters were likely to be with older more sexually experienced males but the power inequality in these sexual experiences remained a problem for us.

Straight Men and Gay Sex

Many straight-presenting men have had sexual experiences with other men and almost all men have experienced some sexual feelings in relation to other men. The following memory from Phillip raises issues about what happens when straight- and gay-presenting men have sex together:

> *Phillip came to Melbourne in 1976 [from Adelaide], and 3–4 years after he got very close to a guy called John. He knew that John was gay and talked to John about being gay. It just seemed like there was no reason not to get into a relationship with John. They were consenting adults.*
>
> *For a month or two, Phillip had a relationship with John, sleeping together, with no actual penetration either way. But certainly a lot of mutual stimulation and so on in various ways. But then Phillip got more uneasy about it as it went on. They were living in the same house and he felt like John was more interested in sticking with him than the other way around. Fairly abruptly, he said to John that he didn't think he wanted to continue in this relationship. Phillip was actually really quite shocked at the pain on John's face at the time. So that relationship stopped and the other intimacy dropped away very quickly after that too.*

Phillip later reported that he and John only see each other very occasionally now and, while they can have a reasonable talk about how they are getting on, it is not the same. Phillip believed that he had not been fair and still feels a sense of guilt about his behaviour: 'I didn't realize how much he was involved, how strongly he was involved. Because we'd talked about me being straight and him being gay a lot. I was basically fairly blind to what I was doing to him.'

The group discussed how Phillip could have handled it differently with more sensitivity and better insight. Phillip commented: 'If I'd communicated a bit more where I was coming from, maybe I would have given him a chance to make his choices, where he wanted to come from. So if I had said up front: "I don't know about this, but I'll try it out."'

There are numerous stories told by gay men about their experience of having sexual relationships with heterosexual men, especially about the latter experimenting with them sexually and then pulling back and leaving them rejected. This is one of the ways that gay men feel abused by heterosexual men; but we rarely hear the story told by the heterosexual man. In this account we again find a lack of acknowledgement of agency or desire on Phillip's part. It seems that the only way he can acknowledge the sexual encounter is to present it as constructed by someone else.

How gay and straight men can talk together and form non-exploitative relationships is a key issue in confronting homophobia and the following memory from Bruce also raised this issue:

> *A friendship had developed between Bruce and a gay man, Robbie. In the second*
> *year of this friendship, it was mutually decided that Bruce and Robbie should go*
> *away for a weekend together down to Queenscliff. Just a friendly thing for two*
> *friends to do. Bruce was unsure about it and there was some sense of obligation on*
> *his part that to deepen the friendship this would be a good thing to do. Spend inti-*
> *mate exclusive time together.*
>
> *So they went down to Queenscliff together and booked into a guest house and*
> *had a nice dinner. During the dinner Bruce was quite aware that other older cou-*
> *ples might be wondering what these two men were doing in this guest house. Bruce*
> *sensed Robbie's uncomfortableness too. But in spite of that they had quite a good*
> *dinner and they went to bed. There were two single beds in the room. In the morn-*
> *ing, they woke up and they were just chatting from the beds and then for some*
> *reason, it wasn't very well thought out but it was fairly spontaneous, Bruce got up*
> *and got into bed with Robbie and lay there and they hugged for a while and talked.*
> *Then Bruce suddenly thought, well this is really a bit strange and he tried to*
> *divorce the actual physical feelings that were there, like skin touching skin. He*
> *tried to keep it just as fairly relaxed conversation. But in his head he was a bit lost*
> *and he then got out of bed and then went and had breakfast.*

Again, there is 'a sense of obligation' present in this memory; this time it is to change the way in which the friendship operated. Bruce indicates a discomfort about how their presence in the guest house might be perceived by other guests. When they are in bed together, with their bodies touching, Bruce gets 'lost in his head' and is thus able to effectively obscure his feelings.

In discussing the memory, Bruce recalled that the episode was not talked about until a year later, when it came up for Robbie, who felt that it was a very significant turn in their relationship because he felt much closer and accepted. By contrast, this was not so for Bruce, for whom 'it was anxious and fraught and non genuine.' In retrospect, he believed that he would have felt more comfortable, in some ways, if they had had sex, 'because then there wouldn't have been that other tension of it, the potential of it happening'. Again, we see a return to the theme of pleasure and danger.

It is 'the potential of it happening' that causes the most discomfort for Bruce. The potential for greater intimacy between gay men and straight men is fraught, perhaps more so for gay men, because, as Humphries (1987: 93) points out, gay men are tied 'to the subordinate desiring role and [straight men] to the superior admired one'.

Sex Between Straight Men

Is a man having sex with another man the ultimate demonstration of over-coming homophobia? Goodman et al. (1983: 126) encourage heterosexual men to get in touch with the gay feelings within themselves and to consider 'making love with someone of the same sex within a certain period of time'. Inglis (1985: 64) similarly suggests that, if heterosexual men believe that homosexuality is a legitimate sexual experience, they should 'include it within the range of their own erotic possibilities, for it is duplicity to do otherwise'.

In response to these challenges, some heterosexual men have felt that they ought to relate sexually to other men, that there is a moral imperative to do so. Michael's memory demonstrates elements of this 'moral imperative':

> *He was 26 years old and living on his own after a threesome of two and a half years had recently broken up. He and another man, John, had lived together with Sarah, with whom they were both lovers. Although the three of them at times had frolicked together in bed and there was a high level of emotional intimacy and touching between he and John, the two of them did not have a sexual relationship. John had had a previous sexual relationship with another man. Michael had not.*
>
> *They both had gay friends, espoused the sexual liberation philosophy of the 70s that everybody had a capacity to be sexually attracted to people of the same sex. They both prided themselves on not being homophobic or heterosexist. They were both 'cool' enough to talk about the possibility of them having a sexual relationship and said that they were not philosophically opposed to it on principle. However, it hadn't happened and the intensity of the threesome had finally exploded. All three of them were now living separately and nursing their wounds.*
>
> *Now John had come around to visit him. There were things unsaid and issues unresolved. He seemed more distressed than Michael. As he talked he began to cry. Michael reached out to comfort him, held him and stroked him as he cried. His crying stopped after a while. He turned to Michael, kissed him on the lips and his hands roamed around Michael's body sexually. Michael felt himself tense up. His mind began racing. Did he want this? Was it the right time? Should he respond sexually, even if he didn't want to? How would John handle a rejection?*
>
> *In the midst of his confusion, he suddenly pushed John away. He said: 'I'm sorry John. I'm not ready for this. You can stay the night if you want to but I don't want to be sexual with you.' He would remember the look of hurt on John's face for a long time to come. John withdrew and, without saying anything, he walked out.*

There is a strong sense of ambivalence about participation in this sexual encounter, with Michael being torn between sub-cultural moral imperatives and wider societal inhibitions. In the midst of all this, he does not appear to know what he wants: 'I'm not ready for this.' Interestingly, again there is no discussion of desire or the lack of it here; he can only discuss social inhibitions.

Michael commented afterwards that there was a view that profeminist men ought to be 'liberated enough' to experiment with sex with men and he had this sense that, perhaps, he was not 'liberated enough' and that he *should* have been more open to it. However, for heterosexual men to have sex with other men for 'political reasons' does not address homophobia at all and it may cause further splitting between the heterosexual and homosexual aspects within themselves.

Overcoming Homophobia

What can we learn about homophobia from the total pool of memories? Interestingly, while the cue for the memories was to recall episodes of discomfort in situations of intimacy with another man, all of the memories involved levels of sexual intimacy. Two of the memories involved adolescent explorations of sexuality, two involved explorations of intimacy with gay men and the final one involved intimacy between two heterosexual men. In all of the memories, there was a sense of obligation that is reminiscent of what one sometimes hears of women's sexual experiences with men.

Five instances of sexual contact between males are of course only a few of the potential encounters that heterosexual men might have but I wonder how prevalent stories such as these would be among heterosexually presenting men. I wonder also what it would mean if more men talked about such experiences amongst other men.

Some of these memories and the stories that flowed from them had never been told before and the disclosures about sexual experiences with other men opened up a new level of intimacy within the group.

For men participating in this experience, there was a repositioning in relation to gay sexuality. Telling these stories in a 'non-confessional' way potentially contributes to breaking down homophobia and heterosexual dominance. By challenging the prohibitions that lead men to 'bury' these experiences, we generate more acceptance and intimacy amongst men and subvert the construction of dominant heterosexuality.

Heterosexual Objectification

Whilst I acknowledge the coerciveness of many men's sexuality, I argue here against the radical feminist view that men's sexuality is *inherently* oppressive to women. I recognize, however, that the process of changing desire is not simply a matter of political will; it will require consciousness-raising and therapy. Here, through memory-work, I explore what this might mean in practice.

Heterosexual men who are aware of sexism and women's oppression often feel torn between their sexual desire and their awareness that their sexual behaviour and expressed fantasies about women may be experienced as oppressive by women (Horowitz and Kaufman, 1987: 81). Most heterosexual men experience their sexual attraction to women through being excited by their bodies. Does such sexual attraction inevitably lead to objectification and fixation? Objectification refers to the process by which the man sees the woman as a thing or an object and fixation to the process of focusing on parts of the female body (Buchbinder, 1987: 65–6). Some men even refer to themselves as 'breast men' or 'legs men'.

Objectification and fixation are seen to be key processes in men's sexual relationships with women, in which often a part of the woman is seen to represent the whole (Kaufman, 1993: 124). It is important to distinguish these processes from sexual and physical attraction. Following Beneke (1990: 178), I posit that 'what is sexist is the inability to simultaneously feel that excitement and accord women the respect and acknowledgement they deserve'.

Cixous has said that 'men have [still] everything to say about their own sex-uality' (cited in Jardine, 1987: 60). Heterosexual men have not often spoken or written reflectively about their sexual desires; they have simply enacted them. Rich (1983: 66) has also challenged men to say why they like pornography, whilst gay men have challenged heterosexual men to be 'up front' about their sexuality (Stoltenberg, 1991: 8).

What follows is an initial attempt to respond to these challenges. Participants were asked to recall a situation where they were conscious of objectifying a woman's body as a basis for sexual arousal. This could be an incident involving use of pornography, staring at a woman who is a stranger to them or using objectifying images while having sex.

Bodies Without Stories

Bruce's memory of objectification describes an experience of sexual arousal that is transformed when the woman's body is given a context:

They were sitting in the darkened theatre, Shane on his left and Sarah, holding his hand, on his right. The holding of hands had an adolescent type of charge about it as they sat surrounded by gay and lesbian couples. The first couple of pieces elicited some giggly smiles from him and any self-consciousness faded. The next piece intrigued him, as he saw an androgynous figure slowly emerge groaning from the trunk of the darkened stage. The puppet-like actor stepped from a box and his eyes zeroed in, 'breasts'. As she writhed and gyrated with loud mournful moans, he wished the light wasn't so teasingly dim. Did he really wish that? The naked woman danced into the light, a clear view of a mud spattered body. Ugly or earthy? Small breasts, cute or misplaced on such a large strong body? He didn't really understand what this performance art was about but watching the breasts and the hip and stomach curves was fascinating enough. The dirt covered woman then crouched on all fours, facing the audience. Her moans and cries became words. She rocked her hips suggestively as Bruce tuned into the lines that she chanted. 'Come on bitch get down, let me into you.' 'Come on bitch get down, let me into you.' He panicked. This woman was replaying to the audience her sexual abuse trauma. He pulled his hand away from Sarah. Maybe no-one had noticed that he was straight.

In this memory, Bruce's objectification of the woman's body is interrupted when her sexual abuse story is made known and he is unable to continue when her nudity is placed in this context. In the discussion afterwards, Bruce said: 'For the first part it was easy to objectify because there was no story. There was nothing. I knew nothing about this woman until that point. And it was only actually revealed when she was in that very sexual pose on all fours.'

Bruce's memory reminded Michael of a story from another man. He had been a habitual user of pornography for arousal and masturbation. On one occasion, he bought a pornographic magazine and discovered that the cen-trefold was a woman that he had known some twelve years earlier as a friend who had disclosed her sexual abuse and the associated traumas to him. The shock of seeing her and the revulsion he felt led him to never use pornography again. Whenever he saw a woman objectified by pornography, he was conscious that there was a story behind it.

Reflecting on this memory, I asked whether, if knowing the stories behind the nude photographs and the naked bodies, we would be less inclined to objectify women? Would it make a significant enough difference to change the way we relate to women when we know their stories? The group believed that it would: by knowing women's stories, it is much more difficult to objectify their bodies and deny their subjectivity.

The following memory by Carl demonstrated similar issues:

> *It was yesterday and Carl was at work and it was a very slow period. On the pile of papers and correspondence on various desks, he noticed an advertisement for a tanning studio. On the picture of this advertisement there was a woman in a single piece bikini, toes pointed. She was blonde and she was in a solar tanning machine. Carl noticed immediately her legs and was unaware of anyone watching him watching this picture. He didn't feel any shame or guilt in doing so. In a sense he felt a sense of freedom, that he was allowing himself to look at this picture so longingly. He moved his eyes upwards noticing her crotch and her bikini. He became less and less interested until he came to her face. Her eyes were shut with a sense of pleasure as she was lying down and he felt disinterested because suddenly these legs were attached to her body and with her person. He felt the unfinished business of relationships gone by with other women and the difficulty, the stress and so forth. Then as his eyes peered towards the whole of her body he felt a sense of sadness and the initial feeling of longing, although still there, was captured in the background of another human being. He looked around to his co-worker as a way of distracting himself from his feelings and made a joke of 'Do you want a free voucher to a tanning studio Bruce?' With that slight joke he was aware of his distraction and he threw the advertisement in the bin.*

In discussing the episode afterwards, Carl said that he was 'turned off' when he realized that the body was attached to a person. He remembered the experience of being sexually attracted to a woman and then, after the relationship developed, that 'things can be very difficult'. As Bruce commented: 'So the arousal bit is easy. The sexual relationship is the hard part.'

Carl reflected that there is a degree of struggle if he is going to relate to this person fully. If he allows himself 'just to objectify' he has limited the parameters of the relationship. Even if he acknowledges that there may be a story behind the woman, he does not want to know; as he commented: 'Either that or I'm so caught up in my objectification that I wouldn't see the story.' In this context, sexual objectification becomes a way of avoiding intimacy for there are no demands being made on men to relate to women holistically.

Pornography and the Sex Industry

The following memory from Michael illustrates the struggle that profeminist men sometimes have with their patriarchally constructed sexuality:

He was walking through the city, having just come from a heavy meeting. It was lunchtime and he was hot and thirsty. As he passed the pub he saw the sign outside announcing topless barmaids inside. He'd passed X-rated movie cinemas with strippers on numerous occasions in the city before. He was never tempted to go in. It was all so sleazy and so much a part of the exploration of his sexuality as an adolescent. He felt angry about the sex industry, about the way his own images of women had been shaped by it in his youth. But now he felt drawn to the pub. Lots of things went through his mind. Things were difficult in his primary relationship at the moment. He was conscious of wanting to be turned on without complications. This wasn't the sex industry. It wasn't sleazy. It was a pub. He often had a drink in pubs on hot days. After hesitating, he went down the steps into the pub. He walked up to the bar. He glanced at her breasts from the distance but avoided staring as he ordered a beer. The men were all gathered around the bar. He looked at them looking at her. Most of them had their eyes targeted at her breasts. Others stole glances when they thought she wasn't looking. He looked at her too, conscious that he was stealing glances rather than staring at her. He knew he had lied to himself. This was sleazy. He felt sleazy. He finished his beer and walked out. As he walked along the street, past some women walking by, he found himself noticing their breasts.

Michael was torn between his attraction to women's bodies and his strong opposition to the sex industry. He tried to rationalize his behaviour, but was forced to recognize his self-deception. He began the discussion of his memory by commenting upon how conscious he was of women's breasts when he came into the daylight again. Having just seen a bare-breasted woman, he felt like having x-ray vision as he walked past women in the street. This experience is consistent with Carl's experience of a participant observation survey carried out in table-top dancing venues:

> We objectified breasts more when we left the venue. In particular breasts, even though the whole body was exposed. I remember one particular situation when I saw a plunging neckline. There was some impulse for me just to try to see more and even entertain the thought of ripping that neckline down and being really shocked by that feeling. I'm not sure where that's come from. I'm still in the stage of integrating that behaviour.

Michael's experience and Carl's disclosure confirm that there is a basis for women's fears about the impact of the sex industry on men's attitudes towards women. The objectification elicited by sex workers potentially reinforces these processes in men who may then enact them with women who are not part of the sex industry.

Pornography is perhaps the most explicit means of objectifying women and fixating on their body parts. The following memory from Tony illustrates his conflicting feelings in using pornography:

> *He was at work and he became aware that one of his co-workers had some Picture magazines in the sleep-over room, in the office that he shares. Part of his office is also a bedroom because he does sleep-over shifts in a refuge. He became irritated*

and fascinated by these magazines being there in his room. He became quite con-
scious about them and particularly as he was aware that there would come a time
later, during the shift, where he would be by himself and he would be going to bed
and there would be all these opportunities to use the pornography and masturbate.
He chose not to masturbate for a long time. But in the end he did. He can't remem-
ber how long it was but he decided he'd just grab one of the magazines and started
reading and ended up masturbating. Afterwards, he felt disappointed with himself.

In discussing the memory later, Tony reported that his disappointment was
to do with having broken his ethical code and a personal commitment to himself as he wanted to perceive himself in a particular way. As he had become
more politically aware of how men relate to women and how he had related to
women in the past, he had wanted to distance himself from that experience. As
a result of using the pornography he began to question the strength of his
personal and political commitments:

What does this really mean, all this stuff that I've espoused? Do I really believe it?
How true is it? What does it say for me and about how I relate to all sorts of
people in my life, particularly women and, in particular, my partner? There was this
constant indecision about will I, or won't I.

Other group members identified with Tony's experience of being involved
in something objectifying and feeling bad afterwards; there was a shared
sense that when you use pornography you let yourself down. Profeminist
men are not alone in this experience, for while many men engage in objectification and fixation, it is not universally approved of, especially not as
commercialized sex.

All four memories presented here illustrate objectifying sexual practices by
men. Two memories describe episodes where the sexually objectifying
responses from the men are elicited in non-sexual contexts. These two memories identify the part played by disconnecting women's bodies from their
lives, enabling objectification to take place. In the other two memories directly
associated with commercialized sex, pornography and topless bars, feelings of
guilt and shame were associated with the objectification. The men were torn
between their desire to objectify and a sense that in doing so they were slip-
ping back into sexual practices they were trying to move beyond. In each of
these episodes, the men 'stumbled' upon the commercialized sex, rather than
consciously seeking it out.

Tony reported that he was also angry because he had not purchased the
magazines or sought them out; rather, they just appeared in his space. He
noticed that newsagents and milk bars were making these magazines more
public these days and he found this a lot more confronting: 'Because I can't
sort of shove these things over into the dark corner of the world or the dark
corner of my brain. I suppose I'm much more likely to bump into them.'

This discussion of the memory is consistent with Beneke's (1990: 171)
notion of intrusive images. He notes that 'advertising is full of images of
women likely to catch men unawares'. Also, sexually attractive women can be

experienced by men to be intrusive leading them to have unwanted erections. We began to reflect on the issue of intrusive images and men being angry at women for turning them on. Michael acknowledged that there have been times when he has felt like that:

> I'll be walking along and I won't be thinking sexual thoughts and I'll see a woman walking towards me. She'll be dressed in a very sexually arousing way, short skirt or a tight T-shirt with no bra. And I'll find myself glancing at her and I will sometimes experience that as an intrusion into my space in some way. I didn't want to feel sexual at that moment and all of a sudden she's presented herself in my space. I mean, it's a relatively mild experience of what I've read of men who are rapists who experience it at that much deeper level. Men who have described their rape as a revenge, a form of revenge on women for arousing them, for exciting them, by being in their space.

Michael said that the woman has 'presented herself in my space.' Men are in women's space all of the time and, with Michael's attitude, it is only a small step to blame women for arousing men and holding them responsible for men's subsequent behaviour. Graves, for example, argues that women who 'wave themselves around' in the workplace are

> using my sexuality as a weapon against me. A lot of male sexuality is visually driven. So anything designed to evoke a visual response is a form of unfair behaviour. It is an intrusion and distraction that is best understood as a form of sexual harassment. (cited in Arndt, 1995: 172–3)

How are we to understand men's anger at women for sexually arousing them? Many men experience women as having sexual power over them but, to the extent that this is true, men have given women this power. Men 'require' women's sexual power to remind them of their heterosexuality and to re-affirm their own masculinity, although they are likely to experience women's sexual power and their own response as 'natural'.

In theorizing the feelings associated with objectification, Carl made the comment that 'feelings have no morality. They're just feelings'. So what you feel is what you feel and there is no point in wanting to repress the feeling or to deny it. But where do feelings come from? If one believes that feelings are socially constructed, what one feels is a product of the culture that has been internalized within oneself. One carries the culture within oneself. If we want to distance ourselves from patriarchal culture, it will require a transformation of some of the feelings that the culture has generated within us.

Challenging the Sexual Objectification of Women

In the light of memories like these, how should profeminist men respond strategically to commercialized sex? We addressed this issue in the discussion following the memory-work in which the question was raised of the extent to which we should develop campaigns and strategies that aim to regulate or prohibit certain practices? The alternative was to run educational campaigns that aim to get men to examine the costs of objectification to their own sexuality and to their capacity for intimacy and connectedness. These questions have obvious implications for how we respond to the debate about censorship and pornography.

In response to this question, Carl argued 'Censorship can link into the denial and disowning process of my own body and therefore it reinforces objectification'. For Carl, the more important issue was the linking of objectification with the sense of ownership or 'power over', rather than objectification on its own. Bruce agreed and argued that prohibiting pornography 'gives too much weight to fantasy'. In his view, it does not allow for people having fantasy lives and it confirms the morally conservative view 'that sex is nasty and naughty'. He was concerned that profeminist men could be seen as moral conservatives.

This is a complex issue because, while it is true that one cannot legislate against fantasy, nor constructively address pornography through the guilt-based repression advocated by the Christian churches, many men's fantasies are shaped by the pornography industry. While such fantasies may 'turn men on', they also function to limit men's feelings when they are with their partners, which is demonstrated by Michael's comment:

> I found that in my early sexual experiences, I was drawing upon pornographic images in my love-making. To the extent that I was doing that, I was objectifying my partner. I was less conscious of her and more conscious of the objectifying images in my mind as I was making love with her.

It is experiences like these that led Michael to give up pornography but he wondered whether that means that we are positing a new morality, to which Bruce responded: 'That's what I feel uncomfortable about. I wouldn't want to see that become the only model.' The question was raised, however, whether we should draw a 'moral line' on some issues in relation to men's sexuality to which Bruce answered:

> It should be done in terms of 'sex is fun', 'intimacy is fun'. Not 'this is the moral line'. I don't think you'd sell it as a moral line. In order to get some more justice, I'd push it much more towards consent. But in order to sell it to men, I wouldn't say 'thou shalt not'. I would try and sell it in terms of it being a much more enjoyable experience.

Carl similarly argued that developing a social ethic was not the best strategy: 'I have a very fundamental belief that men would rather choose intimacy than objectification. I don't believe that if I had a full understanding of both choices that I would choose to objectify.' Some of us did not fully share Carl's optimism. It depends partly upon what a 'full understanding of both choices' means.

Bruce noted that if you are against assault and coercion in sexual relationships with women, you are interpreted as believing that that is all there is to sex. The issue is: how does one challenge sexual violence and coercion in heterosexual relationships without being seen to be challenging heterosexual sex itself? As Segal (1994: 249) reminds us, the prevalence of men's sexual violence does not negate the fact that the majority of heterosexual women experience pleasure in heterosexual sex; women are not simply victims of men's sexual desires. Further, to the extent that men are 'able to accept, encourage, share in and benefit from women's growing autonomy', they will be more able to relate sexually with women in ways that are not oppressive, pathological or disabling. Research also suggests that such men are more likely to be contented (Segal, 1994: 260, 285).

While the articulation and affirmation of positive experiences of heterosexual sex by men who are forming non-patriarchal subjectivities and practices will potentially break the perceived antagonism between enlightened self-interest and social justice, there is still the need for a framework of ethics for accountability.

In this regard, I find Seidman's (1992: 5–6) work useful in his search for a social ethic that goes beyond the polarization between the libertarian celebration of sex as a joyous phenomenon and the romanticist emphasis on the dangers of sex arising from objectification, violence and exploitation. While rejecting a universal moral imperative to guide sexual practice, Seidman, nevertheless, proposes 'sexual responsibility' as a sexual ethic that both affirms variations in sexual conduct while offering standards to regulate moral choice (1992: 199). His recognition of fluid moral boundaries and the importance he attributes to engaged public discourse about morality is in keeping with my emphasis on consciousness-raising and dialogue as ways of personalizing moral issues.

Conclusion

In the preceding chapter, memory-work was used to examine experiences predominantly referring back to childhood and adolescence. The focus here has mainly been on memories from adulthood associated with homophobia and sexual objectification. In comparing the two sets of memories in this chapter, it is interesting that the cue of discomfort with intimacy with other men was read in all instances as sex, whereas the cue of objectification with women elicited incidents that were devoid of intimacy.

In these episodes, profeminist heterosexual men have described their involvement in the reproduction of hierarchical modes of heterosexuality. Reporting these memories, the men disclosed moments in their lives when they either challenged or accommodated to the processes of the reproduction of sexual dominance. They spoke from the dominant position about what it means to repress experiences of intimacy with other men and what it means to objectify women's bodies. They responded to Stoltenberg's

(1991: 9) challenge to speak a form of 'revolutionary honesty' and to say 'This is what I did'. When men share the memories and stories of their part in the reproduction of hierarchical heterosexuality, they are subverting the construction of dominant masculinities. Furthermore, they are engaging in a process of reconstructing their subjectivities and practices in the arena of sexual politics.

PART III

TRANSFORMING MASCULINITY POLITICS

---

7   Men's Movement Politics

Profeminist men's politics is regarded by many commentators as a part of the men's movement which, as previously discussed, is also seen as encompassing men's liberationist, mythopoetic and men's rights groups. Whilst the women's movement is a political movement, the main emphasis in the men's movement has been on personal change and celebrating the diversity of men's experiences.

In response to Canaan and Griffin's (1990: 62) critique that there is no sense of political strategy in profeminist men's work, this chapter examines the political dimensions of the men's movement and the appropriateness of locating profeminist men's politics within it. This examination involves a critical interrogation of the literature of the men's movement and an analysis of dialogues between the research group and interlocutors from the mythopoetic men's movement and the men's rights movement. The dialogues serve both to assess the potential for profeminist men to influence the direction of the men's movement and to act as a catalyst to clarify profeminist subjectivities and practices.

The first part of the chapter engages with issues raised by the men's rights movement, and in the second part of the chapter, I address issues for profeminist men's politics arising from dialogues with the mythopoetic men's movement.

The Men's Rights Movement

No attempt will be made here to comprehensively analyse the men's rights movement as a whole nor to consider all of the issues it has taken up. Rather, the purpose is to identify the premises and claims that critically challenge the profeminist perspective and to engage in dialogue with representatives of the men's rights movement about them. Those issues notably are: blame and victimization, blame and responsibility, women's complicity in patriarchal relations, women's violence, the prevalence of men's violence and violence as a gender issue.

The intellectual sources that I draw upon in my analysis are Goldberg (1976, 1987), Farrell (1986, 1993), Baumli (1985), Lyndon (1992) and Thomas (1993). The local engagement with the issues arises from correspondence, conversations and meetings with Tom Graves and the People's Equality Network.

Blame and Victimization

A key argument of the men's rights movement, that is also widely shared by men in general, is that men are unfairly blamed by women and feminism in that women are portrayed inappropriately as victims and men as perpetrators. Does blaming men for women's oppression indeed portray women as helpless victims and is this ineffective as a response to changing men?

To address these issues, Tom Graves from the People's Equality Network was chosen as an interlocutor as he has been an outspoken critic of feminism and a defender of men whom he sees as being unfairly blamed by women. The People's Equality Network was formed because of some men's 'shared concern and anger at the never ending biased and sexist reporting against men'. They aim 'to expose misleading reporting and biased commentary' about men. Prior to the meeting with the profeminist men's network, Graves sent a letter and some notes outlining his position as a basis for the discussion.

In his notes, Graves argued that people who feel disempowered, may seek to 'export' that sense of disempowerment to others and that such projection of guilt or blame is to deny responsibility for one's own actions. Thus, to blame others is seen as a form of exercising 'power over' and an act of violence. He argues that

> feminism has depended on a premise that men, and men alone, can be blamed for all the world's problems. It can be shown that this has actually *increased* the net level of violence and hence increased the problems complained about. Only by approaching the problem as a *human* problem – not a genderal one – can we resolve any of the chaos that has been created in the past few decades . . . [T]o be profeminist requires men to blame themselves or, less honestly, blame other men for issues that are inherently human problems. I regard it as essential to understand that we will get nowhere unless we formally recognize that the rights and responsibilities of both genders are exactly equivalent and/or exactly symmetrical. (Graves, 1993: personal communication, emphasis original)

Thus, according to Graves, blaming others is to disempower oneself and consequently women have reinforced their own powerlessness by adopting the victim role. He expands on this in his unpublished book:

> Current feminism seems obsessed with laying the blame for all the world's problems squarely and solely on the shoulders of men . . . Blaming is a way of attempting to

export responsibility . . . And blame . . . is also self-disempowering . . . We blame others, claim that only others have the power to resolve the problem on our behalf: but in doing so, we deny ourselves the power . . . Such feminists demand that all men – and only men – should bear the blame and guilt for the actions and inactions of all other people, past or present. (Graves, 1994: 15–16)

Graves says that the most common theme in feminist literature 'has been to portray women as victims of men'. Is it wrong to see women as victims of men? Certainly, a consciousness of victimization 'recognizes the oppressor's responsibility and assigns blame to the oppressor' (Wendell, 1990: 12–13). It enables women to avoid blaming themselves for their oppression, relieves them of guilt, enables them to express anger at their oppressors and provides the basis for empathy with other women and for collective opposition to their oppression.

But are there also negative consequences for women in identifying themselves primarily as victims? The danger in adopting a victim role is that one can block one's personal power. People may not look for what it is that they can do within their own lives to more effectively deal with the consequences of their oppression. However, there is an important distinction between empowering people to take more responsibility for their own lives and blaming them for their oppression.

The opposite danger is that of shifting the focus from the perpetrator to the victim. In encouraging people to empower themselves, the intimidating behaviour of the perpetrator remains unchallenged. For those on the receiving end of abuse to work out how best to avoid, escape or challenge the abuse is one thing. It is a different matter for those in positions of privilege to tell others that they are not taking enough responsibility for the abuse. Stressing the choice of the victim rather than the imposition by the person who hurt or threatened the victim is a form of 'victim blaming' (Ryan, 1976). Such a process focuses 'attention on characteristics of the victims and away from the oppressive actions of individuals who are harming them or the more general social causes of their oppression' (Wendell, 1990: 6).

Thus, victim blaming occurs where blame and responsibility are assigned to the victims of oppression, who are encouraged to adopt the perspective of the oppressor, thereby feeling guilty for their victimization. Accordingly, the men's rights critique of 'victim–feminism' shifts responsibility for the experience of oppression to those on the receiving end.

Blame and Responsibility

Another criticism of blaming men for abusive behaviour is that it is not an effective means of changing them. Men's rights advocates believe that blaming men for the oppression of women is counter-productive to ending sexism. They argue that it is more important to understand *why* it is that men do what they do than to condemn them for their behaviour (Clatterbaugh, 1990: 62, 66).

Goldberg argues that behaviour that arises out of guilt and shame can never be liberating. In his view, blame and guilt are misguided and if the goal is to change men, the strategy is counter-productive: 'I have never seen a person grow or change in a self-constructive, meaningful way when he was motivated by guilt, shame, or self hate' (1987: 5).

This view is echoed by McMillan:

> *If I care to look* I can see the exploitation and objectification of women that is going on in pornography, but that does not mean I am going to stop buying it or enjoying it. I know that Thai girls are sold by their families into prostitution and become virtual slaves, but I still fantasise about going to Asia and fucking women to my heart's content . . . So how do attitudes change? Certainly nothing really changes if the motivation is guilt, the belief that I should change or the fact that somebody else thinks I should. I will on the other hand be motivated to look at the way I operate if *I see good reason for doing so.* (1992: 140–1, emphasis mine)

One wonders what would constitute 'a good reason' in McMillan's view. There certainly appears to be no ethical basis for decision-making in this perspective, whilst those men who do operate from such a position are themselves subjected to criticism:

> There has been a *misdirected* 'men's movement' of sorts . . . Unfortunately it was based on apologising for being a man . . . the agenda and the energy of the male feminists was often overwhelmingly negative, and most healthy men didn't want a bar of it. Imagine joining a movement or attending a group which started from the premise that you were born (and always would be) defective, second rate, child molester and murderer – and had better exercise some self control. It was limited in its appeal . . . Simply blaming men doesn't change anything. (Biddulph, 1994: 21–2, emphasis mine)

Thus, men's rights proponents view profeminist men as being filled with self-loathing. It seems that to criticize hegemonic forms of masculinity and to challenge men's violence and abuse is regarded as essentializing men as bad. To hold men responsible for maintaining patriarchy is to evoke a defensiveness among them. Biddulph explains the 'backlash' against women as a result of men being frightened:

> When feminism is one-sided, it finds just such reaction . . . Any move to change the order of things which does not also address the fact that men are *equally* lost, trapped and miserable will only create its own resistance . . . Blaming men is neither compassionate, accurate or useful. Women who attack men as a group are simply passing on their own abuse . . . it's inexcusable. (1994: 20, emphasis mine)

Faludi (1992: 331) cites Levin, whom she interviewed for *Backlash*, as saying that he took a stand against the women's movement because 'women began calling on men to alter their behaviour'. Also, Bloom is cited as saying that 'the most tyrannical demand of feminism is that men should change too' (cited in Faludi, 1992: 322).

Tom Graves develops the theme that blaming men will not be an effective means of changing them and at the meeting with us this argument was put vehemently, as the following outburst suggests:

> I'm fed up with women's lies . . . There is a significant anger. I do not wish to see men like myself, as I have done, go all out to cripple, not merely themselves, but other men with blaming. Blaming is a form of anger which some aspects of feminism have made into a very fine art. Blaming is a very interesting trap. There is a crucial difference between blame and excuse. There is a crucial distinction between blame and responsibility. The point about blame is to demand that someone go back and change the past. That is a double bind. It is clearly impossible . . . Blame is also a demand that others exclusively must respond to the situation.

The Concise Oxford Dictionary makes no distinction between blame and responsibility, as Graves asserted; it defines blame as to 'fix responsibility on', to 'hold him [sic] responsible for it'. Holding someone responsible does not demand changing the past but it does entail accepting some responsibility for the past and it requires that one resolve how to *make amends* for the past. French gives a useful definition in relation to responsibility: 'To ascribe responsibility is for some person to identify another person as the cause of a harmful or untoward event, because of some action that was performed by that other person' (1991: 3).

Certainly, a victim perspective recognizes the responsibility of the oppressors and it is arguably the best perspective for someone who has recently been victimized. It is, however, important to consider whether holding people responsible for past conduct will affect future behaviour. Can too much blame obscure the blamer's choices? Is it legitimate to use moral reproach as a tool for affecting personal and social change? I believe that it is, because public blaming affirms moral standards, it can influence people's behaviour and contribute to ending oppression.

Braithwaite (1991: 30) proposes that moral reproach or what he calls 'reintegrative shaming' prevents crime and violence. He applies this perspective to violence within families and emphasizes the importance of persuading men 'to internalize an abhorrence of violence, to take pride in respecting the rights of women and caring for others'. Adopting an ethical stance in relation to violence and abuse can become a source of pride for men rather than a source of self-hate as Graves and men's rights activists would have it.

Blaming the Victim

A third theme running through the men's rights discourse is the importance of acknowledging women's 'equal responsibility' for maintaining the relations of patriarchy. As Graves commented during his meeting with the group: 'When I actually look at the undercurrents, I see a great deal of gender equivalence. It is a lot more subtle than it looks. I see a lot of the maintenance of the social structure, both constructive and destructive, maintained by both genders.'

It is generally acknowledged in feminism and in critical theory that sub-ordinated groups internalize oppression and that they contribute to the reproduction of oppressive social arrangements. Exploring the extent to which women themselves collude in maintaining the conventional structures, Coward (1993: 10-11) acknowledges that, in asking about women's complicity, she faces the 'danger of ignoring the pervasiveness of men's power'. Wendell's response to this issue is a timely reminder: 'It is legitimate to be concerned about the victim's contribution to her/his own victimization, *but only when the oppressor's contribution has been thoroughly and honestly examined and described'* (1990: 29, emphasis mine).

Most men have not even begun to acknowledge their individual and collective responsibilities in the maintenance of patriarchy. The emphasis of much of the men's rights' response is that women are equally responsible for the problems in the world and the issues confronting them. They are seen to be equally violent, equally sexually aggressive, equally controlling and equally power hungry. This is, however, different from the recognition that women may at times be complicit in their own oppression.

When we talk about men's violence, men often retort by referring to women's violence as a way of saying 'it is a human problem; it is not just men, but women are also perpetrators'. If women can be perpetrators, it is obviously not men's problem; it is not gender.

When men do experience violence by women, it is difficult to see beyond that experience, to locate violence within a broader historical and social context. It is also a misreading of feminism to suggest that feminism postulates that only men can be violent. Popular media, however, portray feminism in this way and it consequently is perceived by many of its opponents as being based on this premise. The process of emphasizing women's violence when men's violence is discussed is a common theme in discussions with men and it becomes yet another way of individual men denying that they have any connection with the issue.

The view that women are equally violent is clearly evident in the men's rights literature. Domestic violence is said to be 'mutual and shared aggression' (Lyndon, 1992: 166), and men and women are seen as 'equally capable of committing acts of evil' (Thomas, 1993: 140). It is arguments such as these that lead McNeely and Robinson-Simpson (1988: 184–6) to define domestic violence as 'a human rather than a women's issue' and to argue that to label domestic violence as a women's issue 'tends to vilify men simply because they are men [and] creates conditions that diminish the involvement of men in solving the problem'.

The overwhelming research evidence clearly demonstrates that men and women are not equally victims of violence in marriage and it challenges the premises and the methodology of the previously mentioned studies. The much cited self-reporting Conflict Tactics Scale (CTS) used by Straus and Gelles (1990) to measure aggression and violence in the family ignores the relative social and economic power of men and women. It does not address the social, economic and emotional context in which the violence is embedded. Men and women are treated as equals when, in fact, they are not (Darling, 1988: 189). The CTS has also been criticized for omitting rape and sexual assault and for excluding the events precipitating the violence and the sequence of events by which it unfolds (Dobash and Dobash, 1992: 76). Most instances of violence against men are a result of women taking defensive action before being attacked by a male partner (Thorne-Finch, 1992: 210). This is supported by Saunders's (1988: 96) research indicating that when women use violence 'it is more likely to be against a violent partner than a non-violent one'. Finally, women's greater economic dependence and smaller physical size are clear indications why women are more victimized.

There is no doubt that *some* men are victimized by women but the problem of women's violence against men is nowhere near as significant a problem as men's violence against women. For one to argue that marital violence is 'sexually symmetrical', one would have to ignore a large body of research that illustrates that women greatly outnumber men as victims. In instances where women strike the first blow, such an act is unlikely to be the mirror image of one in which her husband initiated the violence. In male victim cases, there is rarely any indication of the kind of chronic intimidation that characterizes the battering of women (Dobash and Dobash, 1992: 74, 80).

Of course, those few men who are harmed by their partners must be responded to but it does not make sense to divert attention away from the large-scale problem of men's violence to focus attention on the minority of male victims (Straton, 1994: 81). Furthermore, men can leave a violent relationship more easily than a woman can because they usually have greater access to jobs and less commitment to child care.

It is important to identify the differences in the patterns of male and female violence which would enable us to describe and explain the overall process of violence within both its immediate and wider contexts.

One of the main differences here, as Braithwaite and Daly (1993: 1) point out, is that, while some women may commit violence, their behaviour is more likely to be interpreted as being pathological. Men's violence against women has been openly supported by a whole range of laws and cultural norms. There is no history of approval for women's violence against men.

The men's rights advocates endeavour to produce male abuse victims so that they can claim that the violence of men and women is equal in all quantitative and qualitative aspects. If they were less interested in discrediting feminism and more interested in responding to the needs of male victims, they would note that men are most likely to experience violence perpetrated by other men (Thorne-Finch, 1992: 211). The implications of the men's rights' position seems to be that, if women can be shown to be violent under certain circumstances, there is no basis to continue to campaign against men's violence, nor to expect men to change unilaterally.

Men and Collective Responsibility

Another theme in the men's rights discourse is that individual men are not responsible for the actions of other men. This is also expressed as 'all men are not the same'. As two participants on a 1992 Australian television programme *Couchman Over Australia* on men's responses to feminism explained:

> I think it is unfair . . . to make generalizations about men along those lines [of being the abuser, harasser, etc.] . . . When commentators do make generalizations about men which are obviously generalizations about all men, rather than just specific men, who obviously do commit these offences, I think that men have to be able to interject and enter the debate. (Phillip Newton)

> Men are cast in the role as oppressors. The burden of guilt is attached to being male, regardless of one's individual conduct. Men are very definitely being seen to blame for the various ills affecting womanhood. (Perry Hoskins)

In response, one unnamed woman in the studio audience said: 'They're guilty by being silent', which was elaborated by another participant, Liz Connor:

> The important thing to say is not that feminism is accusing individual men of being oppressors. Feminism is asking men to own up to the ways that they have been privileged by those systems and structures [which reinforce structural inequities].

Asking men to hold themselves accountable for sexism, when oppression occurs at the level of 'social practice', faces another level of resistance. Here, the excuse for 'wrong-doing' is the assumed 'normalcy and social legitimacy of one's actions'. Men resist change because there is 'nothing wrong with what one is doing' (Calhoun, 1989: 393). But of course, as Calhoun points out: 'Men's benefiting from oppressive social practices provides them with a motive for resisting critical reflection and for exercising self deception about their own motives and about the consequences for women of their actions' (1989: 399).

There is also a danger that emphasizing the social construction of masculinity will displace individual responsibility, as individual men can say: 'It is not anything that I can help. Nor is it anything that I can be held individually responsible for.'

This leads us into the issue of collective responsibility. Some critics have argued that the latter undermines the concept of individual responsibility 'because it makes one person responsible for the actions of another' (French, 1991: 251). It is, however, important for men to think about their position of dominance in society. Why do men find this so difficult to do? Thompson (1991: 14) says that men believe that they have a 'market on the truth' and are sceptical about the validity of other people's experience. As previously discussed, as men take patriarchy for granted, they are largely unaware of how much the social structure yields advantages to them. Further, as they do not notice the talents and accomplishments of women, which are socially deval- ued anyway, they perceive their superior position as just (Goode, 1982: 137).

It is important for profeminist men to find ways to encourage other men to see why they have a collective responsibility to challenge the personal sexism of other men and the institutionalized sexism that continues to advantage them.

The men's rights perspective has managed to generate a lot of support because it refuses to blame men and argues that both sexes are harmed by gender-role stereotypes. Men's rights advocates sometimes expose the failings of hegemonic masculinity and its effects on men, but they ignore or minimize the effects on women of adhering to this dominant form of masculinity. They also deny the advantages and privileges that men have gained by adopting hegemonic masculinity and they appeal to the tendency within men to regard their own victimization as most important and to ignore the effect their behaviour has on women. Profeminist men thus need to respond theoretically and strategically to all of the issues on the men's rights agenda and develop counter arguments in the public arena.

The Mythopoetic Men's Movement

The mythopoetic men's movement, first named as such by Shepherd Bliss in 1986, 'looks to ancient mythology and fairy tales, to Jungian and archetypal psychology and to poets and teachers like Robert Bly and James Hillman' (1986: 38). Perhaps the most significant single contribution to the develop- ment of this movement was the Keith Thompson interview with Robert Bly, first published in 1982. Bly elaborated upon his mythical approach in his 1990 bestseller, *Iron John*, and a series of other mythopoetic books followed shortly after, including Moore and Gillette (1990), Keen (1991), Lee (1991) and Kauth (1992).

Here, I look at the political implications of this trend towards personal and spiritual growth in the men's movement, a key premise of which is that men will only change their behaviour by acknowledging and dealing with their own pain and abuse and by healing themselves. It is claimed that the only way for men to eliminate sexist behaviour is to reclaim their pride as men. These premises are interrogated through an examination of major mythopoetic and men's liberation texts, a discussion with research participants following a viewing of Bill Moyer's film about Robert Bly called *A Gathering of Men*, through reflecting upon a meeting with a local men's ritual group called the Men's Evolvement Network and an examination of pamphlets and work- shop fliers for men's personal growth.

Encountering Robert Bly

In the interview with Keith Thompson, Bly (1987a: 178) talks about the importance of men developing 'Zeus energy' which 'encompasses intelligence,

robust health, compassionate authority, good will, leadership – in sum, positive power accepted by the male in the service of the community'. Men can
get in touch with their male energy by 'learning to visualize the wild man',
which involves going back to ancient mythology.

To begin to formulate our response to the mythopoetic men's movement,
we viewed and discussed the Bill Moyer interview with Robert Bly. A number
of the men identified with Bly's ideas, as presented in the film. Carl said that
if he was confused and searching for something and heard someone talking
in a very simple way, making maxims and using talking stones and a guitar,
he would find himself drawn to it. He also believed that there was usefulness
in 'mending the ties between father and son and other men's relationships'.
Trevor argued that Bly had tapped into some deep spiritual truths, although
he had only a limited view of those truths. The ideas touched Alan's personal
experience, because his father, like Bly's, was an alcoholic and was similarly
absent.

Other men were critical of Bly's ideas. Manuel had concerns about his
over-generalizations and lack of qualification about which men he was referring to. He also thought that there was an ageist quality in some of his
comments about 'the death of the boy' which served to put down young
men. Peter also had a critical response to the film: 'He said fathers have been
told they're inadequate by women for 30 or 40 years. What have women been
told for how long? I felt like it was encouraging a sense of self-pity for men.
Like we've got a pretty bad deal here.' Ben's thought was that, if Bly is meeting an important need in men, we should 'not throw the whole thing out' but
work out the spiritual significance of his work and build on that. Michael
acknowledged that Bly touched some aspect of his experience and that, at
times, he felt drawn to his words: 'I feel that I should listen to what he is
saying. But as I reflect upon my response, I note that he knows how to work
an audience and he knows how to use humour and myth to connect with
men.'

Manuel appropriately asked what exactly Bly is providing for men. What
is the basis of the comfort that he seems to provide for so many men? What
needs is Bly responding to in men? Why are his ideas so popular among men?
As I reflect upon these questions, I come to the view that, in spite of Bly's
claims to the contrary, the promotion of the wild man and the warrior has the
propensity to reinforce traditional masculinities and entrench oppressive masculine behaviour. Accounts of participants in the mythopoetic men's groups
tend to describe patriarchal ways of acting as expressions of their warrior-
hood (King, 1992: 137).

Another concern is the danger that Bly's work may be used to justify men's
violence against women and make it acceptable. He describes an incident
where a teenage boy knocked his mother across the table when she asked him
to set the table and his response to this event was: 'The boy couldn't bring
what he needed into consciousness, but his body knew it. And his body
reacted. The mother didn't take it personally either . . . There was too much
female energy in the house for him' (Bly, 1987b: 16–17).

I thus share O'Connor's (1993: 8) concern that pursuing the masculine may revive misogyny and lead to a further deterioration in men's capacity to relate to women. For men who are unreconstructed male chauvinists, the Wild Man can herald a permission to be even more aggressive, and for those men who have not engaged with feminism, Bly's encouragement to 'toughen up' could exacerbate and deepen their patriarchal consciousness (Tacey, 1990: 787).

In mythopoetic writings, rituals initiating boys into manhood in non-Western cultures are thought to be equally important in the Western context. According to Bly (1990: 1–3), their absence in Western culture is the major reason why men have such difficulty achieving 'true manhood'. Most of these rites of passage for males involve a painful ordeal – beatings, fasting, circumcision and killing an enemy or wild animal and the young men are taught by the elders that men must be able to suffer in silence and be brave (Keen, 1992: 238). Thus, such initiation rituals not only separate the men from the boys but also the men from the women and many of them are expressions of oppressive social organization (Samuels, 1993: 189–90).

Societies from which such myths, folk-tales and rituals derive were often patriarchal and many of them were used by men to reinforce their power over women and to advance patriarchal discourses. Bly uses the myths as though they represent certain truths about the human psyche, but they are culture and time-bound descriptions of certain realities that pertain to particular time and space contexts (Silverstein and Rashbaum, 1994: 9).

Encountering the Men's Evolvement Network

To engage in dialogue with men who follow the mythopoetic teachings we set up a meeting with the Men's Evolvement Network (MEN). This group was chosen as interlocutors because they seemed to best represent the application of mythopoetical ideas in the local context. The group was formed in 1990 and describes its vision as 'to facilitate the process of self discovery by activating in men their full masculine potential'. They state in their newsletter that they are 'open to the inner reaches of the masculine soul' (MEN Newsletter).

The group is led by Andy Hauser and John Byrne, who use storytelling, myth analysis, poetry readings and drumming nights to explore manhood issues. The following excerpts from their newsletter illustrate some of their premises:

> The archetypal masculine is accessed by relating our life issue with the substance of myth, ritual, fairy tale and dream. The door opens to the ageless level of male experience containing 'inherent patterns for our unfoldment'.
> World change begins with the individual . . . By changing our own psyche we change or 'add to' the collective psyche of men thereby making further patterns of unfoldment possible for others. (MEN Newsletter 1994)

Fliers for workshops advertise the following:

Discover the Magic of Being Men: Reclaiming the Male Spirit
We shall explore creative aspects of our fierce energy while remaining centred and supportive of each other. Special emphasis on spiritual warriorship.

Unfolding the Whole Man
Integrating the fragmented 'parts' of manhood and building relationship with the Cosmic or Universal Man.

The Inner Dance of the Masculine and the Feminine
Tap your potential energy, joy, creativity and direction through entering into the heart of relationship mystery by connecting with the polarities within . . . Develop skills for healing the global gender conflict.

Notions like 'archetypal masculine', 'male spirit' and 'universal man' tend to assume an essentialist masculinity. Most essentialists regard biology as the basic cause of all gender differences. Thus, by construing masculinity as part of that essence, the mythopoetic men's movement is likely to conclude that only limited changes in masculinity are desirable and possible. This will reinforce traditional masculinity rather than transform it (King, 1992: 136). Certainly essentialism has played an important role in the reproduction of patriarchy. Men have argued the superiority of men's essential nature over women's essential nature and have claimed privileged access to rationality and universal truth on that basis. As a result, women's experience has been ignored or denied. Thus, the search for a 'true masculine' can become yet another way to continue male privilege with essentialism obscuring the nature of that power. Furthermore, the idea of a masculine essence does not make ethnographic and historical sense as representations of masculinity vary significantly between cultures (Connell, 1992b: 34).

The meeting with the Men's Evolvement Network took place in their group premises during one of their regular meetings. As we arrived and before introductions took place, we found ourselves immediately involved in their ritual space. The lights were dimmed, we were asked to remove our shoes and the MEN members took percussion instruments and began to drum, tap and rattle them. Other men moved to the rhythm and began to dance and sway, whilst we were left to work out our responses to this ritual. Some of us danced, some tuned in to the rhythm, while others sat motionless with dance and sounds surrounding us. The music and sounds moved to a crescendo as those with drums belted out rhythms with increasing volume. After some twenty minutes this ritual came to a close and the men formed a circle with a lighted candle in the centre and began to introduce themselves, affording us the opportunity to do the same.

As they shared their thoughts and feelings about the meeting, it was apparent that there was a high level of anxiety on their part about our visit. It also became apparent that many of them had preconceptions about us that involved political correctness, ideology and manifestos. They were at pains to emphasize that they were not 'political'. Rather they were concerned with their own personal journey and supportive friendships with a few men with little or no concern about the wider social impact of their journey. Other men in the group argued that men should address their personal needs before becoming involved in social activism. These views contrasted, however, with the actions of the facilitators to promote an alternative masculinity through the establishment of a men's centre and through the public media.

In response to my inquiry about how they handled accounts of sexist or abusive behaviour, some of the men present said that they saw no place for a moral stance on acceptable male behaviour. One man argued quite aggressively that all men who abuse have been abused themselves and that consequently moral imperatives and legislative changes against violence and abusive behaviour would not connect with such men. They will only change their behaviour by acknowledging and dealing with their own pain and abuse and by healing themselves. I responded that I believed that we needed to separate the healing journey men may need to go through from attempting to stop violent and oppressive behaviours and that, if any ambivalence about this prevailed, men would find justifications for their violence.

I challenged the emphasis on men's pain in the context of men's violence to which one man responded that it was understandable and appropriate that men should quickly assert their own hurts or injustices when reminded or confronted with men's violence against women. He talked about the way in which women express their anger, while another man talked about the experience of being oppressed by a woman. Murmurs of agreement from other MEN members were forthcoming and it seemed that men's bonding through the putting down of women emerged quickly on the night.

The starting point for our reflection of the meeting with MEN was whether their experience constituted a place to start for many men. Ben believed that it was, as a lot of men involved in the mythopoetic men's movement may be open to looking at other issues if they can be presented to them in such a way that they can see the connections: 'When they can actually see that being dominating, being patriarchal is stuffing up their relationships, then that may be the next step.' Harry, on the other hand, saw no potential to connect these men to profeminist issues. In his reflections on the meeting with MEN, he saw no responsiveness to the issues we raised. Rather, in his view, they demonstrated a range of defensive positions.

So we were presented with two different responses to the mythopoetic men's movement: to work closely with them to help them connect their personal issues to a broader political context or to publicly challenge them as part of the backlash against women.

Spirituality, Politics and Social Change

The MEN members contrasted their spiritual approach with what they saw as our emphasis on intellectual and political dimensions implying that profeminist men had no spirituality. We discussed this as we reflected on our meeting with the group.

Bruce believed that they were trying to claim the territory of the personal and the spiritual, the inference being that anyone who talks intellectually is, by definition, unconnected to the spiritual:

> I think we can talk intellectually and personally and spiritually and with energy in what we have to say, without using those sorts of mythical and poetic terms. This is the idea that if words are used in any sort of analytical way, they are therefore devoid of spirit.

He further commented that, while they laid claim to the personal, they maintained that they were not dealing with the political. Criticism of intellectual and theoretical frameworks is common among men who identify with the mythopoetical and men's liberation groups. Phillip identified the lack of context in their perspective:

> There's all that stuff about hurt and wounding and all that sort of stuff. But the thing that they don't have is a social context or even a sort of ethics. OK, I'm trying to deal with this, but it's my responsibility to put it in a social context. As a male, I've got to start talking about my patriarchal position and behaviour after that.

For many of us, to reject many of the premises of the mythopoetical men's movement does not necessarily imply rejecting spirituality. The question is, though, how does spirituality relate to our social change work? I mentioned that Bly has been very effective in moving from the spiritual to the political. We may not like the message he communicates but he has written about it in a way that has struck chords of recognition in thousands of men. I wondered whether an equally powerful alternatively based spiritual message could be conveyed to men. Could we construct a spiritual message that would also strike chords of recognition in men and at the same time would lead them to act responsibly in the world?

Bruce remarked that the power of Bly's message was not just about chords of recognition but also about affirmation. The ideas were received fairly happily because they were not very threatening. They affirm what men want to believe about themselves: 'Chords of recognition could actually be quite threatening, like feminism for instance. I recognize things within feminism, as it is described in my experience, and I don't like what it says.' Bruce said that feminism confronts him and challenges him to do things differently, but to get a positive response from most men, one has to be affirming. The distinction between recognition and affirmation in educational work with men is an important one but the question then becomes: Can feminism be an affirming experience for men?

In light of our discussion of the limitations of Bly's mythopoetic approach, we began to question whether it was tapping into the spiritual at all. Peter suggested that if someone has something akin to a spiritual experience in the context of a Robert Bly weekend retreat, they may erroneously associate it with his teachings. Ben similarly referred to Bly's teachings as 'a McDonald's version of spirituality'. If men are out of touch with their bodies and estranged from their fathers, an emotional experience in the context of an intensive workshop could be experienced as 'spiritual' by some men.

Thus, the therapy and healing that takes place on mythopoetic weekends is not necessarily 'spirituality'. Getting our emotional needs met in a group setting is not in itself the basis of a spiritual experience. As Upton comments: 'There's so much stress in our lives nowadays, that if we're ever able to get away for the weekend, think about something more interesting than our jobs, and actually relax a little, we think we've had a mystical experience' (1993: 219). It could be said, then, that the mythopoetic movement is more of a ritual enterprise than a spiritual one, especially in light of the lack of discussion of ethics.

The discussion of spirituality left us with further questions: How does spirituality relate to making changes in the world? How do we build a bridge between the spiritual and the political? For Ian, political commitment was fuelled by his spirituality. There was a spiritual dimension for him 'in making sense of this social structure and wanting to change that too'. His energy to strive for change derives from his spiritual commitment which is consistent with Beams's (1991: 37) view that 'to be of use, men's spirituality needs to lead us into the struggle to join women in creating non-hierarchical structures'. This discussion points to the need for profeminist men to articulate an alternative spiritual path that is grounded in the politics of social justice.

Does Childhood Abuse Lead to Oppressive Adult Behaviour?

The mythopoetic men's writings are located within the wider tradition of masculinity therapy and personal growth for men. In such writings, it is argued that change in men's social relationships with women and with other men will only occur after a change in their inner relationships.

Many writers on masculinity believe, though, that emotional conflicts are the most important issues facing men. Numerous self-help books exist aiming to teach men why and how to feel more deeply. In fact, many men in the men's movement argue that the suppression of feelings is a key factor in the formation of masculinities (Farmer, 1991; Lee, 1991; Osherson, 1992; Pasick, 1992).

Pasick (1992: 10–17) defines the problem as men being in a 'deep sleep', which manifests itself in terms of life being out of balance, social isolation, mistrusting our emotions, confusion about dependency/intimacy with women and not taking care of ourselves. Steiner (1986: 112) refers to men's 'emotional illiteracy' to describe men who do not know their own emotions and what causes them, whilst Biddulph (1994: 4) identifies men's major difficulty as isolation, reflected in loneliness, compulsive competition and lifelong timidity.

Some men's liberation writers refer to the notion of men's woundedness. Farmer (1991: 4), for instance, talks about men as the 'walking wounded'. These wounds can be inflicted at any time in a man's life, but Farmer regards childhood injuries as the ones that have the most significant impact. They are the wounds resulting from sexual abuse, from physical or verbal battering, or from absence of intimacy with father or mother. Most of the associated therapeutic approaches involve the search for childhood precedents of our current tragedies.

Kreiner (1992: 52) argues that men 'behave oppressively towards women because they are scared' and Orkin (1991: 9) similarly asserts that men's violence is a result of the abuses they suffer. Men do suffer, but this suffering cannot justify men's treatment of other people. Small boys may not be fully responsible for the choices they make but grown men continue to exercise their choices largely for the benefits they receive (Jukes, 1993: 136), however unconscious the link.

The notion of men as victims undermines attempts to help them to change and analytic therapy is largely ineffective with violent men because it implies that the men's violence is caused by some deeply buried trauma. The latter is partly true but such an approach fails to confront the violent man with his responsibility for his behaviour. The issue of responsibility is critical and it is an issue that mainstream men's movement activists continually shy away from, arguing that any focus on men's oppressive actions reinforces them feeling bad about themselves.

Most of us involved in profeminist politics do acknowledge the importance of enhancing men's lives, although we believe that one way of doing this is by living our lives in ways that make a difference and we resist the tendency to portray men as victims. None of the mythopoetic or therapeutic books mention men's violence against women and most of them ignore issues of power altogether. Osherson (1992: 170) talks about men's power as a 'red herring' because it takes our attention away from men's feelings. Within this framework, the problems in women's lives end up being less important than those of men.

Will a men's movement motivated only by male self-interest encourage men to overcome their restrictive masculinity and do nothing else? Would the men who say they want to change the definition of masculinity, simply want to feel better? Individual, personal or spiritual change will not address the problems of exploitation and power inequality. Spiritual practices will not in themselves reveal the elements in our belief systems that reinforce oppressive social relations. One does not learn political skills in therapy or discover how the world works and personal growth does not necessarily lead to political action.

Furthermore, by focusing on spiritual change, no need is seen to change economic and social structures and men settle for an individualistic solution. This seems inevitable when most personal growth and spiritual paths promise individual liberation and fulfilment, irrespective of social and economic conditions.

In advancing the above critique of the mythopoetic men's movement and the masculinity therapy associated with it, I do not wish to argue that there is no place for personal change and healing in the transformation of men. Unfortunately, however, few men seem to have used insights gained from therapy or personal healing as a basis for political action. Nevertheless, it is important that we continue to explore the relationship between men's psyche and the material and social world, for this will enable us to more adequately address the relationship between personal change in men's subjectivities and simultaneous change in the social relations of gender dominance.

Conclusion

As previously discussed, the men's movement has been portrayed as a new social movement in the sense that, whether men are working for social change and violence prevention, involved in personal growth or part of the backlash against feminism, they are said to be articulating new identities as men. Thus, men's movement politics (and profeminist men's work within it) is constructed as a form of identity politics.

Identity politics considers personal identity as a legitimate place to start for investigations of oppressive social relations, whereby experience is contextualized and related to structural factors. Bromley (1989: 211) sees identity as arising from material conditions which, when interpreted through culturally specific modes of discourse, lead to particular forms of consciousness, in turn enabling people to understand the role material conditions have had in forming their identity. Phelan (1989: 163) argues that 'the most profound and potentially most radical politics come directly out of our own identity as opposed to working to end someone else's oppression'.

Identities are thus said to enable people to become active subjects who define who they are in the world (Epstein, 1987: 30). However, what are the implications when the source of identity is connected to one's privilege rather than one's oppression. It could be said that the men's movement's search for 'authentic maleness' is a new form of 'essentialist identity politics of the privileged' (Fee, 1992: 172).

Thus, the problem is, how does one construct an identity that both acknowledges and at the same time breaks with oppressorhood? In discussing white anti-racists, Frankenberg (1993: 232) considered how one separates an identity of whiteness from the 'white pride' of the right. The same problem was addressed by Memmi (1965) over thirty years ago with the dilemma of the colonizer who rejects his identity as a colonizer, but is unable to form a positive identity which will enable him to form an alliance with the colonized.

Connell (1995: 224) proposes a strategy of 'exit politics': opposing patriarchy and trying to exit from hegemonic masculinity. While he identifies this strategy as the only path that has any potential to change the gender order, he also doubts its ability to achieve this potential. By contrast, I argue that Stoltenberg's (1989) strategy of 'refusing to be a man' and Connell's (1995) notion of 'exit politics' only remain unrealistic political strategies for a progressive gender politics for men, as long as we continue to essentialize men's identities.

I would propose that we have to *destabilize* men's identities and encourage them to create solidarity with women and gay men on the basis of a respect for difference. In constructing a new masculine subjectivity as profeminist men, it is important to conceive of identities as not being 'founded on the notion of some absolute integral self' (Hall, 1987: 45). We have to avoid an identity politics which assumes the essentialist nature of identity and difference. The potential of alliance building and coalition politics as an alternative location for profeminist men to the men's movement is explored in the next chapter.

8　Alliance Politics

In this chapter I explore the potential to develop alliances between feminists, gay men and profeminist heterosexual men. It is premised on the belief that it is important for profeminist heterosexual men to join with feminist women and progressive gay men if we hope to be able to restructure the social relations of gender. As little theoretical and empirical work has explored the possibility for dialogue and coalition between these groups, this chapter endeavours to contribute to the 'prefigurative' aims of the research. The first part explores the main themes arising out of discussions with feminist women and the second part examines outcomes of dialogues between gay and straight men.

Women and Men Talking

Prior to the 1960s, women's movements allowed a supporting but subordinate role for men who shared feminist views, but since that time, most feminists developed more explicitly separatist strategies (Phillips, 1993: 147). While many feminists will continue to be sceptical about men's involvement with feminism, a shift in opinion is occurring that could open up possibilities for profeminist men and women to work together again within a broader feminist movement.

Segal (1987: 245–6) has argued that feminists needed 'to accept that part of their struggle must involve an alliance with men to transform the social inequalities' and she encouraged women to engage with men in progressive social movements of the left including labour parties, unions, community politics, anti-racist movements and the ecological movement. When marginalized groups pursue a separatist strategy, dominant groups are no longer pressured to re-assess their own attitudes and behaviour. Consequently, many feminists have argued that anti-sexist men can have a position in the feminist movement.

Women will bring to this issue their own individual experiences of men, which will range from loving intimacy to violence and abuse. Thus, it is likely that women will continue to be divided between those who will work with men and those who will not. Furthermore, unless men have a committed anti-sexist stance and are responsive to feminist claims, they will not explore the potential to develop alliances with women to construct more socially just gender relations.

I am not suggesting here that men should claim a place in feminism. Rather, while recognizing the need for women to organize independently, men's groups can open their meetings to women, without expecting a recip-rocal response from women's groups. An initial step towards such alliances is the process of dialogue to explore the potential for men and women to work in partnership to transform the social relations of gender. The first part of this chapter examines one such dialogue.

Three feminist women agreed to participate as interlocutors: Wendy Weeks, a social work educator with a long history of involvement in feminist women's services and feminist teaching; Glen Alderson, a facilitator of work-shops on women's empowerment and on surviving men's violence; and Rachel Bloul, a feminist anthropology lecturer with a specific interest in the study of men and masculinity.

Accountability to Women

The question of men's accountability to women has been a contentious issue in profeminist men's politics and this was the first theme to emerge in the dis-cussion with the visitors. It arose when Adam asked the women what they thought about the work that Men Against Sexual Assault was doing. Wendy was first to respond: 'I think one of the things I have respected about the way you [MASA] proceeded was the relationship you set up with the feminist agencies, in terms of using them as critical reference groups for feedback and consultants and so on. I think that was good.'

Glen also commented on this issue:

> I think that one of the things that I particularly like is the thoroughness with which you attempt to stay within the feminist political arena . . . trying to remain conscious about the context in which you work . . . Whenever men gather together, there is always reason to be concerned, as one who lives in occupied territory. That is a very central thing for me. I always have a certain degree of suspicion whenever men gather together. So I think it is good the way that you have kept yourself conscious of all that sort of stuff.

In response to Harry's question about these concerns, Glen went on:

> Because as I said, as a woman I do live in occupied territory. I say this with great love and respect for my profeminist brothers and I do know that there is a growing number of you and I'm delighted about that and I wish to work in absolute coop-eration and with deep respect. However, it is much broader than that and so it is a bit like whenever 'the enemy' gets together there has to be some concern. The old patterns are so hard to break, when men get together in men's groups. They are so deeply ingrained. For five thousand years you have been trained as the dominant ones and so it is very understandable that when you would get together, those pat-terns would emerge and that unknowingly, unconsciously and unwittingly, you would perpetuate them.

Harry wondered whether she thought that there was any disruption in those five thousand years during which time men have acted differently. She acknowledged that there had been 'pockets of change' by men and she saw groups like MASA as an inspiration to other groups especially its account-ability to women's groups.

The form of men's accountability to women has been the subject of con-troversy with some arguing that men should develop formal lines of accountability to particular feminist groups. For example, the Pornography Action Group in the United States declares its allegiance to 'feminists who are actively accountable to those who have been victimized by pornography and prostitution' (Men Against Pornography, 1992). Similarly, the Family Centre in New Zealand is based on a clear commitment to privilege particu-lar groups with lesser power ensuring that the dominant group is directly accountable to the least powerful (Hall, 1994: 7).

On the other hand, in reference to the idea of a formal structure of accountability to particular feminists, Kimmel (1993: 7) argues that it substi-tutes one voice for the multiple voices within feminism. In his view, it is inappropriate for men to decide who are the *real* feminists. MASA has made a commitment to consult both with groups that may likely disagree with their approach and those that are more supportive thus requiring us to take responsibility for the decisions we make.

Relating Profeminism to Men's Experience

All movements have to appeal to the self-understanding of those for whom they speak if they are to be effective (Phelan, 1989: 149). How to do this, when one is working with a privileged group, became the second theme to emerge in the group. In this vein, Wendy raised the issue of how profeminist men can connect with other men whose experiences have been patriarchally constructed. She asks: 'How can a profeminist men's movement become cul-turally relevant, when of course the culture is patriarchy?' How can we develop strategies of change that are culturally acceptable, when we are in and against that culture?

Peter acknowledged that 'profeminist men have not captured other men's hearts'. Does the language of 'profeminist' and 'gay affirmative' alienate other men? Certainly, the gay-affirmative position has been controversial within MASA and a number of men left the movement feeling that such a stance would alienate men who would otherwise have become involved in challenging men's violence against women. There is also the additional prob-lem of the counter-cultural language of profeminist activism. The dilemma is that pitching a culturally acceptable message of change for men who are homophobic and anti-feminist may not challenge their heterosexual domi-nance and misogyny.

Connell (1992b: 36) has proposed a clear profeminist agenda for men that includes the sharing of child care, support for affirmative action, equal oppor-tunity, women's control over reproduction, pay equity and challenges to men's violence against women. A similar agenda has formed the basis of MASA's political intervention in the men's movement. But in adopting such a strategy

there is a danger that profeminist men will be viewed as moralistic and judgemental. Proposing a political strategy will not in itself politicize men.

How do we ground profeminist political work in men's experience without
reproducing men's dominance? One proposed strategy is to relate to men's
pain and to show them how their lives are also damaged by patriarchy. This
means respecting men's emotions but, in addition, showing 'how a sociological analysis of gender inequalities cannot only be guilt and shame alleviating,
[but also] ultimately more empowering than any psychological view'
(Schwalbe, 1993: 72). This again raises the question of *why* should men
change.

Why Should Men Change?

The question of why men should change was the third theme to arise from the
discussions and, being identified by both women and men in the group as a
very important issue, we returned to it on many occasions. Phillip began the
discussion by arguing that change has to be linked to the personal growth of
men, albeit within a feminist framework of what such growth means. Some of
the violent men that he works with 'want to be less dominant' and are motivated to change for themselves. Glen agreed that this was important:

> Because if there isn't anything in it for you, why the hell are you going to do it? A
> few very altruistic and terribly wonderful men here gathered in this room might
> well be prepared to change patriarchy because they are terrific blokes. But the rest
> of them will not.

Questions were raised about what these reasons for change might be.
Wendy did not think that men got a lot out of patriarchy, nor that 'men are
all wilful about their bad characteristics'. She believed that many violent men
'loathed themselves' about their violence:

> I think men are in very bad shape in our culture at the moment. We have the high-
> est suicide rate among young men in the OECD countries. We have an enormous
> problem with unemployment and redundancies. We have had a rural crisis and
> where men have been made redundant, enormous numbers of male suicides and
> male withdrawals for depression.

Many men feel ashamed about their loss of worth as income providers and
she noted the anomie of young men who do not know what to do with their
lives and she wanted the men's movement to address these issues. Pat agreed
with Wendy's view, arguing that 'patriarchy is probably offering fewer men,
fewer rewards, so it is alienating more and more men'.

According to Glen, the main reason why men should change was to regain
a sense of place and belonging. She believed that there had been a time when
men and women lived in harmony with each other and with the earth and
men should work against patriarchy, to regain that harmony. She believed
that 'men and women all long deeply to belong in the right place. There is a

place for men and there is a place for women and we have got to find it again.'

Peter supported this view; for him, 'being a profeminist man is primarily a spiritual thing', and all through his childhood and teenage years there was always part of him that was trying to make more space for himself. In his experience, 'patriarchal values crowded that space out'; patriarchy did not nourish that space.

Similarly for Pat: 'We are not the keepers of the wisdom to sustain life on this planet. It has been a profound relief that I don't have to work out the plot.' It was important for him to act in ways that were both powerful and strong as a man but he placed himself at the service of women whom he trusted, to preserve life. It was enough for him 'to try and walk outside of patriarchy'.

Rachel preferred a more sociological interpretation, although she agreed that men's loss of place was an important issue. In her view, men were socialized to operate in the public but the public was disappearing. When men lost their connection to the public, they lost everything, which would be a good reason for men to change:

> because the things that they are good at, the things that make you feel good about being a man were being the master of the public. But the public sphere is disappearing. You go to work to your 9–5 job. You are a master of nothing. You're the slave there. I suppose that is a contradiction. The ideology of masters and the slave job. That would give a good reason for men to change.

Lack of emotional fulfilment in men's lives is often cited by writers on masculinity as a basis for men to change and Peter articulated this very clearly when he said that his profeminism was primarily a spiritual thing and that patriarchy failed to nourish that part of him. Pat mourned the loss of a sense of place. Many men's lives are plagued by psychological pain and a spiritual vacuum. Twenty years ago, Henderson (1977) appealed to the American 'left' to broaden socialism to include emotional and spiritual fulfilment which was a message that went largely unheeded. However, profeminist men can learn from these mistakes.

Feeling Good About Being a Man

Men's lack of emotional and spiritual fulfilment relates to the desire for men to feel good about being men, but how and what does this contribute to social change? This question elicited the fourth main theme in the group. Wendy said that she did not believe that 'men will be good to women until men are content within themselves and strong and powerful as people'. Glen also reflected that if we had a world in which men felt good and proud of themselves as men, they would not go around killing women and children. Both pondered whether men act so oppressively because they are living out some kind of inner tragedy and, if men would feel better about themselves, they would be less likely to oppress women. The assumption here is that if men felt personally powerful, they would be less likely to engage in 'power-over' behaviours.

Glen spoke about the danger of profeminist men 'emasculating them-selves' and 'wasting their male energy'. Men needed 'to find their own non-patriarchal power and become powerful men that are working in rela-tionship with women to change the world'. She contrasted this vision with men 'cutting their balls off' for women. In her experience, men who did that eventually resented it and became misogynist, which 'comes back in the face of women and I have had that experience'. She is suspicious of men who give up their masculinity for women. Wendy also emphasized the importance of men 'celebrating a strong form of masculinity that is not dominating'. The notion of men finding non-patriarchal strength and power, 'while keeping their masculinity' was a strong theme in the discussion.

Rachel, who had been quiet for some time during this discussion, asked Glen what she meant by men keeping their masculinity.

> *Glen*: I mean it as a positive image of one's gender.
> *Rachel*: That is going to be a bit difficult. [Laughter from some men]
> *Wendy*: I don't feel that negative about men and I don't think all evil resides with men and all good resides with women.
> *Rachel*: I don't mean that necessarily, but it is a bit difficult to find something right now for men to be proud of.

Glen spoke about what she saw as 'the spiritual challenge for men', part of which involved men finding their relationship with the earth. She believed that there was a fundamental goodness in men that had been largely destroyed by patriarchy, and men have to find that again and be proud of it: 'because if you can't be proud of who you are then how on earth are you going to be good for the world?'

In response to Glen's invitation to men to connect with the earth, Harry related an experience of a workshop where men were encouraged to do just this and to get in touch with their male power, but he was surprised to find that it elicited violent, dominating responses which is consistent with some criticisms of mythopoetic men's retreats, as discussed previously.

Adam talked about the importance of men developing 'non-patriarchal spiritualities' and the difficulty of separating them from the New Age men's groups that have no political context. He saw it as a priority to adapt spiritual perspectives to a profeminist political analysis.

It seems significant that during the discussion about men's power, apart from Adam's comment, we remained silent. Upon reflection, we probably missed an opportunity for an important conversation about the connections between femininity, softness and passivity in men. I know that feminine qual-ities in men are being stigmatized but there is a difference between a highly developed feminine side with a preference for nurturance and connectedness and that of passivity and accommodation to others' wishes and demands. It would have been good to have aired these issues further.

I did, however, raise some concerns about other aspects of this view suggesting to me an essentialist premise about masculinity. Glen's comments seemed to imply that male energy or the male essence is somehow being distorted by the social construction of patriarchy and I spoke against the idea of an inner male energy or a masculine essence. If we are talking about evolving non-patriarchal masculinities, they have to be as socially constituted as the patriarchal masculinities. It is not a matter of taking back the mask and getting to the true essence.

This issue was not further explored in the dialogue with the women, but Bruce also challenged the essentialist premise in subsequent discussion following the meeting with the women. He was surprised by some of the things that were said about men becoming estranged from their 'true masculinity' and the problem of men not feeling comfortable about being men. This view is consistent with Bly's (1990) argument that profeminist men have lost their personal power, part of a widely shared perception that men are 'made soft' by profeminism and thus disempowered.

An important discussion ensued about what we understand by 'power'. Peter commented that 'you can be soft and powerful'. There was recognition that, sometimes, profeminist men talk about men's power as the problem. Michael commented that 'we all need personal power, which is quite different'. By personal power, he meant 'men having agency and not at the expense of others'.

Bruce recalled the experiences of one of the participants in the Men's Evolvement Network meeting who had talked about his earlier involvement with profeminism and how it was full of guilt and self-flagellation. He had said that 'if you hear women saying that the problem is men and you believe that, then you feel guilty about it'. Michael commented that most men have, at some time, felt guilty about something they have done and suggested that perhaps we do not want to 'own' the times when we were 'bad'. Peter related to this notion: 'When men say they don't want to be shamed by women, it is not the women shaming them, but the women reminding men of what they are ashamed of.'

We discussed whether there was any place at all for guilt in men's responses to feminism. Much of the men's movement denies any positive role for guilt and the men's rights movement refer to themselves as the 'no-guilt wing' of the men's movement. I wondered whether guilt could be an important catalyst to shatter complacency in men and start them on a journey of change, leading on to more positive motivations.

Harry, reporting on his responses to the atrocities in Bosnia, raised the issue of collective guilt or guilt by association:

I literally want to disavow my connection. Yet, I see that I am like these men. Given the opportunity, I would be pressed in the fear of war, not to act in that way in concert with the rest of the platoon. I don't believe that I am that brave. I don't believe that I am that different.

These atrocities are committed by men; you are a man; you are horrified but there is a point of association there as well. The theme of guilt and shame in men's lives is a strong one in discussions of men and feminism. Can men respond to feminist challenges without feeling guilt or shame? As already discussed, most men's movement writers see profeminism as negative for men and profeminist men as 'apologizing for being a man'.

In contrast to profeminist men being seen as guilt and shame inducing, I would submit that it is important to distinguish between productive guilt and neurotic guilt; the former motivates us to change and the latter makes us feel ashamed of ourselves. To make such a distinction we have 'to see unjust gender arrangements as historical conditions', leading to a 'responsibility for working to change sexist social arrangements [and accept] . . . deserved guilt if we do not' (Schwalbe, 1993: 69).

Most men seem to feel that they either let the feminists force them to hate themselves or they 'assert themselves against this self-hatred and repress the feminist critique'; no third way is seen to be possible (Upton, 1993: 146). The third way is to think sociologically, to not take feminist criticism personally, to not 'experience this criticism as an indictment of their moral worth as men' (Schwalbe, 1993: 70). To achieve this, we need to develop an ethic to assist us in determining whether the guilt or shame we feel is a result of actions for which we are culpable. We cannot address these issues without clarifying ethical and moral questions.

This analysis became clearer to me after the group meeting and it is an issue that warrants further discussion among men and between men and women. Furthermore, in light of the above, we were taken by surprise by the emphasis that Wendy and Glen placed upon men feeling good about themselves. As discussed in Chapter 7, one of the goals of the men's liberation movement has been to make men feel good about being men. The Jungian-inspired part of the men's movement has aimed to help men revalue their identity by celebrating what they see as the goodness of their masculine energies.

In a meeting of the men's group subsequent to meeting with the women, we discussed the relationship between feeling good about oneself as a man and non-oppressive masculinity and I wondered whether we were trying to construct a positive image of manhood? Bruce saw cross-purposes in the debates between how to feel good about being a man and breaking down injustices and hierarchical structures in society. He challenged the notion that, if men felt good about themselves, they would not act oppressively: 'I think there are lots of men who just want to feel good about being men and view the hierarchical society as not that bad, really.'

Michael suggested that there may be a connection from a different perspective in that one may feel good about being a man, by taking a stance against oppressive social structures. Many profeminist men have commented that they have gained a sense of pride and felt better about themselves through their anti-sexist activism.

Bruce noted that both 'hurt men' and 'men who are doing just fine, thanks' act their feelings out in terms of anti-social behaviour. He suggested that some powerful men who exploit others feel great about themselves: 'They are just doing it because they are horrible.' Ian agreed because, he said, there were many different ways that people could choose to feel good about themselves, for example a man owning a multi-million dollar business, whose way of feeling good about himself was 'to be really dreadful to everybody around him', enjoying his power and control over other people.

In this latter view, there is no necessary relationship with feeling good about oneself as a man and non-oppressive masculinity, particularly if this sense of self-worth is not tied to any ethical commitments. Further, why *should* one have to feel good about being a man? Samuels is one of the few male writers to publicly acknowledge that he feels ambivalent about it (1993: 198).

As discussed in Chapter 4, we need to understand more fully *when* it is that men feel like they are men and examine the bases upon which they come to feel good about themselves 'as men'. Given that men's self-esteem is formed on the basis of their access to social power and privilege (Cline and Spender, 1987), if power and resources are distributed equitably, it is likely to result in a perceived loss of self esteem. Profeminist men need to address the spiritual and emotional consequences of this loss of power and to critique mainstream notions of empowerment.

Rational Man and the Feeling Man

The spiritual and the emotional, as discussed previously, is often pitted against the rational and the intellectual and this became the fifth theme in our discussions with the women. Two views on rationality and emotions were expressed. Pat, speaking with some aggression in his voice, said that he thought that we had become so reliant on our brain that we did not 'trust our gut or our instinct'; we had put too much 'into this intellectual stuff of working it out in our head' and patriarchy disconnects our head from the rest of us.

Bruce disagreed, arguing that men acted far too much from the gut and had a lot of muddled thinking. He believed that men spent a lot of the time acting out of feelings, without much clear thinking, to which Pat responded that 'clear thinking [was] another patriarchal trick'. Wendy joined the discussion by arguing that the human mind had the capacity to transcend patriarchy. She supported Bruce's view that many men do not mediate their oppressive behaviour through their minds: 'They never even used their mind to put it to their gut to find out what their gut was all in a mess about. So I think Bruce has got a powerful point.'

Pat responded that he was 'trying to jump out of intellectual analysis as being the only way'. He thought that one of the paucities of men's lives was that they spent too much time talking to each other and not enough time singing and playing together: 'I am trying to jump out of what I would call a mind set.' He rose from his chair, as he concluded, as if to demonstrate a physical jumping out of a patriarchal 'mind set'.

On her part, Glen distinguished between 'reacting from unconscious repressed feelings' and 'reacting from our feelings when we are in good shape'. The question is, though, how do men know the difference between the two? It is just as likely, if not more so, that men's feelings will be as distorted by patriarchy as men's intellect.

There seems to be some leaning towards the kind of anti-intellectualism encountered in the mythopoetic men's movement. Mythopoetic philosophy asserts that men are taught to live in their heads, that is, to be rational to the point of being emotionally numb. Socio-political analyses of gender are said to encourage men 'to think and talk in an abstract intellectual manner, from the head and not from the heart' (Schwalbe, 1993: 70). My own experience has been that even mentioning the notion of patriarchy at mythopoetic gatherings is to open oneself to the criticism of being 'too intellectual'. It is true that men are socialized to be rational and 'reasonable' but it is important to distinguish between reason itself and patriarchal traditions of reason that lead men to denigrate significant aspects of their experience (Seidler, 1989: 17).

The dialogue with the women opened up a number of important issues for profeminist men. The women's responses to some of these questions were surprising to us but this was not always made evident during the discussions with them but it became more apparent in the following reflective meeting. The men expected a stronger challenge to the traditional men's movement focus on personal healing. Instead, there were at times parallels between the women's views of how men change and the ethos of the traditional men's movement. The danger of profeminist men losing touch with their masculinity was emphasized in a way that was reminiscent of the mythopoetic men's movement.

These three feminist voices were not intended to be representative of feminist views on men and masculinity; different women would have raised different issues for discussion. What was significant about the dialogues was that men and women were talking together about these issues and through these discussions we learned about how to better conduct such dialogues in the future. Such learning is a necessary precondition for future alliances and coalitions.

Gay and Straight Men Talking

The men's movement has not attracted a high level of gay support and the profeminist men's movement is no exception in this regard, with some gay men arguing that many profeminist analyses 'ignore the power and privilege that heterosexual men have over gay men' (Clatterbaugh, 1990: 138).

At a meeting in Melbourne in 1987, convened to revive an anti-sexist men's group, gay men voiced some of their anger at profeminist heterosexual men for their avoidance of issues of concern to gay men. Anecdotal evidence was also available to MASA that gay men had left the group because of what they perceived as unexamined assumptions about men's sexuality. Gay men clearly want more acknowledgement by the men's movement of homophobia and they want more recognition of the tragedy of AIDS (Hennessy, 1994: 15–16). Humphries (1987: 13) suggests that heterosexuals should start writing about heterosexuality rather than simply assuming it and Parker (1987: 137) asks heterosexuals to 'explain their sexuality rather than being constantly forced to explain ours to them'.

We had begun to examine some of our own issues to do with homophobia, through memory-work and we had problematized our heterosexuality by examining the way in which we objectified women. We believed that the next step should involve opening up a dialogue with some gay men about how heterosexual profeminist men and gay men might be able to work together.

Straight Men Learning From Gay Men

We came to the dialogue with a premise that, as straight men, we had things to learn from gay men, although some of us were unclear about what issues might emerge. I was mindful, however, of Kinsman's (1987: 105) claim that if heterosexual men were really interested in transforming the social relations of gender, we would 'have to stop seeing gay liberation as simply a separate issue for some men that has nothing to say to us'. As Dowsett (1987: 11) confirms: 'gay men have a lot to say to straights about existing male capacities for genitally and non-genitally focused sex.'

Finding gay men who would talk to us was not an easy task because there is a debate within the gay movement about whether gay men should reach out to heterosexuals to assist in challenging homophobia. Some gay men were hostile to the very idea of talking to straight men and one man who had expressed initial interest in such a dialogue withdrew at short notice, saying that he did not feel safe entering into such an exchange.

In beginning a dialogue with gay men, it is perhaps inevitable that we will make mistakes and we need to acknowledge that making mistakes is part of the learning process. Tom, one of the gay interlocutors who did talk with us, identified this:

> You're not going to be able to see or understand everything. Fallibility is a starting point. It is just as similar in dealing with the issues of women. Subconsciously or whatever, you're going to stuff up in terms of how you react, even though you think you're not, you're going to do it.

While Kupers (1993: 56) extols the virtues of 'a free and open exchange between men and women, straight and gay' as offering 'a golden opportunity to examine our gender relations and move forward together', he appears unmindful of the potential costs to gay men (and women). And while Jung and Smith (1993: 168) 'invite both heterosexual and gay people to make the borders of their respective communities more permeable', the implications of doing so are quite different for heterosexuals and gay men.

Heterosexual men must demonstrate to gay men that they are prepared to confront their own heterosexual privilege. There is not a lot of evidence of heterosexual men taking a public stance against their dominance and it is therefore understandable that there was wariness on the part of gay men to having a dialogue. In the end, two representatives from Gay Men and Lesbians Against Discrimination (GLAD) agreed to participate in an open exchange.

GLAD formed in 1990 and its major focus has been on issues of equal opportunity. The two representatives who attended as interlocutors were Mark Riley and Tom Moore. Mark works with the AIDS Council and the gay men's health centre on Beats Outreach for men who have sex with men, while Tom works in a refuge for homeless men.

We wanted to explore the potential of a dialogue around issues of mutual concern as well as issues of tension and conflict. What issues would lead to disagreement and opposition? How would those issues arise? What activities could we engage in that would be mutually beneficial?

Being Allies of Gay Men

What can heterosexual men do as allies of gay men and how do we deal with our privileges when attempting to publicly defend gay men? Thompson (1992: 247) says that gay men want heterosexuals to not always tell others about their heterosexuality. On the other hand, for heterosexual men to be both open about their own heterosexuality and their gay-affirmative stance is to challenge homophobia from a clear position of privilege.

In this way, heterosexual men's support for gay rights is a way of 'affirming their social identities' as non-homophobic heterosexual men (Herek, 1990: 329). But then again there are clearly times when it is appropriate to allow others to wonder about one's sexual identity. Profeminist heterosexual men are often thought to be gay because they are seen to 'take the women's side'; why else would they be interested in 'women's issues'?

Whichever way one responds to this debate, affirming the validity of gay sexuality is an important act for heterosexual men. In 1992, MASA adopted a 'gay-affirmative' position as one of its guiding principles; it was defined as 'a commitment to confront our homophobia by developing and maintaining more intimate and supportive relationships with other men and to work with lesbian and gay organizations to end all forms of discrimination based on sexual orientation' (Douglas, 1993: 6). Thus, in addition to acknowledging gay men, it also requires taking a stand against discrimination and prejudice and actively supporting gay struggles and defending gay men from attack.

This public position has been controversial; many men who might be opposed to violence against women and who might otherwise support MASA can also be homophobic. Some men left MASA because of its overt gay-supportive stance, arguing that it detracted from the basic goal of ending men's violence against women and one interstate branch of MASA withdrew from national networking meetings for similar reasons. Thus, in taking such a public stance against homophobia, we had to confront it within our own network as well.

How do gay men respond to heterosexual men stating that they are gay-affirmative? This was one of the initial questions raised in the discussion and Mark thought that 'it's pretty amazing really because there aren't many groups that would even consider a position'. He said that he thought that for heterosexual men to come out and openly state that they were gay-affirmative was quite a major step. Tom was more circumspect about the implications, saying that as a member of a minority he has developed a moral conscious-ness. He has been denied a voice for so long and has had to fight so hard to get it that when someone else volunteers to take on the role of speaking out it raises all sorts of issues for him: 'We don't want to give it away. Perhaps one is not so much a minority any more. So there must be some level of legitimacy happening. There being another voice is not necessarily a good or bad thing. You're there, so it needs to be dealt with.'

The same question is raised by a profeminist stance and it relates to the broader issue of what it means when a privileged group speaks in support of an oppressed group. Who has the right to speak for whom? What are the con-sequences when one speaks from the dominant position? Discussions about alliances led to a consideration of queer theory.

Queer theory is a term coined within the gay and lesbian community to avoid the distinctions between lesbian and gay sexualities and to develop 'a common front or political alliance between gay men and lesbians' (De Lauretis, 1991: v). Such a term is now seen to encompass all sexual dis-sidence, including sadomasochistic games (Altman, 1993: 47), transsexuals, bisexuals and even heterosexuals who are attached to the gay and lesbian community (Galbraith, 1993: 24–5). Tom raised some problems with queer politics; it was too broad because, in addition to including gay men and les-bians, it could also include people of transgender 'and their friends and acquaintances'. Presumably it was good to be talking with others, but 'for many lesbians and others in the community, it's potentially awful, because it denies the existence of a voice'. He said that some voices were not being heard as a result of queer politics.

Galbraith (1993: 23–5) argues strongly against the notion of a queer com-munity, saying that it does not exist. He is concerned about the moves to broaden the coalition to include bisexuals and people of transgender and even 'queer heterosexuals'. While some are happy to retain the term as long as it just refers to gay men and lesbians, others are also critical of any attempt to diffuse their single identities.

The situation of gay men is substantially different to the situation of les-bians. While lesbians are critical of the women's movement for its homophobia, they are also critical of the gay movement for its sexism (De Lauretis, 1991: vii). Altman (1993: 47) argues that gay men and les-bians have too little in common to make a coalition. However, while queer politics may pose particular political problems for lesbians and gay men, it does not represent the only form of coalitional identity. To reject queer politics is not necessarily to reject alliances.

Sexism and Misogyny in the Gay Movement

The tension between gay men and lesbians led into issues of sexism and misogyny within the gay movement. I asked Mark and Tom whether this was perceived to be an issue. Mark spoke at length about the efforts of women to get parity on the board of one of the gay groups in Melbourne and the resistance by the men to this proposal. He said:

> I suppose this is the sort of issue that I share in common with you. There are many issues around being men and male that a lot of gay men have no idea about. It's just not important to them.

> *Tom*: It's that moral ownership thing again. Because we're gay we're not all these other things?

Originally, the term 'gay' encompassed both lesbians and homosexual men, but by the end of the 1970s, lesbians concluded that the word 'gay' no longer defined their struggles and the social marginality of lesbianism in the outside world was reproduced within the gay movement (Burgman, 1993: 163). Gay and lesbian organizations are as much in need of affirmative action as other male-dominated organizations and it is clear that gay men are not immune from being sexist because they are gay.

In our discussions with the feminist women, Glen was critical of profeminist men for not sufficiently challenging our gay brothers' sexism and misogyny. Some feminists have been extremely critical of gay men's sexism and regard gay sexuality as 'sexist sexuality'. Stanley (1982: 190) talks about gay men being 'more sexist, and certainly more phallocentric, than many heterosexual men'. Jeffries (1990: 145) similarly argues that the principles of gay liberation are in conflict with the principles of women's liberation.

There are thus some tensions between feminism and gay liberation, as demonstrated by Tom's challenge to our self-definition as profeminist men. He said that the title suggested that we were defining ourselves in terms of our relationship with women rather than defining ourselves as men.

> I suppose why I mentioned it, is that perhaps it doesn't recognize some of the problems feminism has. Feminism, as much as I love and appreciate it, isn't perfect. Some brands of feminism, for instance, would have incredible difficulty dealing with drag queens. Is a drag queen patriarchal? Is it challenging or is it suppressing notions of gender? What about people who are transgender, or specifically men who choose to become women and take on a women's identity? Why, for instance, don't you hear of people who are transgender who are feminists?

Certainly, drag queens are sometimes regarded by feminists as 'the epitome of gay men's innate hatred of women' (Bristow, 1989: 67). Is misogyny a feature of gay culture? Edwards's (1990: 123) response is that 'feminism is probably incompatible with a positive gay male identity' and he is critical of feminists who put the blame on gay men for sexism. Owen (1987: 219) also criticizes some feminist criticisms of gay male misogyny as being homophobic. Thus, many elements of gay culture pose problems for feminist women, and consequently, profeminist men, namely inter-generational sex, gay pornography, sadomasochism and public sex.

Beats and Public Sex

The issue of beats and public sex came up in our discussions, with Mark reporting that he was interested in discovering the reason 'why men do beats'. Why do men go into parks and toilets and try to solicit other men for sex? He commented that a lot of these men are married with a home and children, but then they have this other world where they go off and have sex with other men in toilets. 'They'll never meet and it'll never ever be discussed with anyone else.' For Mark, the fact that he could 'talk about this in a group like this is quite revolutionary because the whole notion of beats is a secret world. It's unexposed.' In opening up the discussion about beats, Mark indirectly responded to a previously unanswered question about what gay men want heterosexual men to know about their experience.

Tom commented that, in talking about beats, a discussion of public and private notions of sexuality is opened up. The unacceptability of public sexuality lead police into strategies of entrapment but, he emphasized, public sexuality itself is not a bad thing: men and women walk down the street hand in hand and kiss in public. It only becomes a 'bad thing' when you are talking about gay and lesbian sexualities: 'It's very difficult for a straight man to see. Because if you are a straight man, who is in a relationship with a woman, it's very difficult to see what's not there when you're frame setting.' Tom identified the unexamined 'normalcy' of heterosexuality locating the discussion of public sex in a wider context because he is continuously confronted with public heterosexuality.

Another issue that often arises amongst heterosexual men is 'why are gay men apparently so obsessed with sex?' Edwards (1994: 105) offers the explanation that sexual opportunities create the activity but *are* gay men more 'promiscuous' than heterosexual men? Garfinkel (1985: 175) reminds us that 'gay men are first male . . . the sexual promiscuity of gay men reflects the male approach unimpeded . . . With men it is green lights all the way. There seems to be no barriers to the sexual advances and seduction. This aspect of the public nature of gay men's sexuality alienates many heterosexual men. 'Why do they have to flaunt it in our face all of the time?' is the often-posed question about the Gay and Lesbian Mardi Gras in Sydney.

In response to this kind of criticism, Kirk and Madsen (1989: 305) propose a self-policing social code because, in their view, the present gay lifestyle makes them look bad to straight men. Such a code includes, among other items, rules about not having sex in public places, not making passes at strangers who may not be gay and not talking gay sex and gay raunch in public. However, such a code seems to be shaped more by the desire to conform to existing heterosexist norms than to validate gay and lesbian sexual identities.

The session with the gay men illustrated some tensions between heterosexual profeminist men and gay men. There is a reluctance on the part of many gay men to engage in an open dialogue with heterosexual men. Concern was expressed that a heterosexual, gay-affirmative stance may marginalize gay men's voices. Attempts to form coalitions between gay men, lesbians and gay-affirmative heterosexuals through queer politics has also been controversial within the gay community. Tensions between feminism and gay liberation, with charges of misogyny from feminists and of homophobia from gay men, have implications for alliances between profeminist men and gay men. Issues of public sex, inter-generational sex, gay pornography and gay and lesbian sadomasochism also pose moral and political dilemmas for profeminist heterosexual men. Furthermore, confronting homophobia in men poses more significant challenges than confronting men's sexism and misogyny. In spite of these issues, however, I believe that alliances between profeminist heterosexual men and progressive gay men are possible as profeminist men confront their homophobia and become more knowledgeable about gay politics and the importance it has in challenging both patriarchy and heterosexual dominance.

Conclusion

When we met with these interlocutors, we were mindful that we spoke from positions of unequal power. There are views that inequality of power prevents the conditions for real dialogue to develop in this culture at this time (Ellsworth, 1989: 316).

In this view '*any* attempt to establish reasonable and consensual discourse across difference inevitably involves the imposition of dominant groups' values, beliefs and modes of discourse upon others' (Burbules and Rice, 1991: 401, emphasis original). If participants have to be equals first, a non-oppressive dialogue between women and men and heterosexual men and gay men will not be possible. At this level, heterosexual men's credentials can never 'be acceptable enough' (Grob, 1991: 139). Boulet argues that the notion of preconditions for dialogue can be paralysing because no action can take place before the preconditions are met. In his view, the only way forward is to enter into the dialogue and grapple with the contradictions in the unequal power situation (personal communication).

I accept the view that equality in dialogue is at the moment not possible but I believe that dialogue should nevertheless occur. I also believe, though, that it is important for members of dominant groups to *earn* the right to dialogue. This is done by:

learning to listen attentively to marginalized people; it requires educating oneself about their histories, achievements, preferred social relations and hopes for the future . . . it requires critical examination of the dominant institutional beliefs and practices that systematically disadvantage them; it requires critical self examination to discover how one unwittingly participates in generating disadvantage to them. (Harding, 1993: 68–9)

In acting as allies to women and gay men, profeminist men face a number of challenges. It has been recognized that when heterosexual men become involved with women's and gay campaigns, they 'often slip into authority positions' (Luxton, 1993: 352). There is a thin line between being a constructive ally and taking over another group's struggle. Even when men are sensitive to these issues, their involvement is more likely to be acknowledged and praised.

It is inevitable that allies will sometimes 'get it wrong'. They must overcome this fear by being willing to learn from women and gay men and committing themselves to challenge their own internalized domination. Straight men will also have to accept that their offers of alliances will sometimes be rejected. This will at times lead them to be estranged from those they would want to support. Profeminist men also need to learn from the insights and challenges of feminists and gay men who see no potential for such alliances.

9   The Politics of Men's Interests

The question of whether it is in men's interests to change towards gender equality has dominated debates in sexual politics during the last twenty years. To explore this question further, the research group invited Anthony McMahon as an interlocutor, because, at the time of the study, he was undertaking research on men's resistance to changing the division of domestic labour.

In a background letter to the group, Anthony argued that men continue to exploit women's domestic labour because it is in their interests to do so: 'Men thus directly benefit from such services, and are also freed to pursue their purposes in the public sphere, where patriarchal relations are also in their interests.'

Anthony began his discussion with the group by noting that men still do not share housework and child care equally with women. He outlined and criticized three arguments advanced to explain men's limited participation:

- structural arguments: as men do not have much time and earn more, it is rational for them to concentrate on their work;
- cultural arguments: as men accommodate to stereotypes promoted through the media;
- psychological arguments: that because of the ways boys are brought up, they fear relationships and intimacy and are unable to nurture babies.

Anthony challenged the view that men are constructed with a need to dominate and says that it is more useful to ask: 'What are men getting out of domination?'

> So I'm arguing that men are doing this in a perfectly straightforward rational way in their own interests and they're aware that they're doing so too, I think, on the whole . . . I think that men have got into a favourable situation about the organization of the household and they want to perpetuate it.

In his view, there is no general male interest in changing gender relations; men support patriarchy because they get something out of it:

> If there is anything in what I'm saying at all, then what are the implications for pro-feminist men, with whom I count myself as one? Profeminist men have always been few in number and perhaps this isn't odd. If patriarchy is in men's interests why should we want to dismantle it?

Anthony acknowledged that men suffer in various ways through over-work, marriage breakdown, death on the roads and drug addiction. Because men are cut off from the joys of having children as well as from their emo-tions, they lose out by not being more involved in family life. He also accepted that, because of class and race relations, some men are oppressed as workers or as blacks and that there are sometimes negative side-effects to the exercise of power. Patriarchy is contradictory and it does not work perfectly in men's interests but he argued that these amendments do not detract from his general proposition.

If patriarchy is in men's interests generally, how can men be profeminist? Agreeing that a few men may come to identify with women, he posits that this will not form the basis of a mass movement. Rather, the only basis for men to challenge patriarchy is ethical: 'Rather than trying to misleadingly argue that change is in the interests of all men, I think it would be better to be honest and say, well it may not be in our interests in a material sense but it's the right thing to do in any case.'

Men's Interests and Domestic Labour

Following Anthony's presentation, Alan challenged his thesis that it is not in men's interests to change their involvement in domestic labour. Due to changes in men's and women's participation in paid labour, men are spending more time at home and thus learning to value the benefits of a positive home environment. Over time, he has found that through his own desire for a tidy house, he has become motivated to do housework. In his view, 'men are learning new ways to value themselves' and this is part of a process of change. There was support for this view in the group, as all of us have endeavoured to assume our share of responsibility for housework.

For Anthony this was too optimistic: 'I've got the figures to say that it's not changing much and that you're something of an exception', and according to him, there was considerable evidence that men generally resist changes in the division of labour.

In the preceding exchange, Alan spoke vigorously against Anthony's crit-icism about change; he wanted to believe that he was part of a process of change for men, however slow that change might be. But he has to do battle with statistics on the general trends of change. I could also sense Alan's frustration as he tried to convey that his coming to value child care and domestic tidiness was based on his ability to conceive of his interests differ-ently.

Alan's experience (and that of other men in the group) is consistent with studies of couples who *do* share the domestic labour equally and where men articulate benefits to themselves deriving from a change in the division of labour. Such benefits include being closer to one's children, a sense of accom-plishment when doing well as parents, creation of a bond between parents and a sharing of the economic load. Furthermore, such studies also show that the more housework a husband does, the lower the chances that the wife has considered divorce (Goodnow and Bowles, 1994). Thus, quite apart from whether they represent the vanguard of future trends, some men *are* constructing their interests differently in relation to domestic labour. What enables such men to do so? I endeavoured to address this issue by challenging Anthony's conception of men's interests.

Beyond Men's Material Interests

I challenged Anthony's definition of interests as being limited to subjective, material and rational conceptions of what men want. I proposed that it was possible to conceive of men having interests that went beyond the material self-interests he described even if they may not be what most men would say they wanted at this point in time. It is rather postulating a concept of men's interests that needs to be prefigured and lived out. I further suggested that once one actually made practical changes in gender relations, then it becomes in one's 'interests' to be in equal relationships with women and not to occupy positions of dominance and privilege.

Anthony was sympathetic to that point of view but 'that's something that has to be constructed doesn't it? It's not here with us. It's an idea. It has to do with a vision and has to be enacted', to which my response was that 'women's interests have to be constructed by feminism too' as they do not automatically perceive their interests through a feminist framework. Anthony thought that there must be differences 'because women's interests being constructed by feminism wasn't very difficult and it arose out of a lot of pain'. He asked for an example of what these ideal interests are, to which I referred to changes in my needs in the context of changes in relationships. Challenges to my dominance enabled me to construct my needs differently. Peter gives an example of this process for him: 'There was a stage in my background when I realized a lot of my sexual needs reflected a particular emotional need and that the actual need for sex, as much as I did it at home, stopped. I didn't need sex so much because I was finding other ways to have intimacy. For me that's how I changed my sexuality.'

Anthony related to these examples, at the personal level: 'I can't stand getting into a relationship that's unequal too. And really, if we are disagreeing with each other it would be along the lines of, well I'm pleased you're like that and I'm pleased I'm like that. But just how many men are going to be like this?' He questioned whether we can extrapolate from our own experience and assume that a lot of men will feel this way. He returned to the empirical evidence demonstrating that there is little change occurring and thus discounting the notion that men have interests in moving towards equality, therewith overriding his own personal experience that has led him to value equal relationships.

Ian acknowledged that the majority of men perceive their interests as supporting patriarchy but he challenged the notion that one could extrapolate from that and say it is in *all* men's interests to do so. Indeed it is no more legit-imate to make such inference than it is to extrapolate from the personal experience of men who are changing. Even if the majority of men think it is in their interests to maintain things as they are, it does not necessarily follow that maintaining the status quo *is* in their interests. Large numbers of women see their interests as being within traditional roles in the family and the com-munity, which does not mean that their perceptions of their interests are necessarily liberating or fulfilling either. We thus returned to the question of how we construct our interests.

Why Are So Many Men Discontented in Patriarchy?

In the follow-up meeting, some participants discussed Anthony's proposition that there is no pain in men's lives that might lead them to review their inter-ests. Adam pointed out that the psychologically oriented men's movement has shown 'that even quite well-off middle-class, white men in society can be deeply dissatisfied with relationships and life styles and want to change'. Whilst the direction of this change is not necessarily going to be profeminist, they still have an interest in wanting to get out of their dissatisfied, alienated life. The task for us, he said, is to construct a proposition that it is in men's interests to oppose patriarchy. How do we show that it can be in men's inter-ests to create different relationships to power?

Tony also challenged the view that profeminist men are not able to develop solidarity on the basis of a shared interest in changing gender relations. For him 'there is something really liberating about the idea of being a profeminist man. It's like becoming whole, expanding the horizons.' It became a way for him to challenge the power relations that he was and is enmeshed in. As Peter agreed that it is in men's interests to reconstruct the hierarchical power relationships that govern men's relationships with women, Harry entered the discussion with pain in his voice: 'I would want to say it is in my best interests that my daughters don't live in a world where 50 per cent or more of the people are oppressed because in the end we are not going anywhere together.' He acknowledged that he is part of what they have to struggle against and such a struggle does not permit them to know him or him to know them. Thus, one of the costs of dominance for him is lack of intimacy between fathers and daughters. Ben also argued that it is in men's interests to move beyond patriarchy 'because I think that most men want to have relationships that are not abusive' but narrow conceptions of self-interest inhibit men's sense 'of more fundamental interests'. Notions of 'ideal interests' and 'fun-damental interests' require problematizing, which I will return to later in this chapter.

Ethical Masculinity Politics

The group was divided on Anthony's challenge that the only basis for men to change was an ethical commitment. Bruce believed that an ethical stance 'involves some degree of repression' and asked how we prevent ourselves from becoming moral crusaders: 'There is a moral tone in that idea of committing yourself to the long haul regardless of whether or not it meets your interests.'

Alan wondered whether even calling ourselves profeminist meant that we were relating our analysis too much to women's interests:

> Whereas, for me, the richness or the possibility of change are when men start examining what they might not be getting out of life. It's OK for me to operate on an ethical system. And I suppose I do. But ultimately, if I was honest, I do things because I find them rewarding. We really get focused on this issue of men changing for the sake of women. And I just don't think we are ever going to get a large-scale movement amongst men on that basis.

The focus should be on what is missing in men's lives, but what would then differentiate our work from the men's liberation movement and the mythopoetic movement? As Bruce said: 'We can change in certain ways to actually suit our interests even more.'

According to Harry, for men to challenge patriarchy there is a need for a moral stance, because we still carry 'deeply ingrained behaviours' that support patriarchy: 'There has to be something that actually causes you to work against those parts of you that support patriarchy.' Ben also said that having an ethical stance was important for him in becoming involved in profeminist work, but when he is talking to other men, he does not emphasize the ethical dimensions of his work. Ben is differentiating here between interests as a reason for change and interests as a component of an overall strategy for change. The reasons for change may be that gender inequality is unjust, but in developing a strategy, it may be appropriate to emphasize the various gains men may derive from change. He believes that those who take an ethical stance alienate people and, from his experience in environmental politics, he observed that people became involved 'not because they have read about it or they have been told that it is morally good not to wreck the environment but because they have a particular connection, at a particular point in time with a particular place that touches them at some level'. He concluded from this that men need to have something that '*shakes them up*', and one way to do this is find ways '*to help men to hear the stories of women*'. Bruce disagreed because it involved asking people to experience other people's pain.

Michael commented that, while he has been motivated by ethical and moral considerations about change, he wanted to believe that it was also in his interests. One cannot sustain personal change that is solely derived from a moral and ethical basis. If it does not ultimately meet your needs, 'you will not be in there for the long haul'. Having an ethical stance about some issues may, for a time, involve a repression of needs, as Bruce suggests, but through the transformation in our relationships over time, it may be possible to construct and create different needs and interests. This was an issue we did not fully explore in the group but it is necessary to elaborate upon it in more detail here.

Deconstructing the Unitary Interests of Men

One of the questions I had when beginning this book was whether it was in men's interests to change. I now realize that a more relevant question is: how are men's interests constructed and how can they be reconstructed? Do men have 'objective' interests that arise as a consequence of being men in a patriarchal society? Anthony argues in his doctoral thesis that:

> If men are able to dominate women and in particular to receive benefits from the exploitation of their labour, it is not at all clear that we need to theorize specific psychological mechanisms which produce a desire for domination. (McMahon, 1994: 244)

Interest theories, such as the above, are premised on the assumption that men are rational and that they will act to advance their own interests through a process of rational calculation. Thus, men's interests are seen to flow directly from their location in social structure, assuming that there are unitary interests between men. The view that it is not in men's interests to change is based upon 'categoricalism, . . . the assumption that men as a category are driven to oppress women as a category' (Sibeon, 1991: 32–5).

Consequently, simply because the status quo benefits some men disproportionally, does not necessarily mean that all men will act in ways to maintain the benefits. Membership of collectivities, such as white, upper-class men, may predispose particular men to think and act in particular ways, at particular times and in particular situations, but it does not necessarily predetermine the nature of their interests. Persons do not have 'objective' interests as a result of their location; rather, they *'formulate* a sense of having particular interests' and may behave on the basis of this formulation (Sibeon, 1991: 32, emphasis mine). Men formulate their interests and they do so within the context of the available discourses in situations in which they are located and which they co-produce.

Interests can thus be very wide-ranging, from doing something because it will make one feel better, to doing it because if one does not, it will be diminishing one's integrity as an ethical being. If one is going to address the question of whether it is in men's interests to change, one has to distinguish *which* interests one is talking about and assess their relative importance to different men. If we reject the idea of unitary interests for all men, there is space to explore unintended consequences of patriarchal domination (Marshall, 1994: 150).

Clearly, there is a level at which patriarchy *is* in some men's interests, as these interests are currently constructed. However, while men may construct interests towards their own material well-being, as evident in Anthony's position, they may also construct ideal interests that are formed by support for more abstract principles (Jonasdottir, 1988: 36). From this, we may conclude that men's interests cannot be ascertained on the basis of what a theory of patriarchy says they are. Indeed, 'interests feature as elements of discursive availability' (Clegg, 1989: 180).

This understanding has been corroborated in assessments of women's interests. This notion is constructed by feminist theorizing and consciousness-raising and it does not flow automatically from 'women's natural interests' (Grant, 1993: 103). Women 'do not simply know their material interests but have to form conceptions of them' (Watson and Pringle, 1992: 66). Women's interests are thus historically produced and are capable of redefinition and we can therefore argue that men's interests have to be (re)constructed as well.

Conclusion

People are capable of learning from the level of fulfilment that flows from the pursuit of their 'interests' and on this basis, they may decide to pursue alternative interests (Menzies, 1982: 93). As men begin to articulate dissatisfaction with their own lives, numerous discourses are available to enable them to make sense of these dissatisfactions in ways that are quite compatible with the patriarchally constructed interests of men. The political task for profeminist men, therefore, is to articulate notions of non-patriarchal interests of men. How do we construct discourses that challenge patriarchal frameworks of meaning?

To encourage men to change their perception of what constitutes their self-interests is to be involved in the reconstitution of their social and personal identities (Benton, 1981: 181). To be successful, these alternative conceptions of interests must be based, to some extent, in the life experiences of men. The question is, how does one invite these alternative conceptions within the framework of patriarchy?

Various suggestions have been proposed, from promoting universal interests to save the planet, through to appealing to men's interests as fathers of daughters and offering men the promise of greater intimacy and connectedness through redefining their relationships with women. While I believe that the above constitute the 'emancipatory interests' of men, they are not self-evident to most men. Political strategies are required to create the discourses in which reasons for change will motivate men to reposition themselves.

I would propose that two related ways towards the reconstruction of men's interests are: first, through the encouragement of social empathy in men by increasing their understanding of the consequences of men's structural power and privilege; and, second, through the reconceptualization of men's pain based on a new conceptualization of need.

How does one articulate a moral stance that challenges men to consider the social justice implications of their behaviour in the world without alienating them? Understanding the experiences of an oppressed group does not appear to be sufficient, unless it involves 'some kind of transformation experience, particularly of the sort that results in the unsettling of the person's self and position' (Babbitt, 1993: 256). To change one's sense of self-interest involves a process of becoming unsettled and strategies are thus required for this purpose.

Thompson (1991: 14, 16) argues that if men deny their own feelings and their own pain, they will not be able to acknowledge the pain of others; men will be unable to recognize their privilege unless their pain and their hurt have been validated. Of course the acknowledgement of men's pain on its own is not enough; the plethora of masculinity therapy books and workshops for men are testimony to that. Rather, what is required are strategies for connecting men's pain to their position in the social relations of gender.

Furthermore, the concept of 'men's interests' has to be critically interrogated (beyond that which is attempted here) in the same way that the concept of 'need' is being constantly reappraised in the light of Marxist (Doyal and Gough, 1991), phenomenological (Ife, 1995) and postmodern (Yeatman, 1994) investigations. Indeed, in contrast to those who equate men's interests as the enactment of men's wants, the logic of interests is closer to the logic of needs (New, 1996: 90). Just as we require a discussion of human needs that recognizes their historical and social influences as well as the spiritual dimensions of human existence, so we require a theoretical articulation of men's interests that can encourage men to see beyond the options that are available to them within the prevailing patriarchal discourses.

When men do become actively involved in social and political projects to challenge the social relations of gender, they create themselves as subjects in their ethical activity and so further reconstitute their interests. They change and their interpretative background changes and thus they evaluate their desires and their interests differently (Babbitt, 1993: 252). When this occurs, ethics are not at odds with self-interest; rather, it changes our sense of what constitutes our self-interest. Such a view enables us to move away from a repressive view of ethics as simply something that stops us from doing what we want towards a reconstitution of our self-interest as ethical beings.

10 Conclusion: Postmodern Masculinity Politics

In the introduction to this book, I indicated that my aims were twofold: to theorize masculinities and male power in order to inform a profeminist men's politics; and to develop strategies in order to promote these processes of change. In conclusion, I will outline the implications of this research for each of these aims.

Understanding what it means to be profeminist will theoretically inform profeminist men's politics. Studying profeminist men's experiences and dilemmas, as a submerged voice within the hegemonic discourses of masculinity, will also further our understanding of the potential and limitations of men's capacity to change. Giving voice to such experiences is part of the process of subverting dominant masculinities.

Changes by women interrupt men's positioning in discourses as well as women's and thereby contribute to opening up alternative subject positions for men. I have examined how one group of men, who are supportive towards feminism, are responding to the feminist challenge. I have endeavoured to identify the extent to which individual men can detach their own subjectivities and practices from the social structures and ideologies of male dominance. I propose that the formation of male subjectivities that challenge patriarchal masculinities constitutes the first step in the development of profeminist activism among men.

Theoretical Issues

I have suggested that one of the most central issues for women's prospects for equality is whether men can and will change. As we saw, the three main feminist responses to this question – that men have too much to lose to be reliable allies, that men should reject domination for ethical reasons to do with responsibility and justice and that men should support women's struggles because it is in their enlightened self-interest to do so – should not be seen as mutually exclusive positions. Although, whilst challenging feminist essentialist arguments that men are inherently violent, dominating and sexually coercive and feminist materialist arguments that maintain it is not in men's interests to change, I am cautious about feminist and men's studies arguments that are overly optimistic about potential and actual changes in men.

While pointing out that it is important that men should respond to the demands of women for both ethical and enlightened self-interest reasons, my research suggests some new ways of understanding men's responses to these questions.

As an activist committed to social change in gender relations, prior to undertaking this research, it had been difficult to find a theoretical framework to guide such work. Although I located myself within a feminist sociological tradition, feminist theorists had not articulated ways of transforming masculinity as part of the process of changing gender relations. In order to understand better the extent to which men can reconstruct their subjectivity, a theory that is able to embrace both micro- and macro-levels of analysis was required.

In the process of constructing such a framework, I adopted ideas from postmodern, critical and feminist perspectives, enabling me to identify ways in which men have come to position themselves within the context of specific discursive frameworks. The dominant discursive frameworks of masculinity are patriarchal but I maintain that men can reposition themselves subjectively in relation to patriarchal discourses and through evolving profeminist subjectivities and practices can resist succumbing to such masculinities.

In articulating a postmodern feminist framework and adapting it to explore the formation of profeminist subjectivities and practices among men, I have tried to provide a new language with which to understand the process of change for men, a language which enables us to ask new questions providing new insights into men's potential to change.

Methodological Issues

In researching men's subjectivities and practices from a profeminist perspective, I have taken note of the feminist critique of 'masculinist' and 'male stream' research. It is essential to articulate one's own structural location and subject position within gender relations and I acknowledge having written as a white, heterosexual, middle-class, middle-aged, academic man. Within this position, however, I can articulate a profeminist man's standpoint as a location from which to research men's subjectivities and practices. Such a standpoint has required me to engage self-consciously and self-critically with men's dominant position in the gender order, similar to recent attempts by Frankenberg (1993) and others to develop a white, anti-racist standpoint from which to research white women's lives.

Furthermore, men can learn from and use the methodological approaches associated with feminist research. Accordingly, I have explored the experiences and dilemmas of profeminist men through three participatory methodologies: anti-sexist consciousness-raising, collective memory-work and dialogues with allies and opponents of profeminism.

Consciousness-raising enabled the men to explore issues in relation to their own lives and to link these issues to the wider social and political context. It was not used to explore our 'true nature', but as a way of changing our subjectivity by positioning ourselves in alternative discourses that we produced together. Through our discussions, we strengthened a profeminist discursive framework as an alternative subject position.

Memory-work provided an opportunity to reframe some of the content of our memories. The process of recalling memories enabled us to elevate unconscious elements of our experiences to the conscious, as the immersion within a discourse involves elements of the unconscious as well as conscious remembered subjectivity. Such remembering facilitates a process of challenging dominant social relations. By asking men to reflect on their understandings of the ways in which they accommodated to or resisted the dominant constructions of masculinity, through the process of memory-work we were able to understand the ways in which new subject positions could be created.

Finally, dialogue constituted an important part of the methodological approach of this research. Group discussions allowed the research participants greater control over the research process and thus provided a more democratic way to produce knowledge. Furthermore, the process of dialogue itself contributed to the development of new subjectivities and in this case allowed for collective positioning in the ongoing public debates about profeminist men's politics.

The combination of the three methods provided a basis to bridge the gap between the individual and the social, and the subjective and the structural. They have enabled me to avoid the dangers of psychologizing our masculine subjectivities at the expense of structural change. They also grounded the discussion of political strategies in the subjective realities of our lives as men. The three methods combined enabled the group to move through different temporal aspects relevant to the process of change: through anti-sexist consciousness-raising, we explored the future by discussing how men might be different; through memory-work, we explored the past by examining our personal histories of how we became the men we are; through dialogues with allies and opponents of profeminism, we explored the political possibilities for ways forward in the present.

The combined purposes of this research intended to produce a praxis of how men can change and the methodological approaches employed became some of the very strategies being sought. That is, the methods used in this research each represent pedagogical strategies for profeminist politics for men. Thus, in addition to contributing to theorizing men's subjectivities and to the insights about issues and dilemmas in profeminist men's lives, this research has contributed to the development of these methodologies, both as research tools and as strategies for change in gender relations.

Personal Issues

For men who support feminism, there are numerous dilemmas about how to act personally and politically; they rest within men's psyches, within men's relationships with other men and within men's relationships with women in intimate partnerships as well as in workplaces and in political campaigns. This research identifies some of the key dilemmas profeminist men experience in trying to live out their commitment.

In telling their stories, the men in this study provide new narratives that have the potential to influence future stories; they are living out changes in gender relations. They struggle to maintain a balance between anti-sexist activism focused on the oppression of women and activities aimed at enhancing their own lives. The process of anti-sexist consciousness-raising and memory-work helped us to explore these dilemmas and to articulate alternative ways of resolving them. The memory-work made more visible the discursive threads by which our masculinities were produced and it assisted us to identify forms of resistance to dominant masculinities.

These profeminist men's experiences with their fathers accorded with the findings of other research in this area; they had endured experiences of physical abuse, emotional withdrawal, unrealized expectations and a sense of betrayal. They did not seek, however, an uncritical reconciliation with or forgiveness of their fathers as most masculinity literature would suggest they should. Rather, they chose to dis-identify with their fathers and sought alternative discourses of masculinity from which to construct notions of non-patriarchal manhood. Hence, in the context of abusive and emotionally distant fathering, boys should not be encouraged to identify with their fathers as sources of male socialization. This has implications for how both profeminist men and feminist women should respond to current debates about the 'new father' and the increased involvement of men in family life.

The early capacity for these men to identify as boys with the oppression of their mothers also played a significant role in their later ability to identify with the experiences of women. Through the memory-work on relationships with mothers, it became evident that these men experienced a lot of ambivalence in these relationships which also accords with other research into this area. They, along with other men, received strong messages that they should distance themselves from their mothers or else risk being ridiculed as 'mothers' boys'. They demonstrated a resistance to this devaluation, however, as they struggled to own the positive influences their mothers had upon their lives. Such experiences seem to suggest that there needs to be a challenge to the prevailing orthodoxy that boys need to distance themselves from their mothers to become men. Rather, it is proposed that boys need to be supported and encouraged to form loving relationships with their mothers as part of the process of learning to relate to women as equals. For such changes to occur, however, challenges are required to both the ideology of mother-blaming and to the devaluation of women.

Heterosexual men's identities entail a definition of gay men and women as the 'other', and to construct non-patriarchal subjectivities and practices, I propose that men should confront the processes of homophobia and the sexual objectification of women that inform heterosexual dominance and misogyny. Homophobia and patriarchy are inextricably linked. In sharing stories of sexual and emotional intimacy with other men, the heterosexual men in this study began to break down the processes that pressure men to conform to hegemonic masculinities. The implications of these memories are that heterosexual men should be encouraged to disclose their experiences of sexual and emotional intimacy with other men as part of the process of normalizing love between men.

Under hegemonic masculinity, objectification is one of the key processes in the way men relate to women sexually. It is one of the elements of men's heterosexuality that limits the potential to develop nurturing and egalitarian sexual relationships with women. In talking about the processes of objectification they had engaged in, the men in this study heightened their awareness of the ways in which their sexuality is socially constructed. The implication of these experiences is that, for men to construct non-patriarchal heterosexualities, they will have to be prepared to examine critically sexual responses that the dominant ideologies have essentialized and normalized.

Political Issues

Profeminist men's politics has been positioned as a 'wing' of the men's movement. Because such a movement has been encouraging of diversity and difference, profeminist men's work has existed alongside both mythopoetic and men's rights perspectives. Profeminist men face strategic decisions about the extent to which they should work within the men's movement in an attempt to encourage a more profeminist positioning among men. The meetings with interlocutors from the People's Equality Network and the Men's Evolvement Network represented an attempt to clarify these strategic issues. The participants in this study engaged in dialogue across ideological differences when they met with these interlocutors.

The men's rights critique of 'victim-feminism' attempts to shift responsibility for the experience of oppression to women themselves, and this is another form of victim blaming. Given the often deep-seated misogyny and sexism in men's rights groups, it seems unlikely that respectful and critical dialogue will be possible with these men.

The men's rights polemic against feminism and women must, however, be publicly engaged with by profeminist men and it is therefore still important for them to listen carefully to anti-feminists as part of the process of learning their arguments and understanding the constitution of patriarchal subjectivities. Such an engagement means that male disadvantages highlighted by the men's rights writers, for example men's ill health, custody arrangements, sexual abuse, work stresses, youth male suicide and men's experience of powerlessness, must be acknowledged and addressed. This can best be done by contextualizing these disadvantages within the power relations of class, race, age and sexuality, and so on, on the one hand, and the contradictory effects of patriarchal power, on the other. Another implication is that profeminist men, at times, may have to distance themselves from feminist essentialist arguments that posit an inherently violent male nature and also from some radical feminist portrayals of men as a homogeneous category of oppressors.

In terms of the wider men's movement's focus on men's emotional hurts, I suggest that profeminist men should remain open to dialogue and be sensitive to men's need for healing and personal fulfilment in their lives, whilst rejecting the view that men's oppressive behaviour can only be understood as a result of men's hurts or deprivations. We should also challenge the view that men's attempt to address their hurts and the restrictions they feel as men is a sufficient way to address the consequence of exploitation in women's lives. Men's personal growth will not automatically lead to political action in support of gender equality. It could even assist men in accommodating women's demands in a more modernized patriarchy. For those men who are concerned about the women in their lives, the above-presented dangers inherent in the men's movement must be made clearer through dialogue.

Profeminist men are seen by many men as guilt and shame inducing and, along with feminist women, they are accused of male bashing. There is an important distinction between holding men responsible for their individual and collective behaviour and blaming them because they are men. Moreover, an ethical and political stance that does not recognize the subjective experiences of men is unlikely to engage men and we need to find ways to articulate such a perspective that will not estrange them. Proposing a profeminist political strategy will not in itself politicize men. It is therefore important that profeminist men continue to talk to 'ordinary' men and find ways both to communicate the moral/ethical reasons and to appeal to their enlightened self-interests as to why men should reposition themselves in relation to feminism.

In relation to alliances and coalitions, several issues were explored in discussions between profeminist men and feminist women and gay men. Such discussions are a necessary part of forming alliances, the latter representing an important strategy in the transformation of gender relations. Understandably, both feminist women and gay men are cautious about such alliances and these are not partnerships that profeminist men could or should determine but rather they should remain open to any initiatives that come from within these movements. The dilemmas of accountability and issues of trust and power inequality when men and women enter into dialogue and alliance have been discussed and I propose that men must prove themselves worthy of dialogue before they are trusted as potential allies.

Profeminist heterosexual men have been criticized by gay men for ignoring their heterosexual privilege and for not addressing their own and other men's homophobia. In suggesting some ways of addressing this challenge, I have discussed the practical politics of taking a gay-affirmative stance and potentially alienating many heterosexual men who, whilst open to confronting their violence and their sexism, are not yet open to confronting their part in heterosexual dominance. The tensions between gay men and feminist women, especially feminist claims of misogyny amongst gay men and gay claims of homophobia amongst feminist women, have been noted along with the problems associated with queer politics as a coalitional identity.

Some feminist women and gay men will choose not to work with men and these decisions must be respected. Some have been too bruised by heterosexual men to consider dialogue and alliances. Furthermore, there is the issue of which feminist women and which gay men profeminist men should dialogue and work in alliance with. Which feminisms are profeminist men to support? Which sections of the gay movement are profeminist men to affirm? There are no easy answers to these questions. They will ultimately be determined by the practicalities of particular political situations at particular times and I have documented two such specific instances of dialogue.

One of the questions I had when I began this research was whether it was in men's interests to change gender relations. I argued against the claims by McMahon (1994), that it is not in men's interests to change, by pointing out that men's interests are formulated and constructed within the context of patriarchal discourses. While men continue to locate themselves within those discourses, it is likely that they will pursue their interests in the ways suggested by McMahon. I believe that it is possible for men to reposition themselves in those discourses and consequently come to formulate their interests in different ways.

Various questions are raised in this context: How will this reformulation of interests take place? Will it inevitably occur as a result of contradictions within patriarchy? Is it possible to educate men to come to conceive of their interests differently? Is it likely that large numbers of men are going to reformulate their interests in the ways suggested by this book? The prospects for change are not encouraging. Clearly, the deconstruction of men's internalized domination is not a simple matter.

Part of the process involves articulating a vision of gender justice that is compelling enough to persuade other men to reinterpret their interests. The profeminist men in this study present some attempts to enact that vision. Our struggles provide information that may assist those men who choose to reposition themselves within the patriarchal discourses. The process of self-transformation described in this book can contribute to social transformation through prefiguration. As previously discussed, our choices today will form the basis of the collective politics of the future.

Furthermore, the choices we make today will be partly dependent upon the available discourses and subject positions which in turn will be a product of political struggles. Thus, profeminist men's work needs to operate on both the personal and the social level. It is both an individual and a collective project. Such a project is but a part of the wider struggle to be undertaken in alliance with feminist women and other progressive social movements.

Because heterosexual men are increasingly having to manage their sexual and gender identity, they do not have to identify with reactionary politics. Because their subjectivity is contradictory, it is amenable to change and therefore they can come to recognize the justice of gay people and women. Through what Ferguson (1993: 159, 180) calls 'mobile subjectivities', heterosexual men can come to feel empathy for different positions and loosen their connection to heterosexual dominance and patriarchy. This book has endeavoured to contribute to the loosening of those connections.

Appendix: Methodology

The nature of my research interests and my commitment to praxis and change suggested a participatory approach to this project. Thus, I invited self-defining profeminist men to participate in a collaborative inquiry group to link the process of personal transformation to the collective politics of change in gender relations.

While it is generally accepted that men cannot do feminist research, they are encouraged to evolve approaches based on feminist standpoint epistemology to research men's lives. Wadsworth and Hargreaves (1993: 5) suggest that the methodological approaches of feminism will be relevant to men who are seeking to transform subordinating practices, whilst Maguire (1987: 71) also encourages men to use participatory research to uncover their own modes of domination of women.

In addition to feminism, my exploration of participatory approaches to research draws upon emancipatory action research. This form of action research requires a group process to enable the development of a learning community to generate a critique of the context in which the group operates (Carr and Kemmis, 1983: 171–2). This learning community is further transformed into a critical community that subjects its own values and practices to scrutiny. Torbert (1991: 232) has defined this process as a 'practical community of inquiry', where people are 'committed to discovering propositions about the world, life, their particular organizations and themselves that they will test in their own actions with others'. Thus, such a group process of action research involves dialogue, discussion, argumentation, critical reflection and theorizing from experience.

Emancipatory action research is at least partly based on a theoretical framework associated with Habermas's (1972) work, in which the participants aim to move from illusory beliefs that may be irrational and contradictory, to a more enlightened understanding of the impact of social structures on their lives. Through the research process, people come to distinguish between what Habermas defines as instrumental and technical knowledge and critical knowledge which derives from the process of reflection and action.

From a postmodern position, Gore (1993: 152–4) has criticized action research for failing to achieve its emancipatory intentions and for reproducing forms of domination because it functions within 'regimes of truth'. With Lather (1991: 1–2), however, I believe it is possible to reconcile emancipatory discourses and modernist strategies like consciousness-raising with a critical appropriation of important elements of postmodernism. They are not antithetical to each other as some postmodern critics suggest.

Within the participatory approach I have outlined, I chose three research methods to carry out the intentions of this research: consciousness-raising, collective memory-work and sociological intervention. All three methods involve group work, a precondition for participatory research and a preferred methodology for enacting the action component of the research process. Furthermore, the combination of the three methods provided a basis to bridge the gap between the individual and the social and between the subjective and the structural. Together, they avoid the danger of psychologizing masculine subjectivities at the expense of structural change, while at the same time grounding the discussion of political strategies in the subjective realities of men's lives.

Consciousness-Raising as Research

Consciousness-raising is a method that reflects both my theoretical analysis and my commitment to activism. It enables participants to explore material about themselves in ways that are searching and insightful and while such a method focuses on the personal, it does not separate the exploration of subjectivity from the wider historical and political issues (Hollway, 1982: 11–13). Consciousness-raising is also a part of my biography and one of the processes through which I became aware of gender domination. As a method, it has a history, both in the contemporary women's movement and in the liberation struggles in Latin America.

Because feminist consciousness was not universal among women, one had to *become* a feminist (Bartky, 1975: 425–6). Hence, MacKinnon (1982: 535) describes consciousness-raising as the 'quintessential expression' of feminism. The metaphor of 'raising' comes from the idea of 'bringing up' into consciousness experiences that have previously only been known at the unconscious level. It involves 'becoming aware at a conscious level, of things that we knew but had repressed' (Eisenstein, 1984: 35). This understanding and analysis are seen as first steps towards social change (Weiler, 1991: 457–8).

Some postmodernists argue that consciousness-raising is a modernist political project based on the 'meta-narrative' premise that people can come to recognize ideological and material domination and can struggle collectively towards egalitarian and socially just relations (Gore, 1993: 121–2). However, I argue with Janmohamed (1994) that it can be reconceptualized in postmodern terms. The process of consciousness-raising can encourage people to develop 'a relationship of non-identity with their own subject positions [which] requires an ejection of the introjected subject positions of dominant groups' (1994: 244–7). Thus, consciousness-raising becomes a process of assisting people to redefine their subject positions. McLaren and da Silva (1993: 58) also position Freire's work within a postmodernist perspective, whilst Freire (1993: x) himself has recently acknowledged that his understanding of subjectivity, power and experience resemble some forms of postmodernism.

For my purposes, I find it useful to adopt Weedon's (1987: 85) view of consciousness-raising, not as a method to discover one's 'true nature' but as 'a way of changing our subjectivity through positioning ourselves in alternative discourses which we produce together'. Thus, consciousness-raising plays a role in destabilizing identity rather than creating a unified sense of self (Sawicki, 1991: 104), which means it challenges previously held conceptions of the self and creates the possibility for senses of the self to be reconstructed.

In adapting the process of consciousness-raising to work with members of a dominant group, Wineman (1984: 187) used the concept of 'negative consciousness' to describe the process by which people become conscious of their oppressor roles and react against them. According to him, 'equal relations can be experienced as more rewarding than top-down relations', which constitutes the positive foundation for negative consciousness. When one dehumanizes people, one denies one's own capacity for emotional connectedness. Lichtenberg (1988: 99) similarly argues that, once egalitarian relations are achieved, they can be as attractive to the dominator as they are to the subordinated. It is this recognition that enables the process of consciousness-raising to further the aims of this project.

Collective Memory-Work

Memory-work is a method that builds upon, yet goes beyond consciousness-raising. The method was developed by Frigga Haug (1987: 60) to gain greater understanding of the resistance to the dominant ideology at the level of the individual, as well as how women internalize dominant values and how their reactions are colonized by dominant patterns of thought. Haug describes memory-work as a method for the unravelling of gender socialization. Her argument is that it is essential to examine subjective memories if we want to discover anything about how people appropriate objective structures (Haug, 1992: 20).

By sharing and comparing memories from their own lives, Haug and her groups hope to uncover the workings of hegemonic ideology in their subjectivities. Her particular concern is 'with the ways in which people construct their identities through experiences that become subjectively significant to them' (1987: 40–52). The premise is that everything we remember is a significant basis for the formation of identity.

By illustrating the ways in which people participate in their own socialization, their potential to intervene in and change the world is expanded. By making conscious the way in which we have previously unconsciously interpreted the world, we are more able to develop resistance against this 'normality' (Haug, 1987: 60) and thus develop ways of subverting our own socialization.

Memory-work is carried out by a group of co-researchers who choose a topic or theme to investigate. It involves at least three phases.

First, written memories are produced according to certain rules.

Individuals are asked to write a memory of a particular episode, action or event in the third person without any interpretation or explanation. Writing in the third person encourages description and avoids rationalization.

Second, the written memories are collectively analysed. After writing the memories, the co-researchers meet to read and analyse them. All group members express their opinions and ideas about the memories and looks for similarities, differences and cultural imperatives. Memories are compared and contrasted with each other and appraised and reappraised by both the writer and others in the group so that the common elements are identified. Members of the group thus collectively interpret, discuss and theorize the memories. It is through this process that new meanings are created.

Third, memories are reappraised and analysed in the context of a range of theories. This involves rewriting the memories following the collective theorizing (Crawford et al., 1992: 40–51).

Memory-work is an example of what McLaren and da Silva (1993: 73–5) call 'remembering in a critical mode'; it becomes a form of 'counter-memory'. The purpose of this critical mode of remembering is 'not only to understand the past but to understand it differently'. By recounting histories of oppression, suffering and domination, those who occupy positions of dominance can find ways to recognize their privilege and form alliances with the oppressed.

Memory-work has much in common with narrative approaches to research. Profeminist men's narratives can be read as counter narratives because they reveal that the narrators do not think, feel or act as they are supposed to. In this context, narrative analysis also becomes a form of consciousness-raising that has both 'therapeutic and transformational possibilities at the individual, familial and societal levels'(Gorman, 1993: 257).

Memory-work is also consistent with postmodern approaches to research in that it enables us to identify how subjectivities are constituted discursively out of contradictions within discourses (Shotter, 1993: 409). It further emphasizes the partiality of subject positions and the potential for agency that arises out of challenges from alternative subject positionings (Stephensen et al., 1995: 2).

Sociological Intervention(s) in Masculinity Politics

Alain Touraine's (1977: 142–53) sociological intervention, a participatory research method specifically designed for the study of social movements, involves work with a number of activists organized in groups. The objective is to create a research situation which would, in some way, represent the nature of the struggle the participants are involved in. Thus, the researcher forms groups of individuals who are involved in and identify with a social movement with the aim of engaging in some form of self analysis. The incentive for individuals to become involved in the intervention is an awareness of disharmony between the ideals of the movement and its organizational practices.

Touraine discusses the importance of having different, even opposing, aspects of the struggle represented in the group so that the tensions and conflicts of the movement can be brought out. Interlocutors, who confront the group with alternative analyses, are brought in to prevent the group from centring in on itself. The interlocutors are other participants in the movement, situated at different levels and engaged in different activities from those of the research participants (1977: 159–62).

Confronting the group with both its partners and its opponents brings out the field of their struggle. Through the dialogues, the members of the group have to answer to interpretations that differ from their own and to modify the image they previously had of their opponents. This enables participants to overcome their rationalizations and encourages them to look critically at their own ideologies. The dialogues that take place model the main components of the struggle and after the meeting with the interlocutors, the group reflects upon the encounter and analyses the action. The group works because it has to resolve the tensions between its experience and its ideology and between its own view of the situation and that of the interlocutors (Touraine, 1977: 175).

At the end of the intervention, the researcher is presented with a diversity of arguments, debates and conflicts, out of which he or she must develop a set of hypotheses which will account for these statements and they are put to the test in discussion with the group. The researcher then makes an interpretation of the struggles facing the social movement. Is it a social movement or not? What directions does the movement take? What are its main problems and its most important conflicts and choices? How can its evolution be defined? When the intervention is completed, the participants return to action, where they match the conclusions of the intervention with their new experiences. On the basis of these new experiences, they return to re-examine the issues with their internal problems and increase their capacity for action (Touraine, 1977: 181–205).

These three participatory group research methods of consciousness-raising, collective memory-work and sociological intervention together strengthened the concerns of this project to link the discursively produced subjectivities of the profeminist participants to the prefigurative practices of profeminist action.

Bibliography

Adair, M. (1992) 'Will the real men's movement please stand up?', in K. Hagen (ed.), *Women Respond to the Men's Movement*. San Francisco: Harper.

Alary, J. (1990) *Community Care and Participatory Research*. Montreal: Nu-Age Editions.

Altman, D. (1993) 'Queer versus gay', *Outrage*, June: 46–7.

Arcana, J. (1983) *Every Mother's Son: The Role of Mothers in the Making of Men*. London: Women's Press.

Arndt, B. (1995) *Taking Sides*. Sydney: Random House.

Babbitt, S. (1993) 'Feminism and objective interests: the role of transformation experiences in rational deliberation', in L. Alcoff and E. Potter (eds), *Feminist Epistemologies*. New York: Routledge.

Bailey, M. (1993) 'Foucauldian feminism: contesting bodies, sexuality and identity', in C. Ramazanoglu (ed.), *Up Against Foucault*. London: Routledge.

Barrett, M. (1980) *Women's Oppression Today*. London: Verso.

Barrett, M. (1987) 'The concept of difference', *Feminist Review*, 26 (July): 29–41.

Bartky, S. (1975) 'Toward a phenomenology of feminist consciousness', *Social Theory and Practice*, 3 (4): 425–39.

Bathrick, D. and Kaufman, G. (1990) 'Male privilege and male violence: patriarchy's root and branch', in F. Abbott (ed.), *Men and Intimacy*. Freedom: The Crossing Press.

Baumli, F. (ed.) (1985) *Men Freeing Men: Exploding the Myth of the Traditional Male*. Jersey City: New Atlantis.

Beams, J. (1991) 'A meditation on men's spirituality', *Changing Men*, 23 (Fall/Winter): 30–1.

Beane, J. (1992) 'First loves', *Changing Men*, 24 (Summer/Fall): 26–9.

Beneke, T. (1990) 'Intrusive images and subjectified bodies: notes on visual heterosexual porn', in M. Kimmel (ed.), *Men Confront Pornography*. New York: Crown Publishers.

Benhabib, S. (1992) *Situating the Self: Gender, Community and Postmodernism*. Cambridge: Polity Press.

Benjamin, J. (1988) *The Bonds of Love: Psychoanalysis, Feminism and the Problem of Domination*. New York: Pantheon.

Benson, T. (1981) 'Talking our way out of it: the rise and fall of a men's group', in R. Lewis (ed.), *Men in Difficult Times: Masculinity Today and Tomorrow*. Englewood Cliffs: Prentice-Hall.

Benton, T. (1981) 'Objective interests and the sociology of power', *Sociology*, 15 (2): 161–84.

Biddulph, S. (1994) *Manhood*. Sydney: Finch.

Biernbaum, M. and Weinberg, J. (1991) 'Men unlearning rape', *Changing Men*, 22 (Winter/Spring): 22–4.

Bliss, S. (1986) 'Beyond machismo: the new men's movement', *Yoga Journal*, November/December: 36–40, 57–8.

Bly, R. (1987a) 'What men really want: interview with Keith Thompson', in F. Abbott (ed.), *New Men, New Minds*. Freedom: The Crossing Press.

Bly, R. (1987b) *The Pillow and the Key: Commentary on the Fairy Tale of Iron John, Part One*. St. Paul: Ally Press.

Bly, R. (1990) *Iron John: A Book About Men*. New York: Addison Wesley.

Bouchier, D. (1983) *The Feminist Challenge*. London: Macmillan.

Boulding, K. (1990) *The Three Faces of Power*. Newbury Park: Sage.

Bradshaw, J. (1982) 'Now what are they up to?: men in the men's movement', in S. Friedman and E. Sarah (eds), *On the Problem of Men: Two Feminist Conferences*. London: The Women's Press.

Braidotti, R. (1987) 'Envy or with my brains and your looks', in A. Jardine and P. Smith (eds), *Men in Feminism*. New York: Methuen.

Braithwaite, J. (1991) 'The political agenda of Republican criminology'. Paper presented at the British Criminological Society Conference, York.

Braithwaite, J. and Daly, K. (1993) 'Masculinities, violence and communitarian control'. Paper presented at the 2nd National Conference on Violence, Australian Institute of Criminology, Canberra, 15–18 June.

Brenkman, J. (1993) *Straight Male Modern: A Cultural Critique of Psychoanalysis*. New York: Routledge.

Bristow, J. (1989) 'Homophobia/misogyny: sexual fears, sexual definitions', in S. Shepherd and M. Wallis (eds), *Coming on Strong: Gay Politics and Culture*. London: Unwin Hyman.

Brittan, A. (1989) *Masculinity and Power*. Oxford: Blackwell.

Brod, H. (1987) 'The case for men's studies', in H. Brod (ed.), *The Making of Masculinities*. Boston: Allen and Unwin.

Brod, H. (1988) *A Mensch Among Men: Explorations in Jewish Masculinity*. Freedom: The Crossing Press.

Brod, H. (1994) 'Some thoughts on some histories of some masculinities: jews and other others', in H. Brod and M. Kaufman (eds), *Theorising Masculinities*. Thousand Oaks: Sage.

Bromley, H. (1989) 'Identity politics and critical pedagogy', *Educational Theory*, 39 (3): 207–23.

Brown, L. (1992) 'Essential lies: a dystopian vision of the mythopoetic men's movement', in K. Hagen (ed.), *Women Respond to the Men's Movement*. San Francisco: Harper.

Buchbinder, D. (1994) *Masculinities and Identities*. Melbourne: Melbourne University Press.

Buchbinder, H. (1987) 'Male heterosexuality: the socialised penis revisited', in B. Young (ed.), *Who's On Top? The Politics of Heterosexuality*. Toronto: Garamound Press.

Burbules, N. and Rice, S. (1991) 'Dialogue across differences: continuing the conversation', *Harvard Educational Review*, 61 (4): 393–416.

Burghardt, S. (1982) *The Other Side of Organizing*. Cambridge: Schenkman.

Burgman, V. (1993) *Power and Protest: Movements For Change in Australian Society*. Sydney: Allen and Unwin.

Calhoun, C. (1989) 'Responsibility and reproach', *Ethics*, 99 (January): 389–406.

Callinicos, A. (1985) 'Postmodernism, poststructuralism and post marxism?', *Theory, Culture and Society*, 2 (3): 85–101.

Canaan, J. and Griffin, C. (1990) 'The new men's studies: part of the problem or part of the solution', in J. Hearn and D. Morgan (eds), *Men, Masculinities and Social Theory*. London: Unwin Hyman.

Carey, M. (1992) 'Healing the mother wound', *Dulwich Centre Newsletter*, 3 and 4: 65–9.

Carlin, K. (1992) 'The men's movement of choice', in K. Hagen (ed.), *Women Respond to the Men's Movement*. San Francisco: Harper.

Carr, W. and Kemmis, S. (1983) *Becoming Critical: Knowing Through Action Research*. Geelong: Deakin University Press.

Carrigan, T., Connell, R.W. and Lee, J. (1987) 'Hard and heavy: towards a new sociology of masculinity', in M. Kaufman (ed.), *Beyond Patriarchy*. Toronto: Oxford University Press.

Chodorow, N. (1978) *The Reproduction of Mothering*. Berkeley: University of California Press.

Christian, H. (1994) *The Making of Anti-sexist Men*. London: Routledge.

Clatterbaugh, K. (1990) *Contemporary Perspectives on Masculinity*. Boulder: West View Press.

Clegg, S. (1989) *Frameworks of Power*. London: Sage.

Cline, S. and Spender, D. (1987) *Reflecting Men at Twice their Natural Size*. London: Andre Deutsch.

Cockburn, C. (1988) 'Masculinity, the left and feminism', in R. Chapman and J. Rutherford (eds), *Male Order: Unwrapping Masculinity*. London: Lawrence and Wishart.

Cockburn, C. (1991) *In the Way of Women*. London: Macmillan.

Collinson, D. and Hearn, J. (1994) 'Naming men as men: implications for work, organization and management', *Gender, Work and Organization*, 1 (1): 2–22.

Connell, R.W. (1987) *Gender and Power: Society, the Person and Sexual Politics*. Cambridge: Polity Press.

Connell, R.W. (1990) 'A whole new world: remaking masculinity in the context of the environment movement', *Gender and Society*, 4 (4): 452–78.

Connell, R.W. (1991) 'The big picture – a little sketch: changing western masculinities in the perspective of recent world history'. Paper presented at the Research on Masculinity and Men in Gender Relations Conference, Sydney, 7–8 June.

Connell, R.W. (1992a) 'A very straight gay: masculinity, homosexual experience and the dynamics of gender', *American Sociological Review*, 57 (December): 735–51.

Connell, R.W. (1992b) 'Drumming up the wrong tree', *Tikkun*, 7 (1): 31–6.

Connell, R.W. (1995) *Masculinities*. Sydney: Allen and Unwin.

Connell, R.W. (1996) 'Response' [to B. Blauner and T. Ditz, reviewers of *Masculinities*], *Contemporary Sociology: A Journal of Review*, 25 (2): 172–4.

Connell, R.W., Davis, M. and Dowsett, G. (1993) 'A bastard of a life: homosexual desire and practice among men in working-class milieux', *Australian and New Zealand Journal of Sociology*, 29 (1): 112–35.

Corneau, G. (1991) *Absent Fathers, Lost Sons: The Search for Masculine Identity*. Boston: Shambhala.

Coward, R. (1993) *Our Treacherous Hearts*. London: Faber & Faber.

Craft, N. (1993) 'So much slime, so little time: the transgression of profeminism', *Changing Men*, 25 (Winter/Spring): 18–23.

Crawford, J., Kippax, S., Onyx, J., Gault, U. and Benton, P. (1992) *Emotion and Gender: Constructing Meaning From Memory*. London: Sage.

Crespi, F. (1992) *Social Action and Power*. Oxford: Blackwell.

Daly, M. (1973) 'For us and against us: anti-chauvinist males and women's liberation', *Social Policy*, 4 (3): 32–4.

Daly, M. (1975) *Gyn/Ecology: The Metaphysics of Radical Feminism*. Boston: Beacon Press.

Darling, A. (1988) 'Continuing debate: the truth about domestic violence', *Social Work*, 33 (2) (March–April): 189.

Davies, B. (1989) *Frogs and Snails and Feminist Tales*. Sydney: Allen and Unwin.

Davies, B. (1990) 'Agency as a form of discursive practice: a classroom scene observed', *British Journal of Sociology of Education*, 11 (3): 341–61.

Davies, B. (1993) *Shards of Glass*. Sydney: Allen and Unwin.

Davies, B. (1994) *Poststructuralist Theory and Classroom Practice*. Geelong: Deakin University Press.

Davies, B. and Harre, R. (1990) 'Positioning: the discursive production of selves', *Journal for the Theory of Social Behaviour*, 20 (1): 43–63.

De Lauretis, T. (1991) 'Queer theory: lesbian and gay sexualities', *Differences: A Journal of Feminist Cultural Studies*, 3 (2): 3–18.

Delphy, C. (1984) *Close to Home: A Materialist Analysis of Women's Oppression*. Amhurst: University of Massachusetts Press.

Di Stefano, C. (1990) 'Dilemmas of difference: modernity and postmodernism', in L. Nicholson (ed.), *Feminism/Postmodernism*. New York: Routledge.

Dinnerstein, D. (1976) *The Mermaid and the Minotaur*. New York: Harper Colophon.

Dobash, R. and Dobash, R. (1992) *Women, Violence and Social Change*. London: Routledge.

Dollimore, J. (1991) *Sexual Dissidence*. New York: Oxford University Press.

Douglas, P. (1993) 'Men = violence: a profeminist perspective on dismantling the masculine equation'. Paper presented at the 2nd National Conference on Violence, Australian Institute of Criminology, Canberra.

Dowsett, G. (1987) 'Queer fears and gay examples', *The New Internationalist*, 175 (September): 10–12.

Doyal, L. and Gough, I. (1991) *A Theory of Human Need*. London: Macmillan.

Dworkin, A. (1981) *Pornography: Men Possessing Women*. London: The Women's Press.

Edley, N. and Wetherell, M. (1995) *Men in Perspective: Practice, Power and Identity*. London: Prentice Hall.

Edwards, T. (1990) 'Beyond sex and gender: masculinity, homosexuality and social theory', in J. Hearn and D. Morgan (eds), *Men, Masculinities and Social Theory*. London: Unwin Hyman.

Edwards, T. (1994) *Erotics and Politics: Gay Male Sexuality, Masculinity and Feminism*. London: Routledge.

Ehrenreich, B. (1983) *The Hearts of Men*. New York: Pluto Press.

Eisenstein, H. (1984) *Contemporary Feminist Thought*. London: Unwin.

Eisenstein, Z. (1979) 'Developing a theory of capitalist patriarchy and socialist feminism', in Z. Eisenstein (ed.), *Capitalist Patriarchy and the Case for Socialist Feminism*. New York: Monthly Review Press.

Eisenstein, Z. (1988) *The Female Body and the Law*. Berkeley: University of California Press.

Ellsworth, E. (1989) 'Why doesn't this feel empowering?: working through the repressive myths of critical pedagogy', *Harvard Educational Review*, 59: 297–324.

Emihovich, C., Gaier, E. and Cronin, N. (1984) 'Sex-role expectation changes by fathers for their sons', *Sex Roles*, 11 (9/10): 861–8.

Epstein, S. (1987) 'Gay politics, ethnic identity: the limits of social constructionism', *Socialist Review*, 17 (3/4): 9–54.

Evans, M. (1990) 'The problem of gender for women's studies', *Women's Studies International Forum*, 13 (5): 457–62.

Faludi, S. (1992) *Backlash: The Undeclared War Against Women*. London: Chatto and Windus.

Farmer, S. (1991) *The Wounded Male*. New York: Ballantine.

Farrell, W. (1975) *The Liberated Man*. New York: Bantam.

Farrell, W. (1986) *Why Men Are The Way They Are*. New York: McGraw-Hill.

Farrell, W. (1993) *The Myth of Male Power*. New York: Simon and Schuster.

Fee, D. (1992) 'Masculine identity and the politics of essentialism: a social constructionist critique of the men's movement', *Feminism and Psychology*, 2 (2): 171–6.

Ferguson, K. (1993) *The Man Question: Visions of Subjectivity in Feminist Theory*. Berkeley: University of California Press.

Figes, E. (1972) *Patriarchal Attitudes*. London: Pantheon.

Firestone, S. (1971) *The Dialectic of Sex*. London: The Women's Press.

Flax, J. (1993) *Disputed Subjects*. New York: Routledge.

Forrester, J. (1992) 'What do men really want?', in D. Porter (ed.), *Between Men and Feminism*. London: Routledge.

Foster, H. (1983) 'Postmodernism: a preface', in H. Foster (ed.), *Postmodern Culture*. London: Pluto Press.

Foucault, M. (1972) *The Archaeology of Knowledge.* London: Tavistock.

Foucault, M. (1978) *The History of Sexuality (Volume One): An Introduction.* London: Penguin.

Foucault, M. (1980) *Power/Knowledge: Selected Interviews and Other Writings 1972–1977.* New York: Pantheon Books.

Frankenberg, R. (1993) *White Women, Race Matters: The Social Construction of Whiteness.* London: Routledge.

Franks, H. (1984) *Goodbye Tarzan: Men After Feminism.* London: Allen and Unwin.

Freire, P. (1993) 'Foreword', in P. McLaren and P. Leonard (eds), *Paulo Freire: A Critical Encounter.* London: Routledge.

French, M. (1991) *The Spectrum of Responsibility.* New York: St Martin's Press.

Friedan, B. (1981) *The Second Stage.* London: Abacus.

Frosh, S. (1994) *Sexual Difference: Masculinity and Psychoanalysis.* London: Routledge.

Fuss, D. (1987) *Essentially Speaking: Feminism, Nature and Difference.* New York: Routledge.

Galbraith, L. (1993) 'Who are we now?', *Outrage*, June: 23–6.

Garfinkel, P. (1985) *In a Man's World.* New York: New American Library.

Giddens, A. (1976) *New Rules of Sociological Method: A Positive Critique of Interpretative Sociologies.* London: Hutchinson.

Giddens, A. (1977) *Studies in Social and Political Theory.* London: Hutchinson.

Giddens, A. (1984) *The Constitution of Society: Outline of the Theory of Structuration.* Cambridge: Polity Press.

Giddens, A. (1991) *Modernity and Self Identity.* Cambridge: Polity Press.

Giddens, A. (1992) *The Transformation of Intimacy.* Cambridge: Polity Press.

Gilding, M. (1982) 'Men's groups: their radical possibilities', *Gay Information*, 9/10: 35–9.

Giroux, H. (1990) *Curriculum Discourse as Postmodernist Practice.* Geelong: Deakin University Press.

Gitlin, T. (1989) 'Postmodernism: roots and politics', *Dissent*, 36 (Winter): 100–8.

Goldberg, H. (1976) *The Hazards of Being Male: Surviving the Myth of Male Privilege.* New York: Signet.

Goldberg, H. (1987) *The Inner Male.* New York: Signet.

Gomez, J. (1991) *Psychological and Psychiatric Problems in Men.* London: Routledge.

Gondolf, E. (1987) 'Changing men who batter: a developmental model for integrated interventions', *Journal of Family Violence*, 2 (4): 335–49.

Goode, W. (1982) 'Why men resist', in B. Thorpe and M. Yalan (eds), *Rethinking the Family: Some Feminist Questions.* New York: Longman.

Goodman, G., Lakey, G., Lashof, J. and Thornes, E. (1983) *No Turning Back: Lesbian and Gay Liberation for the 80's.* Philadelphia: New Society Publishers.

Goodnow, J. and Bowles, J. (1994) *Men, Women and Household Work.* Melbourne: Oxford University Press.

Gordon, M. (1993) 'Why is this men's movement so white?', *Changing Men*, 26 (Summer/Fall): 15–17.

Gore, J. (1993) *The Struggle for Pedagogies.* New York: Routledge.

Gorman, J. (1993) 'Postmodernism and the conduct of inquiry in social work', *Affilia*, 8 (3): 247–64.

Grant, J. (1993) *Fundamental Feminism: Contesting the Core Concepts of Feminist Theory.* New York: Routledge.

Graves, T. (1994) 'Recovering From Whiplash: On Ending the Gender War'. Unpublished Manuscript, Melbourne.

Griffin, S. (1981) *Pornography and Silence.* London: The Women's Press.

Griscom, J. (1992) 'Women and power: definition, dualism and difference', *Psychology of Women Quarterly*, 16: 389–414.

Grob, L. (1991) 'Male female relations and the dialogical imperative', in L. Grob, R. Hassan and H. Gordon (eds), *Women's and Men's Testimonies of Spirit.* New York: Greenwood Press.

Gurian, M. (1994) *Mothers, Lovers and Sons*. Boston: Shambhala.

Gutterman, D. (1994) 'Postmodernism and the interrogation of masculinity', in H. Brod and M. Kaufman (eds), *Theorizing Masculinities*. Thousand Oaks, CA: Sage.

Habermas, J. (1972) *Knowledge and Human Interest*. Boston: Beacon Press.

Hagen, K. (1992) 'Introduction', in K. Hagen (ed.), *Women Respond to the Men's Movement*. San Francisco: Harper.

Hall, R. (1994) 'Partnership accountability', *Dulwich Centre Newsletter*, 2 and 3: 6–29.

Hall, S. (1987) 'Minimal selves', in *ICA Documents*, no. 6, London.

Hamilton, M. (1977) *Fathers' Influences on Children*. Chicago: Nelson Hall.

Hanmer, J. (1990) 'Men, power and the exploitation of women', in J. Hearn and D. Morgan (eds), *Men, Masculinities and Social Theory*. London: Unwin Hyman.

Haraway, D. (1988) 'Situated knowledges: the science question in feminism and the privilege of partial perspectives', *Feminist Studies*, 14 (3): 575–99.

Harding, S. (1986) *The Science Question in Feminism*. Ithaca: Cornell University Press.

Harding, S. (1987) 'Is there a feminist method?', in S. Harding (ed.), *Feminism and Methodology: Social Science Issues*. Bloomington: Indiana University Press.

Harding, S. (1992) 'Subjectivity, experience and knowledge: an epistemology from/for rainbow coalition politics', *Development and Change*, 23 (3): 175–93.

Harding, S. (1993) 'Rethinking standpoint epistemology: what is strong objectivity?', in L. Alcoff and E. Potter (eds), *Feminist Epistemologies*. New York: Routledge.

Hartmann, H. (1981) 'The unhappy marriage of Marxism and feminism: towards a more progressive union', in L. Sargent (ed.), *Women and Revolution*. Boston: South End Press.

Hartsock, N (1990) 'Foucault on power: a theory for women?', in L. Nicholson (ed.) *Feminism/Postmodernism*. London: Routledge.

Haug, F. (1987) *Female Sexualisation: A Collective Work of Memory*. London: Verso.

Haug, F. (1992) *Beyond Female Masochism: Memory-Work and Politics*. London: Verso.

Hearn, J. (1987) *The Gender of Oppression: Men Masculinity and the Critique of Marxism*. Sussex: Wheatsheaf.

Hearn, J. (1992) *Men in the Public Eye*. London: Routledge.

Hearn, J. and Collinson, D. (1994) 'Theorizing unities and differences between men and between masculinities', in H. Brod and M. Kaufman (eds), *Theorizing Masculinities*. Thousand Oaks, CA: Sage.

Hekman, S. (1990) *Gender and Knowledge: Elements of a Postmodern Feminism*. Cambridge: Polity Press.

Henderson, J. (1977) 'Emotions and the left', *Issues in Radical Therapy*, 18 (Spring): 10–12.

Hennessy, K. (1994) 'Loosen the homophobic grip', *Changing Men*, 27 (Winter): 14–16.

Henriques, J., Holloway, W., Urwin, C., Venn, C. and Walkerdine, V. (1984) 'Constructing the subject', in J. Henriques, W. Hollway, C. Urwin, C. Venn and V. Walkerdine (eds), *Changing the Subject: Psychology, Social Regulation and Subjectivity*. London: Methuen.

Herek, G. (1987) 'On heterosexual masculinity: some psychical consequences of the social construction of gender and sexuality', in M. Kimmel (ed.), *Changing Men*. Newbury Park: Sage.

Herek, G. (1990) 'The context of anti-gay violence: notes on cultural and psychological heterosexism', *Journal of Interpersonal Violence*, 5 (3): 316–33.

Herzog, E. and Sudia, C. (1971) *Boys in Fatherless Families*. Washington DC: US Department of Health Education Service.

Hirschmann, N. (1992) *Rethinking Obligation: A Feminist Method For Political Theory*. Ithaca, NY: Cornell University Press.

Hite, S. (1987) *Women and Love*. London: Penguin.

Hite, S. (1994) *The Hite Report on the Family: Growing up Under Patriarchy*. London: Bloomsbury.

Hollway, W. (1982) 'Identity and gender difference in adult social relations'. PhD dissertation, University of London.

Hollway, W. (1989) *Subjectivity and Method in Psychology: Gender, Meaning and Science*. London: Sage.

hooks, b. (1984) *Feminist Theory: From Margin to Centre*. Boston: South End Press.

hooks, b. (1989) *Talking Back: Thinking Feminist Thinking Black*. Boston: Sheba.

hooks, b. (1991) 'Essentialism and experience', *American Literary History*, 3 (1): 172–83.

hooks, b. (1992) *Black Looks: Race and Representation*. Boston: South End Press.

hooks, b. (1993) 'Let's get real about feminism: the backlash, the myths, the movement', *Ms*, 4 (2): 34–43.

Hornacek, C. (1977) 'Anti-sexist men's consciousness-raising groups', in J. Snodgrass (ed.), *For Men Against Sexism*. New York: Times Change Press.

Horowitz, G. and Kaufman, M. (1987) 'Male sexuality: towards a theory of liberation', in M. Kaufman (ed.), *Beyond Patriarchy*. Toronto: Oxford University Press.

Horsfall, J. (1991) *The Presence of the Past: Male Violence in the Family*. Sydney: Allen and Unwin.

Horsfield, P. (1994) 'The church, forgiveness and reconciliation', in S. Bartley and H. Macdonald (eds), *Sexual Assault and other Forms of Violence within the Australian Community*. National Resource and Training Seminar, CASA House, Melbourne.

Humphries, M. (1987) 'Choosing with care: working with non-gay men', in G. Hanscombe and M. Humphreys (eds), *Heterosexuality*. London: G.M.P. Publications.

Humphries, M. and Metcalf, A. (eds) (1985) *The Sexuality of Men*. London: Pluto Press.

Ife, J. (1995) *Community Development: Creating Community Alternatives – Vision, Analysis and Practice*. Melbourne: Longman.

Ingamells, A. (1994) 'Practice and the postmodern'. Paper presented at the Australian Association of Social Work Education Conference, Perth.

Ingham, M. (1984) *Men: The Male Myth Exposed*. London: Century Publishing.

Inglis, A. (1985) 'Sexuality, welfare and political practice'. Social work monograph, University of East Anglia, Norwich.

Intervente, J. (1981) 'Dancing along the precipice: the men's movement in the '80's', *Radical America*, 15 (5): 53–71.

Jackson, D. (1990) *Unmasking Masculinity: A Critical Biography*. London: Unwin Hyman.

Janmohamed, A. (1994) 'Some implications of Paulo Freire's border pedagogy', in H. Giroux and P. McLaren (eds), *Between Borders: Pedagogy and the Politics of Cultural Studies*. New York: Routledge.

Jardine, A. (1987) 'Men in feminism: odor di vomo or compagnons de route?', in A. Jardine and P. Smith (eds), *Men in Feminism*. New York: Methuen.

Jeffries, S. (1990) *Anticlimax: A Feminist Perspective on the Sexual Revolution*. London: The Women's Press.

Jonasdottir, A. (1988) 'On the concept of interest, women's interests and the limitations of interest theory', in K. Jones and A. Jonasdottir (eds), *The Political Interests of Gender*. London: Sage.

Jukes, A. (1993) *Why Men Hate Women*. London: Free Association Books.

Jung, P. and Smith, R. (1993) *Heterosexism: An Ethical Challenge*. Albany: State University of New York Press.

Kaufman, M. (1987) 'The construction of masculinity and the triad of men's violence', in M. Kaufman (ed.), *Beyond Patriarchy*. Toronto: Oxford University Press.

Kaufman, M. (1993) *Cracking The Armour: Power, Pain and the Lives of Men*. Toronto: Viking.

Kaufman, M. (1994) 'Men, feminism, and men's contradictory experience of power', in H. Brod and M. Kaufman (eds), *Theorizing Masculinities*. New York: Sage.

Kauth, B. (1992) *A Circle of Men*. New York: St Martin's Press.

Keen, S. (1991) *Fire in the Belly: On Being a Man*. New York: Bantam Books.

Keen, S. (1992) 'Rapacious normality: the war between the sexes', in C. Harding (ed.), *Wingspan: Inside the Men's Movement*. New York: St Martin's Press.

Kellner, D. (1989) *Critical Theory, Marxism and Modernity*. Oxford: Blackwell.

Kelly, L. (1990) 'Journeying in reverse: possibilities and problems in feminist research on sexual violence', in L. Gelsthorpe and A. Morris (eds), *Feminist Perspectives in Criminology*. Milton Keynes: Open University Press.

Kelly, L., Burton, S. and Regan, L. (1994) 'Researching women's lives or studying women's oppression? Reflections on what constitutes feminist research', in M. Maynard and J. Purvis (eds), *Researching Women's Lives From a Feminist Perspective*. London: Taylor & Francis.

Kimmel, M. (1987) 'Men's response to feminism at the turn of the century', *Gender and Society*, 3 (3) (September): 261–83.

Kimmel, M. (1990) 'After 15 years: the impact of the sociology of masculinity on the masculinity of sociology', in J. Hearn and D. Morgan (eds), *Men, Masculinities and Social Theory*. London: Routledge.

Kimmel, M. (1992) 'Reading men: men, masculinity and publishing', *Men's Studies Review*, 9 (1): 45–50.

Kimmel, M. (1993) 'The politics of accountability', *Changing Men*, 26 (Summer/Fall): 3–4.

Kimmel, M. (1994) 'Masculinity as homophobia: fear, shame and silence in the construction of masculinity', in H. Brod and M. Kaufman (eds), *Theorizing Masculinities*. Thousand Oaks, CA: Sage.

Kimmel, M. and Messner, M. (1989) 'Introduction', in M. Kimmel and M. Messner (eds), *Men's Lives*. New York: Macmillan.

King, B. (1992) 'The men's movement', *Arena*, 99/100: 129–40.

Kinsman, G. (1987) 'Men loving men: the challenge of gay liberation', in M. Kaufman (ed.), *Beyond Patriarchy*. Toronto: Oxford University Press.

Kirk, M. and Madsen, H. (1989) *After the Ball: How America will Conquer its Fear and Hatred of Gays in the 1990's*. New York: Doubleday.

Kitzinger, C. (1987) *The Social Construction of Lesbianism*. London: Sage.

Kivel, P. (1992) *Men's Work*. New York: Ballantine Books.

Klein, R. (1983) 'The "men–problem" in women's studies: the expert, the ignoramus and the poor dear', *Women's Studies International Forum*, 6 (4): 413–21.

Kreiner, C. (1991) 'Interview', *Achilles Heel*, 12: 6.

Kreiner, C. (1992) 'Giving up sexism', in *The Liberation of Men*. Seattle: Rational Island Publishers.

Kristeva, J. (1981) 'Women's time', *Signs*, 7 (1).

Kupers, T. (1993) *Revisioning Men's Lives: Gender, Intimacy and Power*. New York: The Guilford Press.

Lather, P. (1991) *Getting Smart: Feminist Research and Pedagogy With/In the Postmodern*. New York: Routledge.

Leahy, T. (1991) 'Positively experienced man/boy sex: the discourse of seduction and the social construction of masculinity'. Paper presented at the Research on Masculinity and Men in Gender Relations Conference, Macquarie University, Sydney.

Lee, J. (1991) *At my Father's Wedding: Reclaiming our True Masculinity*. New York: Bantam.

Leonard, D. (1982) 'Male feminists and divided women', in S. Friedman and E. Sarah (eds), *On the Problem of Men: Two Feminist Conferences*. London: The Women's Press.

Lichtenberg, P. (1988) *Getting Equal: The Equalizing Law of Relationship*. Lanham, MD: University Press of America.

Lisak, D. (1991) 'Sexual aggression, masculinity and fathers', *Signs: Journal of Women, Culture and Society*, 16 (2): 239–63.

Lloyd, M. (1993) 'The (f)utility of a feminist turn to Foucault', *Economy and Society*, 22 (4): 437–59.

Lorde, A. (1984) *Sister Outsider*. New York: The Crossing Press.

Luxton, M. (1993) 'Dreams and dilemmas: feminist musings on the "man question"', in T. Haddad (ed.), *Men and Masculinities: A Critical Anthology*. Toronto: Canadian Scholars' Press.

Lyndon, N. (1992) *No More Sex War: The Failures of Feminism*. London: Sinclair-Stevenson.

MacKinnon, K. (1982) 'Feminism, marxism, method and the state: an agenda for theory', *Signs: Journal of Women, Culture and Society*, 7 (3): 515–44.

Maguire, P. (1987) *Doing Participatory Research*. Amherst: Centre for International Education, University of Massachusetts.

Marcus, J. (1988) 'Australian women and feminist men', *Hecate*, 14 (2): 98–105.

Marine, G. (1972) *A Male Guide to Women's Liberation*. New York: Avon.

Marshall, B. (1994) *Engendering Modernity*. Cambridge: Polity Press.

McBride, T. (1980) 'The woman within', *Magus*, 4: 26–34.

McLaren, P. and da Silva, T. (1993) 'Decentering pedagogy: critical literacy, resistance and the politics of memory', in P. McLaren and P. Leonard (eds), *Paulo Freire: A Critical Encounter*. London: Routledge.

McMahon, A. (1994) 'Taking care of men: discourses and practices of domestic life'. PhD dissertation, La Trobe University, Melbourne.

McMillan, P. (1992) *Men, Sex and Other Secrets*. Melbourne: The Text Publishing Company.

McNeely, R. and Robinson-Simpson, G. (1988) 'The truth about domestic violence revisited: a reply to Saunders', *Social Work*, 33 (2): 184–8.

Mederos, F. (1987) 'Patriarchy and male psychology'. Unpublished manuscript, Montreal.

Memmi, A. (1965) *The Colonizer and the Colonized*. Boston: Beacon Press.

Men Against Pornography (1992) 'A New Principle of Accountability'. Unpublished manuscript, New York.

Mentor Men's Network (1993) *Connectedness* brochure, Melbourne.

Menzies, K. (1982) *Sociological Theory in Use*. London: Routledge and Kegan Paul.

Mercia, K. and Julien, I. (1988) 'Race, sexual politics and black masculinity: a dossier', in R. Chapman and J. Rutherford (eds), *Male Order: Unwrapping Masculinity*. London: Lawrence and Wishart.

Middleton, P. (1989) 'Socialism, feminism and men', *Radical Philosophy*, 53: 8–19.

Miedzian, M. (1992) 'Father hunger: why soup kitchen fathers are not good enough', in K. Hagen (ed.), *Women Respond to the Men's Movement*. San Francisco: Harper.

Millet, K. (1972) *Sexual Politics*. London: Abacus.

Mitchell, J. (1975) *Psychoanalysis and Feminism*. New York: Vintage Books.

Moi, T. (1985) *Sexual/Textual Politics*. New York: Routledge.

Moi, T. (1989) 'Men against patriarchy', in L. Kauffman (ed.), *Gender and Theory: Dialogues on Feminist Criticism*. Oxford: Blackwell.

Moore, R. and Gillette, D. (1990) *King, Warrior, Magician, Lover: Rediscovering the Archetypes of the Mature Masculine*. San Francisco: Harper.

Morgan, D. (1992) *Discovering Men*. London: Routledge.

Mouffe, C. (1992) 'Feminism, citizenship, and radical democratic politics', in J. Butler and J. Scott (eds), *Feminists Theorize the Political*. New York: Routledge.

New, C. (1996) 'Man bad, woman good? essentialisms and ecofeminisms', *New Left Review*, 216: 79–93.

Nicholson, L. (1990) 'Introduction', in L. Nicholson (ed.), *Feminism/Postmodernism*. New York: Routledge.

Nierenberg, J. (1987) 'Misogyny: gay and straight', in F. Abbott (ed.), *New Men, New Minds*. Freedom, CA: Crossing Press.

Noble, V. (1992) 'A helping hand from the guys', in L. Hagan (ed.), *Women Respond to the Men's Movement*. San Francisco: Harper.

Nordstrom, B. (1992) 'How men grow up: sources of tradition and change'. Paper presented at the 17th National Conference on Men and Masculinity, Chicago.

O'Brien, M. (1981) *The Politics of Reproduction*. Boston: Routledge and Kegan Paul.

O'Connor, P. (1985) *Understanding Jung, Understanding Yourself*. Sydney: Methuen.

O'Connor, P. (1993) *The Inner Man: Men, Myths and Dreams*. Sydney: Sun Books.

Onyx, J. (1993) 'Power between women'. Unpublished manuscript, Macquarie University, Sydney.

Orkin, G. (1991) 'Abuse, violence, counselling', *XY: Men, Sex and Politics*, 1 (3): 9–11.

Orkin, G. (1993) 'What about the workers?', *XY: Men, Sex and Politics*, 3 (3): 22–4.

Osherson, S. (1986) *Finding Our Fathers*. New York: Fawcett Columbine.

Osherson, S. (1992) *Wrestling With Love*. New York: Fawcett Columbine.

Owen, C. (1987) 'Outlaws: gay men in feminism', in A. Jardine and P. Smith (eds), *Men in Feminism*. London: Methuen.

Parker, J. (1987) 'The tables are turning', in G. Hanscomb and M. Humphries (eds), *Heterosexuality*. London: GMP Publications.

Parmar, P. (1990) 'Black feminism: the politics of difference', in J. Rutherford (ed.), *Identity, Community, Culture, Difference*. London: Lawrence and Wishart.

Pasick, R. (1992) *Awakening From the Deep Sleep*. San Francisco: Harper.

Pasick, R., Gordon, S. and Meth, R. (1990) 'Helping men understand themselves', in R. Meth and R. Pasick (eds), *Men In Therapy*. New York: Guilford Press.

Pearson, C. (1984) 'Male sexual politics and men's gender practice', *Women's Studies International Forum*, 7 (1): 24–32.

Pease, B. (1997) *Men and Sexual Politics: Towards a Profeminist Practice*. Adelaide: Dulwich Centre Publications.

People's Equality Network (1994) *Newsletter*, 1 (1), Melbourne.

Phelan, S. (1989) *Identity Politics: Lesbian Feminism and the Limits of Community*. Philadelphia: Temple University Press.

Phelan, S. (1991) 'Specificity: beyond equality and difference', *Differences*, 3 (1): 63–84.

Pheterson, G. (1986) 'Alliances between women: overcoming internalized oppression and internalized domination', *Signs: Journal of Women in Culture and Society*, 12 (1): 146–60.

Phillips, A. (1993) *Democracy and Difference*. Cambridge: Polity Press.

Pleck, J. (1983) *The Myth of Masculinity*. Cambridge, MA: MIT Press.

Pleck, J. (1987) 'American fathering in historical perspective', in M. Kimmel (ed.), *Changing Men: New Directions in Research on Men and Masculinity*. Newbury Park: Sage.

Poovey, M. (1988) 'Feminism and deconstruction', *Feminist Studies*, 14 (1): 51–65.

Potter, J. and Wetherall, M. (1987) *Discourse and Social Psychology*. London: Sage.

Pratt, A. (1985) 'Spinning among the fields: Jung, Frye, Levi-Strauss and feminist archetypal theory', in E. Laute and C. Rupprecht (eds), *Feminist Archetypal Theory*. Knoxville: University of Tennessee Press.

Ramazanoglu, C. (1989) *Feminism and the Contradictions of Oppression*. London: Routledge.

Ramazanoglu, C. (1993) 'Introduction', in C. Ramazanoglu (ed.), *Up Against Foucault*. London: Routledge.

Ramazanoglu, C. and Holland, J. (1993) 'Women's sexuality and men's appropriation of desire', in C. Ramazanoglu (ed.), *Up Against Foucault*. London: Routledge.

Reinharz, S. (1992) *Feminist Methods in Social Research*. New York: Oxford University Press.

Rich, B. (1983) 'Anti–porn: soft issue-hard world', *Feminist Review*, 13 (Spring): 65–70.

Riley, D. (1988) *Am I That Name? Feminism and the Creation of 'Women' in History*. London: Macmillan.

Roberts, R. (1989) 'Challenging heterosexism in social work education', in D. James and T. Vinson (eds), *Advances in Social Work Education*. Sydney: Sydney University.

Roberts, Y. (1992) *Mad About Women*. London: Virago Press.

Ross, A. (1987) 'No question of silence', in A. Jardine and P. Smith (eds), *Men in Feminism*. New York: Methuen.

Rowan, J. (1992) 'Wild men and misogyny: defending the horned god', *Man: Men, Relationships, Community*, 18 (Summer): 36–7.

Rowbotham, S. (1981) 'The trouble with patriarchy', in R. Samuel (ed.), *People's History and Socialist Theory*. London: Routledge and Kegan Paul.

Ruether, R. (1992) 'Patriarchy and the men's movement: part of the problem or part of the solution', in K. Hagen (ed.), *Women Respond to the Men's Movement*. San Francisco: Harper.

Rutherford, J. (1992) *Men's Silences: Predicaments in Masculinity*. London: Macmillan.

Ryan, W. (1976) *Blaming the Victim*. New York: Pantheon Books.

Saco, D. (1992) 'Masculinity as signs: poststructural, feminist approaches to the study of gender', in S. Craig (ed.), *Men, Masculinity and the Media*. Newbury Park: Sage.

Samuels, A. (1993) *The Political Psyche*. London: Routledge.

Sarup, M. (1992) *An Introductory Guide to Poststructuralism and Postmodernism*. London: Harvester Wheatsheaf.

Saunders, D. (1988) 'Other truths about domestic violence: a reply to McNeely and Robinson-Simpson', *Social Work*, 33 (2): 179–83.

Sawicki, J. (1988) 'Identity politics and sexual freedom: Foucault and feminism', in I. Diamond and L. Quinby (eds), *Feminism and Foucault: Reflections on Resistance*. Boston: North Eastern University Press.

Sawicki, J. (1991) *Disciplining Foucault: Feminism, Power and the Body*. New York: Routledge.

Sawyer, J. (1974) 'On male liberation', in J. Pleck and J. Sawyer (eds), *Men and Masculinity*. Englewood Cliffs: Prentice Hall.

Schein, L. (1977) 'Dangers with men's consciousness-raising groups', in J. Snodgrass (ed.), *For Men Against Sexism*. New York: Times Change Press.

Schwalbe, M. (1993) 'Why mythopoetic men don't flock to NOMAS', *Masculinities*, 1 (3 /4): 68–72.

Scott, J. (1988) 'Deconstructing equality versus difference: or the use of poststructuralist theory for feminism', *Feminist Studies*, 14 (1): 33–50.

Sebestyen, A. (1982) 'Sexual assumptions in the women's movement', in S. Friedman and E. Sarah (eds), *On the Problem of Men: Two Feminist Conferences*. London: The Women's Press.

Sedgwick, E. (1985) *Between Men: English Literature and Male Homosocial Desire*. New York: Columbia University Press.

Segal, L. (1987) *Is the Future Female?: Troubled Thoughts on Contemporary Feminism*. London: Virago.

Segal, L. (1989) 'Slow change or no change? socialism and the problem of men', *Feminist Review*, 31 (Spring): 5–21.

Segal, L. (1990) *Slow Motion: Changing Masculinities, Changing Men*. London: Virago.

Segal, L. (1993) 'Changing men: masculinities in context', *Theory and Society*, 22 (5): 628–41.

Segal, L. (1994) *Straight Sex: The Politics of Pleasure*. London: Virago.

Seidler, V. (1989) *Rediscovering Masculinity: Reason, Language and Sexuality.* London: Routledge.

Seidler, V. (1991a) *Recreating Sexual Politics: Men, Feminism and Politics.* London: Routledge.

Seidler, V. (1991b) 'Men, sexual politics and socialism', in V. Seidler (ed.), *The Achilles Heel Reader: Men, Sexual Politics and Socialism.* London: Routledge.

Seidler, V. (1991c) 'Preface', in V. Seidler (ed.), *The Achilles Heel Reader: Men, Sexual Politics and Socialism.* London: Routledge.

Seidler, V. (1992) 'Men, sex and relationships', in V. Seidler (ed.), *Men, Sex and Relationships: Writings from Achilles Heel.* London: Routledge.

Seidler, V. (1994) *Unreasonable Men: Masculinity and Social Theory.* London: Routledge.

Seidman, S. (1992) *Embattled Eros: Sexual Politics and Ethics in Contemporary America.* New York: Routledge.

Shotter, J. (1993) *Cultural Politics of Everyday Life.* Buckingham: Open University Press.

Sibeon, R. (1991) *Towards a New Sociology of Social Work.* Aldershot, Hants.: Avebury.

Silverstein, M. (1994) 'A note from the author's son', in O. Silverstein and B. Rashbaum (eds), *The Courage to Raise Good Men.* New York: Viking.

Silverstein, O. and Rashbaum, B. (1994) *The Courage to Raise Good Men.* New York: Viking.

Smith, M. (1992) 'Postmodernism, urban ethnography and the new social space of ethnic identity', *Theory and Society*, 21 (4): 493–531.

Smith, P. (1987) 'Men in feminism: men and feminist theory', in A. Jardine and P. Smith (eds), *Men in Feminism.* New York: Methuen.

Snodgrass, J. (1977) 'Men's liberation (criticisms)', in J. Snodgrass (ed.), *For Men Against Sexism.* New York: Times Change Press.

Sofia, Z. (1993) 'Position envy and the subsumption of feminism', *Arena Magazine*, 4, (April/May): 34–6.

Soper, K. (1990) 'Feminism, humanism and postmodernism', *Radical Philosophy*, 55 (Summer): 11–17.

Soper, K. (1993) 'Productive contradictions', in C. Ramazanoglu (ed.), *Up Against Foucault.* London: Routledge.

Spelman, E. (1988) *Inessential Woman: Problems of Exclusion in Feminist Thought.* London: The Women's Press.

Spivak, G. (1987) *In Other Worlds: Essays in Cultural Politics.* Reston: Reston Publishing Company.

Stanley, L. (1982) '"Male needs": the problems and problems of working with gay men', in S. Friedman and E. Sarah (eds), *On the Problem of Men: Two Feminist Conferences.* London: The Women's Press.

Staples, R. (1989) 'Masculinity and race: the dual dilemma of black men', in M. Kimmel and M. Messner (eds), *Men's Lives.* New York: Macmillan.

Starhawk (1992) 'A men's movement I can trust', in K. Hagen (ed.), *Women Respond to the Men's Movement.* San Francisco: Harper.

Steinem, G. (1975) 'Introduction', in M. Fasteau, *The Male Machine.* New York: Dell.

Steiner, C. (1986) *When a Man Loves a Woman: Sexual and Emotional Literacy for the Modern Man.* New York: Grove Press.

Stephensen, N., Kippax, S. and Crawford, J. (1995) 'You and me and she: memory-work and the construction of self'. Unpublished manuscript, Macquarie University, Sydney.

Stoltenberg, J. (1989) 'Eroticism and violence in the father–son relationship', in J. Stoltenberg (ed.), *Refusing to be a Man.* New York: Meridian.

Stoltenberg, J. (1991) 'A coupla things I've been meaning to say about really confronting male power', *Changing Men*, 22 (Winter/Spring): 8–10.

Stoltenberg, J. (1992) *Sex and Selfhood: A Facilitator's Guidebook*. Minneapolis: Kundschier/Manthey.

Stoltenberg, J. (1993) *The End of Manhood: A Book for Men of Conscience*. New York: Dutton.

Straton, J. (1994) 'The myth of the battered husband syndrome', *Masculinities*, 2 (4): 79–82.

Straus, M. and Gelles, R. (1990) *Physical Violence in American Families*. New Brunswick: Transaction.

Swigonski, M. (1993) 'Feminist standpoint theory and the questions of social work research', *Affilia*, 8 (2): 171–83.

Tacey, D. (1990) 'Reconstructing masculinity: a post–Jungian response to contemporary men's issues', *Meanjin*, 49 (4): 781–92.

Taubman, S. (1986) 'Beyond the bravado: sex roles and the exploitative male', *Social Work*, 31 (1): 12–17.

Thomas, A. (1990) 'Masculinity, identification and political culture', in J. Hearn and D. Morgan (eds), *Men, Masculinities and Social Theory*. London: Unwin Hyman.

Thomas, D. (1993) *Not Guilty: Men: The Case for the Defence*. London: Weidenfeld and Nicholson.

Thompson, C. (1991) 'Can white heterosexual men understand oppression?', *Changing Men*, 22 (Winter/Spring): 14–16.

Thompson, C. (1992) 'On being heterosexual in a homophobic world', in W. Blumenfeld (ed.), *Homophobia*. Boston: Beacon Press.

Thompson, E. (ed.) (1994) *Older Men's Lives*. Thousand Oaks, CA: Sage.

Thorne-Finch, R. (1992) *Ending the Silence: The Origins and Treatment of Male Violence Against Women*. Toronto: University of Toronto Press.

Tilley, C. (1990) 'M. Foucault: towards an archaeology of archaeology', in C. Tilley (ed.), *Reading Material Culture: Structuralism, Hermeneutics, Post Structuralism*. Oxford: Blackwell.

Torbert, W. (1991) *The Power of Balance: Transforming Self, Society, and Scientific Inquiry*. Newbury Park: Sage.

Touraine, A. (1977) *The Voice and the Eye: An Analysis of Social Movements*. Cambridge: Cambridge University Press.

Touraine, A. (1985) 'An introduction to the study of social movements', *Social Research*, 52 (4): 749–87.

Touraine, A., Wieviorka, M. and Dubet, F. (1987) *The Worker's Movement*. Cambridge: Cambridge University Press.

Townsend, H. (1994) *Real Men*. Sydney: Harper and Collins.

Upton, C. (1993) *Hot Iron: A Spiritual Critique of Bly's Iron John*. Wheaton, IL: Quest Books.

Vorlicky, R. (1990) '(In)visible alliances: conflicting "chronicles" of feminism', in J. Boone and M. Cadden (eds), *Engendering Men: The Question of Male Feminist Criticism*. New York: Routledge.

Wadsworth, Y. and Hargreaves, K. (1993) *What is Feminist Research?* Melbourne: Action Research Issues Association.

Walby, S. (1990) *Theorizing Patriarchy*. Oxford: Basil Blackwell.

Walczak, Y. (1988) *He and She: Men in the Eighties*. London: Routledge.

Watson, S. and Pringle, R. (1992) '"Women's interests" and the post structuralist state', in M. Barrett and A. Phillips (eds), *Destabilizing Feminist Theory: Contemporary Feminist Debates*. Cambridge: Polity Press.

Weedon, C. (1987) *Feminist Practice and Poststructuralist Theory*. Oxford: Blackwell.

Weeks, J. (1990) 'The value of difference', in J. Rutherford (ed.), *Identity, Community, Culture, Difference*. London: Lawrence and Wishart.

Weeks, J. (1993) 'Rediscovering values', in J. Squires (ed.), *Principled Positions: Postmodernism and the Rediscovery of Value*. London: Lawrence and Wishart.

Weiler, K. (1991) 'Freire and a feminist pedagogy of difference', *Harvard Educational Review*, 61 (4): 449–74.

Weir, D. (1987) *Jung and Feminism: Liberating Archetypes*. Boston: Beacon Press.

Wendell, S. (1990) 'Oppression and victimization: choices and responsibility', *Hypatia*, 5 (3): 15–46.

White, M. (1995) *Re-Authoring Lives: Interviews and Essays*. Adelaide: Dulwich Centre Publications.

Wilson, E. (1983) *What is to be done about Violence Against Women?* London: Penguin.

Wilson, J. (1990) *Single Fathers*. Melbourne: Sun Books.

Wineman, S. (1984) *The Politics of Human Services*. Boston: South End Press.

Winter, M. and Robert, E. (1980) 'Male dominance, late capitalism and the growth of instrumental reason', *Berkeley Journal of Sociology*, 24–5: 249–80.

Wolf, N. (1993) *Fire with Fire: The New Female Power and How it will Change the 21st Century*. London: Chatto and Windus.

Wolin, S. (1990) 'On the theory and practice of power', in J. Arac (ed.), *After Foucault: Humanistic Knowledge and Postmodern Challenges*. New Brunswick, NJ: Rutgers University Press.

Worden, O., Levin, C. and Chesler, M. (1977) 'Racism, sexism and class elitism: change agent dilemmas in combating oppression', in A. Sargent (ed.), *Beyond Sex Roles*. San Francisco: West Publishing Company.

Yeatman, A. (1994) *Postmodern Revisionings of the Political*. New York: Routledge.

Yoder, J. and Kahn, D. (1992) 'Toward a feminist understanding of women and power', *Psychology of Women Quarterly*, 16: 381–8.

Young, I. (1990) *Justice and the Politics of Difference*. Princeton, NJ: Princeton University Press.

Index

and standpoint theories 5
strong and weak versions of 24
poststructuralism 24
potential for change 14–17, 23–4,
    29, 37–8
power 8–9
    differential access to 29
    Foucault on 32–3
    inner/outer 9
    institutionalized 9, 22
    integrative 9
    personal 117
    positive 102
    and sexuality 9, 42–3
    structural 51, 134
    threat 9
    see also class power;
        disempowerment;
        empowerment; gender
        power; male power;
        women's power
power inequalities 1, 22, 108, 126,
    141
power relations 32–3, 140
powerlessness 80, 94–5
praxis 37–8, 138, 143
pride as men 52, 101, 118
privilege
    heterosexual 122, 141
    and identity 109
    male 17, 100, 104
    recognizing 134–5, 146
    relinquishing 45
production
    mode of economic 23
    relations of 13, 34
profeminism 3–4, 37, 55
    agenda 19, 39, 66, 101, 113–14
    constructing men's standpoint
        4–7, 49–50, 113–14
    criticism of softening effects of
        117–18
    as a kind of masochism 74, 113
    and patriarchal discourses 44,
        113
profeminist men 1, 30, 137
    accused of male bashing 141
    awareness 3, 5, 55
    collective politics among 3,
        7–8, 38, 42, 44, 55, 101, 136
    dilemmas of commitment
        42–4, 88, 119, 132
    ethical stance 42–4, 49–50, 141
    and father-son relationships
        58–9
    and gay men 126
    motivation 46–7, 49–51
    new questions for 41–2, 48–9,
        55
    research by 6–7
    and the sex industry 86–91
    the site of politics 17–18
    and solidarity problem 110,
        131–2
    and spirituality 105–6
    standpoint of 5–6, 137
psychoanalytic theory 21–2, 68
    feminist 21
psychological focus 17, 21–2, 38
public discourse, about morality
    91
public sex, and beats 125–6
public sphere 23, 29, 32, 128

boys in the 70–1
    disappearing 115
    punishment, physical 63

queer theory/politics 123–4, 126,
    141

race 2, 22, 29, 32, 140
race relations 129
racism, role in development of
    white masculinity 30
radical feminism 12, 13, 15, 26,
    48, 84, 140
Ramazanoglu, C. 12, 33
rape 43, 99
    complicity in culture of 43
    prevention of 38
    as revenge 89
rapists
    relationship with fathers 57
    within 29, 43
rational man, and feeling man
    119–20, 133
Ray 44–5, 47–8
recognition 52, 106
reflection, critical 12, 35, 54, 100,
    127, 143
Reinharz, S. 6
repression 20, 90, 132
reproduction
    materialist account of 23
    women's control over 38, 113
resistance
    levels of men's to change 16,
        45–6, 100
    and power 33
    to dominant masculinity 36–7,
        38, 139, 145
    to feminist analysis 1–2
    women's 9
responsibility 6–7, 16–17
    and blame 93, 95–7
    collective 38, 100–1, 118
    displacement of individual 100
    ethic of sexual 91
    men's domestic 45, 129
    and men's violence 108
Rich, B. 85
rights
    gay 122
    men's discourse 95–6, 97–8, 99,
        100, 101
    women's 2, 17
Riley, M. 122–6
rituals, initiation 103
Robert, E. 23
Robinson-Simpson, G. 98
Rowbotham, S. 13
Rutherford, J. 22

sacrifice, and needs 45
sadomasochism 123, 125, 126
Samuels, A. 119
Saunders, D. 99
Sawicki, J. 33
Schein, L. 41
Sedgwick, E. 76–7
Segal, L. 17, 22, 31, 91, 111
Seidler, V. 48
Seidman, S. 91
self
    decentring the 28, 35–7
    narrative of 41, 145

and subjectivity 53
self-distance 49
self-esteem, male 38, 57, 101, 114,
    118–19
self-help books 107
self-interests
    enlightened of men 16–17, 91,
        141
    and ethics 135
    material of men 15–16
    men's 15–17, 108
    and social movements 52
self-knowledge 5, 103–4, 127
self-reflection, critical 12, 127
separation
    experience of 50
    from mothers 67–8
sex
    between straight men 82–3
    genitally and non-genitally
        focused 91, 121
    lust and power over 42–3
    see also gay sex;
        intergenerational sex
sex industry, profeminist men
    and the 86–9
sex-role theory 19–20, 38, 40,
    57–8
sexism
    among men 77, 126, 140–1
    in the gay movement 124–5
    institutionalized 40–1, 101
    personal 101
sexual abuse
    of children 80, 108
    and objectification 85
    of women 22, 23, 99, 111
sexual harassment 23
    of men by women 89
sexuality 2
    adolescent male 78–81
    alternative construction of
        non-patriarchal 76
    anatomical 28
    assumptions about men's 84,
        121
    feminist examination of men's
        7–8
    power relations of 43, 140
    public and private notions of
        125–6
    socially constructed 140
shame 88, 96, 118
shaming, 'reintegrative' 97
Smith, R. 76, 121
social justice 24, 49, 91, 107, 135
social and material context, and
    men's psyches 22–4, 55, 109,
    115
social movements 8, 23, 111,
    146–7
    and self-interest 52
social policies 77
social power, relinquishing 51, 52
social practices
    oppressive 100
    separating boys from girls 22
socialism 115
socialization
    agents of 66
    gender 19, 38, 145
    subverting one's own 145
socio-biology 34